WHAT WOULD NAPOLEON HILL DO?

The absolute best explanations of Napoleon Hill's seventeen Principles of Success from his original masterwork, *Law of Success*, and his classic bestseller, *Think and Grow Rich*—all brought together, analyzed, annotated, and presented in this one book.

Edited by Bill Hartley and Ann Hartley
with commentary by Bill Hartley

HIGHROADS MEDIA, INC.

ISBN-10: 1-932429-59-X
ISBN-13: 978-1-932429-59-6
10 9 8 7 6 5 4 3 2 1

CONTENTS

PUBLISHER'S PREFACE

What Would Napoleon Hill Do? is by far the most complete version of Napoleon Hill's philosophy of personal achievement ever published. It brings together between the covers of this one book all of the key concepts and the clearest explanations from Hill's masterwork, *Law of Success,* and his classic bestseller, *Think and Grow Rich.*

In compiling this book, the editors had one clear and specific goal: to make Napoleon Hill's Seventeen Principles of Success as easy to understand and as practical to use as possible. The first step was to go through Hill's original publication of the principles—the 1928 edition of *Law of Success*—and examine each of the lessons in the book to find the very best explanations and examples of each one of the principles.

Once these were identified, analyzed, and cross-referenced, the same meticulous approach was applied to each chapter in the original 1937 edition of *Think and Grow Rich.* The selections that resulted from the breakdown of these two books then became the source material from which the new chapters of *What Would Napoleon Hill Do?* were compiled.

NEW CHAPTERS

By creating new chapters, each of which is focused on just one principle, and by assembling each new chapter from the best material selected from throughout the two original books, these new chapters literally become the best of the best. In addition to the material from Hill's two classics, each chapter is also augmented by annotations and commentary drawn from *Think and Grow Rich: The Workbook* and *The Secret Law of Attraction as explained by Napoleon Hill.*

The new chapters in *What Would Napoleon Hill Do?* have been arranged in the most logical sequence so that each new lesson is the natural extension of the one that precedes it. The first four chapters set forth the four basic principles that underlie Napoleon Hill's theory of the Law of Success. The next three chapters teach the actual method for putting the theory to work. Each of the remaining chapters focuses on a specific principle and the explanation of how it fits into the overall theory of the Law of Success.

Because this book advances in such a specific and methodical manner, it is not the kind of business book that lends itself to jumping from chapter to chapter looking for the answer to the problem of the moment. What Napoleon Hill offers is a complete philosophy of personal achievement and success, not a collection of quick fixes. This is a book that will not only change *what* you think—it will change the *way* you think.

NEW TERMINOLOGY

For those readers who are sticklers for proper grammar, punctuation, and spelling, you will find that in a couple of instances we have made the seemingly peculiar decision to capitalize certain words that do not normally require capitalization. The following explains our decision.

As Hill was writing his philosophy of success, he realized there were concepts that he could not properly convey without creating his own terminology, specifically: Cosmic Habit Force, Definite Chief Aim, Infinite Intelligence, and the Master Mind. Although the words that comprise these terms would not normally be capitalized, because they have special significance as Hill uses them, we have chosen to set them off by capitalizing them when they appear in this book.

THE EDITING THEORY

As the excerpts from Hill's books were being assembled into new chapters, the editors approached the written text as we would that of a living author.

There is an editorial note that appears either before or after each excerpt identifying the original source material. You will notice that in some of the excerpts from *Law of Success,* Napoleon Hill uses the term "lesson" to refer to the material. The reason for this is that when Hill was compiling this first book, he considered it to be a course of study, and each chapter in the book was actually called a lesson.

Some editing has been done to bring related sections of text into closer proximity to one another, but in every case the original context has been preserved and the original meaning remains unchanged. In a few instances, alterations have been made to correct scientific information that has since become outdated.

All editorial commentary (with the exception of each new chapter opening) is clearly set off in this sans serif font, making it easily distinguishable from the serif font used for text excerpted from *Law of Success, Think and Grow Rich,* or other books by Napoleon Hill.

THERE IS NO DOUBT THAT THIS BOOK WORKS

One of the great advantages in writing a book based on such classic bestsellers as *Law of Success* and *Think and Grow Rich* is that they teach a system which has worked for literally millions of people all over the world. These books have inspired more successes and made more millionaires than any other books in publishing history.

If Hill's method worked for all of those others, why shouldn't it do the same for you? The only potential impediment standing between you and success is how prepared you are to commit yourself to the Napoleon Hill method.

Remember as you read that the people who enjoy the greatest success are those who don't just learn what Hill says—they embrace it without reservation. They don't try to second-guess Hill. They don't think they're too smart or too sophisticated to follow such simplistic rules. They just commit themselves 100 percent . . . and persevere until they have accomplished their goals.

ABOUT THE EDITORS

For more than twenty years, the publisher/editors of this book, Bill Hartley and Ann Hartley, have not only been deeply involved in the study of Hill's writings, but have also been the leading publishers of his works. As publishers, producers, and editors, they have created and published more bestselling books and audiobooks by and about Napoleon Hill than any other publisher in the world.

Chapter One

THE NEWLY DISCOVERED SEVENTEENTH PRINCIPLE

WHAT WOULD NAPOLEON HILL DO?

For years Napoleon Hill had lectured about his sixteen Principles of Success, only to find that when he wrote about the principles in his latest book, *Think and Grow Rich,* he suddenly began getting letters from readers pointing out that they were seeing another principle he hadn't mentioned.

What would Napoleon Hill do?

He went back, reread his own book, and found that his readers were right. They had led him to the key that had eluded him for almost thirty years!

When writing about Napoleon Hill, there is always a temptation to start by telling the tales of how he raised himself up from backwoods poverty to the boardrooms of the rich and powerful. But with this book, the editors have decided to focus first on Hill's Principles of Success, and let the anecdotal stories emerge naturally when they relate to a particular principle being explained.

The only background that needs to be told here is that it was the famed steel baron and philanthropist Andrew Carnegie who originally commissioned Hill to compile the research that would later become Hill's Principles of Success. You will learn more of the details in later chapters, but the crux of the story is that Hill had been hired to write a magazine article about Carnegie, and the two of them got on so well that what was supposed to have been a three-hour interview turned into a three-day marathon.

It finally ended with Carnegie offering to introduce Hill to the most powerful men in America so that Hill could learn their secrets of success—*if* Hill would promise that he would use those secrets to write a philosophy of success that would be made available to the common person.

Hill agreed, and thus the seeds of *Law of Success* and *Think and Grow Rich* were sown.

When Napoleon Hill wrote his original bestselling masterwork, *Law of Success,* he formatted the book as a series of sixteen lessons, each lesson focusing on one of those sixteen Principles of Success.

Hill's sixteen principles were the result of his twenty years of research into why certain people succeed, including details provided by 16,000 individuals who completed a psychological questionnaire administered by Hill, as well as in-depth interviews with one hundred of the most creative and successful self-made multimillionaires in America. The resulting book—*Law of Success*—was a runaway bestseller.

Nine years later, Napoleon Hill adapted those sixteen principles into a more focused and concise format. When this new, revised version was published under the title *Think and Grow Rich,* the number of people who had submitted psychological profiles to him exceeded 25,000, and Hill's personal interviews and analyses had grown to more than 500 of the most famous entrepreneurs, inventors, businessmen, industrialists, politicians, and leaders of every kind.

Think and Grow Rich has gone on to become the best-selling success book in the history of publishing. It is said that Napoleon Hill has made more millionaires than any other person, and variations on his sixteen principles are found in the work of every modern self-improvement author and motivational speaker.

THE SIXTEEN PRINCIPLES OF PERSONAL ACHIEVEMENT

Following are the sixteen principles in the sequence they appeared in *Law of Success*:

Lesson One: The Master Mind Alliance

Lesson Two: A Definite Chief Aim

Lesson Three: Self-Confidence

Lesson Four: The Habit of Saving

Lesson Five: Initiative and Leadership

Lesson Six: Imagination

Lesson Seven: Enthusiasm

Lesson Eight: Self-Control

Lesson Nine: The Habit of Doing More Than Paid For

Lesson Ten: A Pleasing Personality

Lesson Eleven: Accurate Thinking

Lesson Twelve: Concentration

Lesson Thirteen: Cooperation

Lesson Fourteen: Profiting by Failure

Lesson Fifteen: Tolerance

Lesson Sixteen: The Golden Rule

THERE IS NO DOUBT THE PRINCIPLES WORK

There is no doubt that Napoleon Hill's system works. His mentor, Andrew Carnegie, one of the richest and most successful men who ever lived, introduced Hill to America's leaders in business, government, science, and the arts, and Carnegie persuaded them to reveal to Hill what they considered to be the secrets of their success. These secrets, combined with the results from the large number of people who had completed Hill's psychological questionnaire, gave him a rare insight into the traits that are common to those who achieve great success.

It was from this extraordinary database, plus Hill's extensive studies in psychology, philosophy, and human motivation, that he developed his system based on a specific set of sixteen principles that lead to personal achievement. Through his work as a lecturer and consultant to large corporations and government agencies, Hill was able to test and confirm his theories in real-world circumstances.

By the time Hill published *Think and Grow Rich,* he had spent twenty-nine years immersed in learning about and analyzing success. Through rigorous testing and firsthand observation, he had developed a proven system for personal achievement. Hill also had thousands of people who could confirm that his method had worked for them.

THE NEW SEVENTEENTH PRINCIPLE

Because Napoleon Hill lectured so widely, he was constantly receiving feedback from the people who had read his books and tested the principles. As a result, it was his readers who first made Hill aware of a seventeenth principle which acts as a kind of master controller of the other sixteen. This is how he described it in a lecture he delivered in Chicago in 1962:

After *Think and Grow Rich* came out, I commenced to get telegrams and letters and telephone calls from all over the world congratulating me on account of this book. After this had gone on for about a month, I said to myself, well by golly, I'm going to read that book. Maybe that fella's got something I don't know about.

Then I sat down to read my own book, and I just disassociated myself from it as though I had never seen it before, and about the middle of the book it came to me, the idea that gave me the seventeenth principle of this course: the principle of Cosmic Habit Force.

I had been searching for that down through the years and hadn't found it until I read it in my own book. It wasn't something I had written on the lines and forgotten; it was a thought that came as I read those lines. It was something there between and behind the lines.

What Napoleon Hill realized as he reread his book was that although he had been writing about the sixteen Principles of Success, and using real-life examples that illustrated how those principles worked, he had not explained *why* the principles worked.

During the lectures he gave in Chicago in 1962, Hill elaborated on his reasoning as follows:

I feel exceedingly proud of this philosophy for many reasons. First of all, because it is accepted by all religions even though it does not partake of any of them. Catholics and Protestants, whites and blacks, all the races, all the colors, all the creeds accept this philosophy, and I think that's a miracle in itself.

When I first started out with Andrew Carnegie, he had admonished me to never under any circumstances attach any title of an orthodox nature to this philosophy. He said the minute you do that, you will split your audience.

And when you start the actual writing, never use a word or an illustration that will send a high school boy or girl to the dictionary or encyclopedia.

I have followed those instructions to the letter, with the result that we have a philosophy that is understandable to anybody. Anybody can apply it, and millions of people are applying it all over the world.

However, many readers believed that although it wasn't there in black and white, the advice and lessons and stories in his book, when taken together, suggested that why you succeed or fail has to do with a force at work in the world that allows for the thoughts in your mind to affect what happens in reality.

Recognizing the significance of this possible new principle, Hill went back to his research, studied the interviews and analyses he had assembled over the years, and he saw it too. On further examination it was clear that in almost thirty years of asking people about the reasons for their success, every one of the high-achievers he studied shared one thing in common: whether or not they even knew it themselves, each one used some variation on the power of positive thinking.

NOT AS WEIRD OR CRAZY AS YOU MIGHT THINK

When Napoleon Hill first met Andrew Carnegie, Carnegie was the most successful businessman in the world. Although born into poverty, he had worked his way up through the ranks and built his great fortune through hard work combined with keen business acumen. Napoleon Hill was also born poor, and shared the same work ethic, but in his case it was combined with the inquiring mind of a journalist. Each, in his own way, was a self-made man who had risen from poverty to prominence through his own efforts, guided by a practical approach to life's challenges.

The successful track records of Hill and Carnegie are highlighted here to remind the reader that the seventeenth principle is the creation of two very pragmatic men who took a no-nonsense approach to their work. That they were both serious and successful businessmen is significant because, as you will soon learn, the new seventeenth principle has some similarities to concepts that are more often associated with pop psychology than serious business theory.

Most readers will have some familiarity with the concept of the power of positive thinking. At the time Hill was writing his first book, positive thinking was well known as a basic tenet of the New Thought Movement, whose followers referred to the concept as the Law of Attraction. It has also been popular under a variety of other names including creative visualization, positive affirmation, psychocybernetics, autosuggestion, self-hypnosis, and mind over matter.

Because this technique is so often associated with "get rich quick" schemes, it is rare for someone of Carnegie's or Hill's stature to give it serious consideration as a legitimate business tool. However, what caught Hill's attention when he reexamined his research was not the theory itself but, more importantly, the fact that it kept showing up in his research so often and so consistently. Statistically, the number of occurrences went well beyond chance, which meant that Napoleon Hill could not ignore the fact that it was the common denominator among those who achieved great success.

His curiosity piqued by such a high incidence of correlation, Hill decided not to challenge the assumption that positive thinking worked (his empirical data about the end result was quite clear), but rather to focus his efforts on deducing *why* it worked. Once liberated from the need to prove that positive thinking actually worked, the answer to the question of why it worked came in a flash of insight. Hill realized that the most logical reason why focusing on a particular thought can affect what happens in reality is simply because of the way the human mind naturally responds when it focuses on a thought.

It is the natural habit of the mind to try to solve problems. It tries to make things happen. Fixing things is the human mind's normal, natural response. Concentrate on something, and your mind immediately tries to think of what it can do to make it happen. That is because your mind is just following a basic law of nature.

A law of nature is determined when a certain stimulus produces the same result time after time until it is accepted that it is its nature to produce that result every time, all the time. Every aspect of life relies upon the laws of nature to make sure that if we do A, then B will always be the result.

For thirty years Napoleon Hill had studied thousands of the most successful people and analyzed the relationship between what they believed and the success they achieved. The connection between those who used some form of positive thinking and those who achieved great success happened so consistently that it convinced him the way the mind responded was no accident, but was in fact a predictable law of nature.

The following is adapted from Hill's explanation excerpted from *Napoleon Hill's Keys to Success.*

Every living thing below the intelligence of man lives, reproduces itself, and fulfills its earthly mission in direct response to the power of the Cosmic Force of Habit through what we call instinct.

Man alone has been given the privilege of choice in connection with his living habits, and these he may fix by the patterns of his thoughts. You may control your destiny to an astounding degree—simply by shaping your own thoughts. Once these thoughts have been shaped into definite patterns, they are taken over by the law of Cosmic Habit Force and are made into permanent habits, and they remain that way until they have been supplanted by different and stronger thought patterns.

FORCE OF HABIT OR COSMIC HABIT FORCE

Normally when something follows a law of nature and does what comes naturally, we say it is doing it out of force of habit. However, Hill felt that when referring to the force of habit of the human mind it went beyond the common designation, so he created the term *Cosmic Habit Force.*

To the modern ear, the phrase *Cosmic Habit Force* probably sounds a little too tie-dyed and New Age-y, but Hill came up with it about forty years before Woodstock, and in the dictionary-sense that he uses the words, the name is actually a very apt description for the practice of recognizing habitual actions and predictable responses, and using them to your advantage.

Throughout the entire cosmos there is consistency, regularity, and predictable patterns to things and events. Our solar system revolves around the sun in predicable patterns, and electrons revolve around the nucleus of an atom in fixed orbits that are just as reliable. Balls bounce, flowers grow, and steel is hard because that is the nature of balls, flowers, and steel. Storm clouds never rain milk, things fall down not up, magnets have north and south poles, and cats like to lie in the sun.

As Hill often pointed out, if you plant an acorn, you will always get an oak tree, not a carrot or a pineapple, and it is just as predictable that the human mind tries to make your thoughts come true.

- Every individual thing has a built-in propensity, a natural habit or way of being. Every creature, every object, and every force will follow its natural habit or instinct unless something steps in to change it.

- The human mind has its natural habit or propensity too. It is the natural habit of the human mind to try to transform any thought or desire into the physical counterpart of that thought. That is the Cosmic Force of Habit, or as Hill calls it, Cosmic Habit Force.

- Humans have the unique ability to consciously change their thoughts, so unlike every other thing that follows instinct, you can control what your mind focuses on and, therefore, you can make Cosmic Habit Force work to your advantage.

- Because you can control what you think, you can control your habits. Habits become part of your nature through repetition.

As a result, if you keep repeating certain ideas in your mind, Cosmic Habit Force will take over those patterns of thought and make them your natural reaction.

When you focus on what you desire as intently and as consistently as Hill says you must, you visualize it so realistically that it burns into your subconscious and becomes a part of every thought you have and everything you do. It is there in your subconscious at all times, putting together bits and pieces of every thought or thing you come into contact with, trying to come up with ideas to help you achieve your desire.

THIS IS WHAT SEPARATES HILL FROM THE HOCUS-POCUS

The following is the most important part of this lesson. This is where Napoleon Hill's approach to positive thinking separates itself from the mystical hocus-pocus and New Age thinking. This is where Hill makes it clear that in his method there is nothing magical about repeatedly focusing your mind on what you desire; it is simply a straightforward application of established psychological principles.

The following is excerpted and adapted from *Law of Success*.

Everyone wishes for the better things in life, such as money, a good position, fame, and recognition, but most people never go far beyond the wishing stage. Men who know exactly what they want of life and are determined to get it, do not stop with wishing. They intensify their wishes into a burning desire, and back that desire with continuous effort based on a sound plan.

All riches and all material things that anyone acquires through self-effort begin in the form of a clear, concise mental picture of the thing one seeks. When that picture grows to the proportions of an obsession, it is taken over by the subconscious mind. From that point on, you are attracted in the direction of the physical equivalent of the mental picture.

The subconscious mind may be likened to a magnet; when it has been thoroughly saturated with any definite purpose, it has a decided tendency to attract all that is necessary for the fulfillment of that purpose.

As Napoleon Hill interprets it, positive thinking can indeed help you realize your aim or goal. But visualizing your desire can't put actual dollars in your bank or park a Rolls-Royce in your driveway any more than it can make a cup and saucer suddenly materialize on the desk in front of you.

Hill does say that when you focus your mind it has a tendency to attract what you need to achieve your desire. However, if the human mind is actually capable of attracting something, then whatever it attracts is attracted to itself. And what the human mind is capable of attracting to itself are thoughts, ideas, and plans—not dollar bills, automobiles, or crockery.

When you visualize yourself acquiring money, a car, or any other real object, what you are really doing is confirming to yourself the belief that achieving what you desire is a possibility, and that you are a person who is capable of making it happen.

The vivid images that you create of your desire are burned into your subconscious, where they connect and interact with other bits of information, so that your mind automatically starts coming up with more and better ideas of how you can earn the money to put in your bank so you can buy the Rolls-Royce.

Thinking positively and visualizing things the way you want them to be doesn't create concrete objects; it creates attitudes and ideas. When you change your attitudes and ideas, you naturally go from thinking about what you desire, to thinking about how to get what you desire, to actually making things happen in the real world to achieve your desire.

That is how positive thinking turns into positive results: Thinking prompts you to act, and it is your actions that make the concrete things come true.

For some readers this straightforward, nonmagical explanation of "why" Napoleon Hill's system works will be somewhat of a letdown. Some will be disappointed because they believe that positive thinking is nothing more than keeping a happy thought in mind, while others who have been influenced by certain New Age thinking go to the other extreme and believe that all you have to do is think positively, send out the right vibes, and the universe is going to drop whatever you think about into your lap.

Hill's approach to positive thinking is not the cerebral equivalent of a smiley face, and it's not a mystical, mental mail-order house either. But don't make the mistake of rejecting it because it involves more work than just thinking how nice it would be to have what you want. Hill's method may not be as magical as you'd like, but his method also doesn't make outrageous claims. It doesn't say you have to follow some guru, and it doesn't ask you to suspend your belief in physics. It just works.

Go through it step by step, and you can't help but see how perfectly logical it is.

It is a fact that when you think about something you desire, your natural response is to wonder what you'd have to do to get it. It is also a fact that if you don't believe you are capable of getting what you desire, the chances are you will just give up on it and your self-fulfilling prophesy that you are a loser will have come true.

On the other hand, if you work at convincing yourself to the point of obsession that you are perfectly capable of getting what you want, your new self-fulfilling prophesy will take over and start searching everything you know in both your conscious and your subconscious to come up with ideas about how to satisfy your desire.

And if you don't think that is magic, you are mistaken.

YOU HAVE A HEADSTART

What Would Napoleon Hill Do? is the first book of Napoleon Hill's materials that begins by explaining why Cosmic Habit Force offers the key to the theory that the thoughts you focus on and visualize can be transformed into your reality.

Because Hill did not uncover the law of Cosmic Habit Force until after the original sixteen principles were already published, in later books it was mistakenly included as the last chapter, despite the fact that Cosmic Habit Force is the "master principle" and it makes much more sense to place it at the beginning where it will be learned first and will help the reader to better understand the other principles that rely on it.

By learning at the beginning of this book why Cosmic Habit Force works, you have a great advantage over previous students of Napoleon Hill's method. By knowing in advance that there is a logical explanation that relies on nothing more exotic than common sense, the laws of nature, and well-established motivational psychology, you will be able to approach the rest of the principles with full confidence that Hill's method works and that it will help you achieve the success you desire.

In addition to placing Cosmic Habit Force at the beginning, you will find that in *What Would Napoleon Hill Do?* the other sixteen principles have been arranged in the most logical sequence so that each successive principle builds upon the one that precedes it.

COSMIC HABIT FORCE, STEP BY STEP

Following is a quick recap of the concepts set forth in this chapter.

- Through extensive research, Napoleon Hill identified sixteen principles that lead to success.

- Hill then uncovered a seventeenth principle, which is actually a law of nature that he called Cosmic Habit Force.

- Cosmic Habit Force is the law of nature that everything has its own natural way of being, and all things will follow their instinct or natural habit unless something steps in to change it.

- It is the natural habit of the human mind to try to make whatever thought you hold in your mind come true in reality.

- Because you can control your thoughts, you can therefore control what thoughts you hold in your mind and, as a result, what thoughts become your habitual way of thinking.

- If you intentionally think thoughts about succeeding, it is those kinds of positive thoughts that will become your natural habit.

- The bottom line is: If thinking positive thoughts about succeeding becomes your natural habit, and if your mind naturally tries to make the thoughts you hold in your mind come true, then it will become your habit for your mind to think positive thoughts. Your mind will then do all that it can to help you succeed and make those positive thoughts come true.

Chapter Two

YOUR DEFINITE CHIEF AIM

WHAT WOULD NAPOLEON HILL DO?

Napoleon Hill makes it clear that when you desire to accomplish an important objective, and you want to use his system to achieve that desire, you must begin by knowing precisely what you desire and you must be able to visualize your desired goal so clearly that you can hold the image in your mind.

When you have a Definite Chief Aim, it is more than merely goal-setting. Every single action you take in life boils down to one question: Will doing this help me reach my desire, or won't it?

Whether you are deciding something as grand as what will be the guiding philosophical purpose of your life, or something as nuts-and-bolts as figuring out how to accomplish a particular goal in time to meet a deadline, if you wish to make Hill's method work for you, you begin by identifying and focusing on your Definite Chief Aim.

As you learned in the preceding chapter, it is a law of nature that if you make your mind focus on the image of your desire, your mind's natural habit is to do whatever it can to make your desire into a reality. This chapter will explain the methods for identifying, and then visualizing, a Definite Chief Aim in such a way that your mind can help you achieve what you desire.

DEFINING A DEFINITE CHIEF AIM

In *Law of Success* Napoleon Hill calls it an "aim"; in *Think and Grow Rich* he uses the word "desire." And in both it is also referred to as "a burning desire," "a definite purpose," "definiteness of purpose," as well as other variations using the words "goal" or "objective." For the sake of clarity, in this book the concept of a major desire will be most often referred to as your aim or purpose.

- Hill calls it a "definite aim" to differentiate it from general, every-day, wishful thinking. This kind of aim or desire is very specific, exact, and visualized in detail.

- Hill calls it a "chief aim" to make it clear that although you may have a number of different aims that all contribute to what you want to achieve, this aim is the most important of those aims.

- When Hill first wrote about this concept in *Law of Success,* he referred to it as a "Definite Chief Aim in life," which he envisioned as an overriding philosophical precept that you hold in your mind as a personal ideal that will guide your entire life.

- By the time Hill wrote about a Definite Chief Aim in *Think and Grow Rich,* he had come to realize that the concept was not limited to an all-encompassing personal philosophy of life, but could also be very helpful in accomplishing those desires that we encounter in our everyday lives.

- It is not uncommon to have to deal with more than one issue at any given time, and therefore it is likely that you will have more than one Definite Chief Aim operating simultaneously.

- You may have separate Definite Chief Aims that don't conflict with one another, or you may have a number of lesser desires that all contribute to a larger, overarching Definite Chief Aim.

YOUR DEFINITE CHIEF AIM: FOCUSING ON YOUR DESIRE

The following explanation of the psychological basis of the concept is excerpted and adapted from *Law of Success*, Lesson Two: A Definite Chief Aim.

THE PSYCHOLOGICAL REASON
FOR A DEFINITE CHIEF AIM

The keynote of this entire lesson may be found in the word *definite*.

Far too many people are drifting aimlessly through life, without the slightest concept of the work for which they are best fitted, and with no concept whatsoever of even the need for such a thing as a definite objective toward which to strive.

There is both a psychological and an economic reason for the selection of a Definite Chief Aim in life. Let us first devote our attention to the psychological side of the question. It is a well-established principle of psychology that a person's acts are always in harmony with the dominating thoughts of his or her mind.

Any Definite Chief Aim that is deliberately fixed in your mind and held there, with the firm determination to realize it, finally saturates the entire subconscious mind until it influences the physical action of your body toward the attainment of that purpose.

Your Definite Chief Aim in life should be selected with deliberate care, and after it has been selected it should be written out and placed where you will see it at least once a day. The psychological effect is to impress this purpose upon your subconscious mind so strongly that it accepts this purpose as a pattern or blueprint that will eventually dominate your activities in life and lead you, step by step, toward the attainment of the object behind that purpose.

THE ECONOMIC REASON FOR A DEFINITE CHIEF AIM

Let us now shift our attention from the psychological reason to the economic reason for choosing a Definite Chief Aim.

If a ship lost its rudder in mid-ocean and began circling around, it would soon exhaust its fuel supply without reaching shore, despite the fact that it would have used up enough energy to carry it to shore and back again several times.

The person who labors without a definite purpose backed by a definite plan for its attainment resembles the ship that has lost its rudder.

Every well-built house started in the form of a definite purpose plus a definite plan in the nature of a set of blueprints. Imagine what would happen if you tried to build a house by the haphazard method, without plans. Workmen would be in each other's way, building materials would be piled all over the lot before the foundation was even completed, and everybody on the job would have a different notion as to how the house ought to be built. Result: chaos and misunderstandings, and costs that would be prohibitive.

Have you ever stopped to think that most people finish school, take up employment or enter a trade or profession, without the slightest concept of anything that even remotely resembles a definite purpose or a definite plan?

If success depends upon power, and if power is organized effort, and if the first step in the direction of organization is a definite purpose, then you may easily see why such a purpose is essential.

With the aid of a magnifying glass, you can teach yourself a great lesson about the value of organized effort. Through the use of such a glass you can focus the sun's rays on a definite spot so strongly that they will burn a hole through a plank. Remove the glass (which represents the definite purpose) and the same rays of sun may shine on that same plank for a million years without burning it.

Until you select a definite purpose in life, you dissipate your energies and spread your thoughts over so many subjects and in so many different directions that they lead not to power but to indecision and weakness.

FOCUSING IN ON YOUR DEFINITE CHIEF AIM

In a vague sort of way, nearly everyone has a Definite Chief Aim or purpose: the desire for money. But that is not a Definite Chief Aim as it is used in this lesson. Before your purpose could be considered definite, you would have to reach a decision as to the precise method through which you intend to accumulate that money.

It would be insufficient for you to say that you would make money by going into some sort of business. You would have to decide just what line of business. You would also have to decide just where you would locate. And you would also have to decide the business policies under which you would conduct your business.

Your desire is the factor that determines what your definite purpose in life shall be. No one can select your dominating desire for you, but once you select it yourself, it should become your Definite Chief Aim and occupy the spotlight of your mind until it is transformed into reality, unless you permit it to be pushed aside by conflicting desires.

This lesson is intended to impress upon your mind a clear concept of the value of a definite purpose of some nature, and, as has also been stated, to be sure that you understand the value of organized effort as a means of attaining the necessary power with which to achieve that definite purpose.

The following is how Napoleon Hill wrote about the same concept in *Think and Grow Rich*. This is excerpted and adapted from the chapter called Desire, and it expands on the importance of having a Definite Chief Aim.

BE PREPARED TO BURN YOUR BRIDGES

A long while ago, a great warrior faced a situation that made it necessary for him to make a decision which ensured his success on the battlefield. He was about to send his armies against a powerful foe, whose men outnumbered his own. He loaded his soldiers into boats, sailed to the enemy's country, unloaded soldiers and equipment, then gave the order to burn the ships that had carried them. Addressing his men before the first battle, he said, "You see the boats going up in smoke. That means that we cannot leave these shores alive unless we win! We now have no choice—we win or we perish!"

They won.

Every person who wins in any undertaking must be willing to burn his ships and cut all sources of retreat. Only by so doing can one be sure of maintaining that state of mind known as a burning desire to win, essential to success.

Napoleon Hill loved to tell stories to illustrate his principles, and one of his favorites was the story of how Edwin C. Barnes became so committed to his Definite Chief Aim of becoming the partner of the world's greatest inventor, Thomas Edison. Even though he was dead broke, had no connection to Edison, and no scientific training, Barnes went to the local railroad yards and hopped into an empty boxcar on a freight train headed for New Jersey, where the famous inventor's lab was located . . .

When Edwin C. Barnes climbed down from a freight train in West Orange, New Jersey, he may have resembled a tramp but his thoughts were those of a king!

As he made his way from the railroad tracks to Thomas A. Edison's office, his mind was at work. He saw himself standing in Edison's presence. He heard himself asking Mr. Edison for an opportunity to carry out the one consuming obsession of his life: a burning desire to become the business associate of the great inventor.

Barnes' desire was not a hope! It was not a wish! It was a keen, pulsating desire, which transcended everything else. It was definite.

When he went to West Orange, he did not say to himself, "I will try to induce Edison to give me a job of some sort." He said, "There is but one thing in this world that I am determined to have, and that is a business association with Thomas A. Edison. I will burn all bridges behind me, and stake my entire future on my ability to get what I want."

He left himself no way of retreat. He had to win or perish!

A few years later, Edwin C. Barnes again stood before Edison, in the same office where he first met the inventor. This time his desire had been translated into reality. He was in business with Edison. The dominating dream of his life had become a reality.

Barnes succeeded because he chose a definite goal, placed all his energy, all his will-power, all his effort, everything, behind that goal.

The world in which we live is constantly demanding new ways of doing things, and behind all of this demand for new and better things, there is one quality that you must possess to win, and that is the knowledge of what you want, and a burning desire to possess it.

There is a difference between wishing for a thing and being ready to receive it. No one is ready for a thing until he believes he can acquire it. The state of mind must be belief, not mere hope or wish.

Every human being who understands the purpose of money wishes for it. Wishing will not bring riches. But desiring riches with a state of mind that becomes an obsession, then planning definite ways and means to acquire riches, and backing those plans with persistence, which does not recognize failure, *will* bring riches.

The following section is excerpted and adapted from material that appears in *Think and Grow Rich: The Workbook.* It is designed to help you identify and refine your Definite Chief Aim, and it will teach you a method for firmly planting your Definite Chief Aim in your mind.

DEFINING YOUR DEFINITE CHIEF AIM

In this section the term "a Definite Chief Aim" is used in identifying what you desire when considering major issues such as choosing a career, deciding if you should make a move, taking on a particular job or assignment, launching a new project or product, searching for a new method, or other equally important challenges.

Your Definite Chief Aim is a statement of a specific desire that has been arrived at after serious thought. Although this may not be "the grand guiding philosophical principle of your life," it does mean that in at least this one area you know exactly what you want to achieve, it gives that part of your life focus, and it gives you a target for which to aim.

Those who know what they are aiming for and where they are going do not waste their time and energy trying to accomplish too many things at once. Nor do they bounce from one desire to the next, quickly abandoning anything that doesn't bring immediate satisfaction.

Those who know what they want concentrate their efforts on a Definite Chief Aim, exerting all of their powers to attain that end. When it is accomplished, they reset their sights and take on another Definite Chief Aim, which becomes their new burning desire.

WRITING YOUR WAY TO YOUR DEFINITE CHIEF AIM

Following is an exercise that will go a long way toward helping you to define your Definite Chief Aim or purpose. By doing this exercise and writing out your answers, you will find that you are clarifying your thinking and making your ideas more specific.

1. Write an explanation of where you would like to go and what you would like to see in your lifetime.

2. Write a description of the kind of person you would like others to think you are.

3. Write an explanation of the kind of knowledge you wish to acquire in life.

4. Write an explanation of the skills you would like to master.

5. Write a description of your ideal job.

6. Write a statement of how much you would like to earn each year.

7. Write an explanation of what you would be willing to give in return for that amount.

8. Write an explanation of what success for you would mean in terms of your home and family.

9. Write an explanation of why success would make you a better person.

This exercise is designed to open your mind about your purpose in life and what you want to achieve. When you feel that you have a clear idea of your Definite Chief Aim or purpose, it is time to narrow your focus and define the goals and objectives that make up your aim or purpose.

DEFINING YOUR GOALS OR OBJECTIVES

In this section, the words *goals* and *objectives* refer to those lesser desires that contribute to the achievement of a larger Definite Chief Aim. These are the individual steps that you have to take in order to get to your Definite Chief Aim.

Your goals and objectives should answer the question "What specific steps must I take to acquire or achieve my Definite Chief Aim?"

Once you have accomplished a goal, it should naturally open the door to your next new goal.

Even though your goals and objectives are often nothing more than a "to-do" list, you should still write out the list.

WRITING OUT YOUR GOALS AND OBJECTIVES

1. First, write My Definite Chief Aim as a heading. Under the heading make a list of the tasks that need to be done in order to achieve your desire. Those are your goals or objectives.

2. Opposite each goal write a one-sentence explanation. If you can't express it in a single sentence, it is not a goal, and you need to break it down further.

3. Every goal should be broken down into specific tasks. The more you break it down, the more achievable that goal will seem, as it becomes clear that each of the smaller tasks can be handled easily.

4. Make all of your goals measurable. Each goal should allow you to easily determine if and when you have accomplished it. In order to be measurable, each goal should include specifics such as: (a) How much time will it take to do, and when is the deadline up? (b) What are the quotas, thresholds, minimums, or maximums that must be achieved?

5. Examine your goals to determine if they are challenging and yet obtainable. Goals should be realistic but they should also stretch your knowledge, skills, and self-discipline.

6. Examine your goals to determine if they are stated in a positive fashion. A goal that is stated as a negative may focus your attention on what you fear rather than on the result you seek.

WRITING THE STATEMENT OF YOUR DEFINITE CHIEF AIM

The following should provide everything you need to write out the statement of your aim or purpose. First there is a seven-point review of the steps you must take to clearly know your desire. Later in the chapter you will find a blank form that you can use as a template for creating the statement of your Definite Chief Aim or purpose.

1. Fix in your mind exactly what you desire as your Definite Chief Aim or purpose. Write it out in a clear, concise, positive statement.

2. Determine exactly what you intend to give in return for what you desire. Will it be your time, your money, your privacy, your independence? What about your sense of security? How much control will you give up in exchange for success? Remember, there is no such reality as "something for nothing."

3. Next, write out the exact amount of money or other benefits you will receive by carrying out your aim or purpose.

4. Then set the time limit for its accomplishment, choosing an exact date when you want to possess what you desire.

5. Create a definite plan for carrying out your desire and begin at once, whether you are ready or not, to put this plan into action. Do it now—right now.

6. Read your written statement aloud at least twice daily. Read it just before retiring at night and read it after arising in the morning. As you read, see and feel and believe yourself already in possession of the money.

7. To guarantee success, set specific times to review your progress and determine whether you are on the right track.

The review process requires that in evaluating your progress toward your stated desire you must be completely honest with yourself. The main purpose of the evaluation is for you to decide if you need to change your Definite Chief Aim. Therefore it will be of no value to you if you are overly generous in your personal assessment.

You should select your Definite Chief Aim only when you truly believe that you are capable of accomplishing it. However, it is possible that as you gain experience and wisdom you may have to change your plans. Revisions in your Definite Chief Aim should never be made for something as minor as having failed to meet a deadline. Changes in your plan should only be made after you have seriously evaluated your Definite Chief Aim and it is clear that there is a valid reason why it cannot be accomplished as it was planned.

Napoleon Hill says that changing your Definite Chief Aim does not mean that it was wrong. It simply means that what you desired could not be accomplished in the way you had planned it.

In Hill's view that is not failure. He says that you have never failed until you have given up in your own mind. All that happened is that you have had a temporary defeat. The answer to temporary defeat is to redefine your Definite Chief Aim, create a new plan, and immediately start taking action to accomplish the revised Definite Chief Aim.

The following is excerpted and adapted from *Think and Grow Rich,* Chapter 7: Organized Planning.

IF YOUR FIRST PLAN FAILS—TRY ANOTHER!

If the first plan that you adopt does not work successfully, replace it with a new plan; if this new plan fails to work, replace it in turn with still another, and so on, until you find a plan that does work. Right here is the point at which the majority of people meet with failure, because of their lack of persistence in creating new plans to take the place of those that fail.

The most intelligent person living cannot succeed in accumulating money—nor in any other undertaking—without plans that are practical and workable. Just keep this fact in mind, and remember when your plans fail, that temporary defeat is not permanent failure. It may only mean that your plans have not been sound. Build other plans. Start all over again.

Temporary defeat should mean only one thing: the certain knowledge that there is something wrong with your plan. Millions of people go through life in misery and poverty, because they lack a sound plan through which to accumulate a fortune.

Your achievement can be no greater than your plans are sound. No one is ever whipped, until he quits—in his own mind.

James J. Hill met with temporary defeat when he first endeavored to raise the necessary capital to build a railroad from the East to the West, but he, too, turned defeat into victory through new plans.

Henry Ford met with temporary defeat, not only at the beginning of his automobile career, but after he had gone far toward the top. He created new plans, and went marching on to financial victory.

We see men who have accumulated great fortunes, but we often recognize only their triumph, overlooking the temporary defeats that they had to surmount before "arriving."

No follower of this philosophy can reasonably expect to accumulate a fortune without experiencing "temporary defeat." When defeat comes, accept it as a signal that your plans are not sound, rebuild those plans, and set sail once more toward your coveted goal.

If you give up before your goal has been reached, then you are a "quitter." A quitter never wins—and a winner never quits.

Lift this sentence out, write it on a piece of paper in letters an inch high, and place it where you will see it every night before you go to sleep and every morning before you go to work.

REVIEWING THE PROCESS, MAKING THE PLAN

If you are going to follow the Napoleon Hill plan, once you have established your Definite Chief Aim you must write it down and lay out a specific step-by-step action plan that will keep you on track.

The sample on the following page illustrates how an individual whose desire is to own his own business might write out his Definite Chief Aim, and then identify the goals and objectives that must be accomplished to get there.

My Definite Chief Aim

My Definite Chief Aim is: To own my own discount specialty food store that will be profitable enough annually over the next twenty years that my wife and I can afford to maintain our home mortgage, cover our automobile and insurance payments, and continue to support our current lifestyle while sending our children through college.

In order to do this I will give up my current job as Director of Marketing for *[company name]*.

In the past five years I have set aside *[insert amount of money]*, which my wife and I have agreed we shall loan to our new specialty food store to be used as the working capital with which to launch the business.

For the first two years I fully expect to give the business my complete attention, devoting at least ten hours per day, six days per week to the management and operation of the store. Knowing that the business will take up much of my time, I will make it a point to find time every day to do something special and unexpected for my wife and children, and I will strive daily to make sure they know that this is our family's business, that we are all in this together—and I will make sure they know how important it is that they are helping me to succeed at my Definite Chief Aim.

I will make it a part of my daily business to attract to me the type of people who have a sense of excellence about their work and who want to excel in their job.

In return for their help, I will give each employee and supplier the full benefit of my years of experience. By helping others, I will benefit by attracting good people to work with and for me.

During the first five years of operation I will pay myself a monthly salary of *[insert specific amount of money]*. In addition, I will earn an annual bonus of *[insert specific percentage]* of the earnings calculated as revenue from operation, less costs and expenses, taxes, and depreciation.

By the end of the second year I will have repaid *[insert specific amount of money]* against the original sum lent to the company.

By the end of *[insert year]* I will have repaid 100 percent of the money lent to the company by me and my wife.

Our exit strategy is to sell the store and our home at the end of twenty years and use the proceeds to retire to Scottsdale, Arizona.

Goals and Objectives

My first goal is to find an appropriate building that is at least *[specify floor space]*, at a rate of *[specify cost per square foot]*, that must be in an area such as *[detail the factors that govern where you want to operate a small specialty food store]*.

A simultaneous, noncompeting second goal is to make exclusive agreements with regional suppliers who can provide gourmet foods at a wholesale cost that will allow me to price goods at least 25 percent less than the gourmet section of the major food chains in the region, while still maintaining a contribution to overhead of 25 percent.

My objectives for the second goal are: (1) Call the owner of the 99 Cents Only Stores to see if he will provide the names of low-price specialty goods suppliers. (2) Surf the Internet for names of overstock and closeout companies. (3) Call Farmer's Co-op to arrange to meet at Saturday's Farmer's Market to discuss securing options on future berry crops.

[signature] _____

[date] _____

On the following page is a blank form that you may want to use as a guide for creating your own personalized statement, inserting the appropriate number of goals for your own particular Definite Chief Aim or purpose.

MY DEFINITE CHIEF AIM OR PURPOSE

My Definite Chief Aim or purpose is:

_____

_____

_____

_____

I will accomplish this by _____ [MONTH] _____ [DAY] _____ [YEAR]

My first goal toward my Definite Chief Aim or purpose is:

_____

_____

_____

I will accomplish this by _____ [MONTH] _____ [DAY] _____ [YEAR]

My second goal toward my Definite Chief Aim or purpose is:

_____

_____

_____

I will accomplish this by _____ [MONTH] _____ [DAY] _____ [YEAR]

My third goal toward my Definite Chief Aim or purpose is:

_____

_____

_____

I will accomplish this by _____ [MONTH] _____ [DAY] _____ [YEAR]

[SIGNATURE] _____

YOUR DEFINITE CHIEF AIM: PLANTING THE SUGGESTION

The following is excerpted and adapted from *Law of Success,* Lesson Two: A Definite Chief Aim.

HOW TO IMPRESS YOUR DEFINITE CHIEF AIM ON YOUR SUBCONSCIOUS

Let us go back, for the sake of clarity and emphasis, to the psychological principles upon which this lesson is founded.

The presence of any thought or idea in your consciousness tends to urge you to transform that feeling into appropriate physical action that is in perfect harmony with the nature of the thought.

Stating this principle from another angle: You choose a Definite Chief Aim and make up your mind that you will carry out that aim or purpose. From the very moment that you make this choice, this aim or purpose should become the dominating thought in your consciousness, and you will be constantly on the alert for facts, information, and knowledge with which to achieve that purpose. From the time that you plant a Definite Chief Aim in your mind, your mind begins, both consciously and unconsciously, to gather and store away the material with which you are to accomplish that purpose.

The principle of psychology through which you can impress your Definite Chief Aim on your subconscious mind is autosuggestion, or suggestion that you repeatedly make to yourself.

Although the technique of planting a thought in your mind has been commented on often in both this and the preceding chapter, the above excerpt from *Law of Success* is the first time that it has been referred to by its proper psychological term: *autosuggestion*. The following, excerpted and adapted from *Think and Grow Rich,* Chapter 4: Autosuggestion, elaborates on the concept of autosuggestion and its relationship to the subconscious mind.

AUTOSUGGESTION: THE MEDIUM FOR INFLUENCING THE SUBCONSCIOUS MIND

Autosuggestion is a term that applies to all suggestions and all self-administered stimuli that reach your mind through any of the five senses. Stated in another way, autosuggestion is self-suggestion. It is the means of communication between that part of the mind where conscious thought takes place, and that part of the mind called the *subconscious mind.*

Through the dominating thoughts that you permit to remain in your conscious mind (whether these thoughts be negative or positive is immaterial), the principle of autosuggestion voluntarily reaches the subconscious mind and influences it with these thoughts.

The subconscious mind resembles a fertile garden spot, in which weeds will grow in abundance, if the seeds of more desirable crops are not sown therein. Autosuggestion is the agency of control through which an individual may voluntarily feed his subconscious mind on thoughts of a creative nature, or, by neglect, permit thoughts of a destructive nature to find their way into this rich garden of the mind.

The preceding section was how Hill explained the basis of autosuggestion in *Law of Success*. The following, excerpted and adapted from *Think and Grow Rich*, Chapter 12: The Subconscious Mind, expands on the previous explanation.

THE SUBCONSCIOUS MIND

The subconscious mind consists of a field of consciousness, in which every impulse of thought that reaches the conscious mind, through any of the five senses, is classified and recorded.

It receives and files sense impressions or thoughts, regardless of their nature. You may voluntarily plant in your subconscious mind any plan, thought, or purpose that you desire to translate into its physical or monetary equivalent. The subconscious acts first on the dominating desires that have been mixed with emotional feeling, such as faith.

The subconscious mind works day and night.

You cannot entirely control your subconscious mind, but you can voluntarily hand over to it any plan, desire, or purpose that you wish transformed into concrete form.

The following is excerpted and adapted from *Think and Grow Rich*, Chapter 4: Autosuggestion.

THE SECRET OF MENTAL POWER

Skepticism, in connection with all new ideas, is characteristic of all human beings.

But if you follow the instructions outlined, your skepticism will soon be replaced by belief, and this, in turn, will soon become crystallized into absolute faith.

Many philosophers have made the statement that man is the master of his own earthly destiny, but most of them have failed to say why he is the master. The reason man may be the master of his own earthly status, and especially his financial status, is thoroughly explained in this chapter.

Man may become the master of himself and of his environment because he has the power to influence his own subconscious mind.

The actual performance of transmuting desire into money involves the use of autosuggestion as an agency by which one may reach, and influence, the subconscious mind. Keep this thought in mind, and you will, at all times, be conscious of the important part the principle of autosuggestion is to play in your efforts to accumulate money through the methods described in this book.

THE POWER OF HABIT

The following comments by Napoleon Hill on the importance of using autosuggestion to create good habits are excerpted and adapted from *Law of Success*, Lesson Two: A Definite Chief Aim.

Having, myself, experienced all the difficulties of one who didn't completely understand how to use autosuggestion, let me tell you a little of what I learned about the principles of habit and autosuggestion.

Habit grows out of doing the same thing or thinking the same thoughts or repeating the same words over and over again. Habit may be likened to the groove in a record, while the human mind may be likened to the needle that fits into that groove. When any habit has been well formed, the mind has a tendency to follow the course of that habit as closely as the needle follows the groove in a record.

Habit is created by repeatedly directing one or more of the five senses of seeing, hearing, smelling, tasting, and touching in a given direction. After habit has been well established, it will automatically control and direct your actions and responses.

When you were a child, you learned how to write by repeatedly directing the muscles of your arm and hand over certain letter outlines, until finally you formed the habit of tracing those outlines. Now you write quickly and easily, without tracing each letter slowly. Writing has become a habit with you.

The principle of habit will take hold of the faculties of your mind just the same as it will influence the physical muscles of your body. The object in writing out and repeating a self-confidence formula is to form the habit of making belief in yourself the dominating thought of your mind until that thought has been thoroughly embedded in your subconscious mind, through the principle of habit.

IS THERE ANY PROOF THAT IT WORKS?

There is another aspect of autosuggestion that should be explained before moving on to the next chapter, Self-Confidence and Faith in Your Abilities. As Hill has made clear, the subconscious will accept a negative suggestion just as readily as it will accept a positive one. It makes no distinction between good and bad, positive and negative, right and wrong. Similarly, it makes no distinction between true and false. It is a fact that if you keep telling yourself something over and over, such as "I am confident and outgoing when I meet new people," even if it is not true, if you do it often enough and with sincere emotion, your subconscious will come to accept it as reality.

As you will learn, this theory has been tested and proven by every kind of motivational professional, from psychiatrists to athletes to NASA astronauts, and as a result it has become one of the basic tenets of contemporary motivation theory, usually stated as follows: The subconscious mind cannot distinguish between what is real and what is vividly imagined.

One of the most frequently cited studies supporting this concept was done with a group of basketball players. The players were divided into three teams, and the players on each team were tested on their ability to make free throws. The teams were then separated for a period of time and each team was given instructions which they were told would improve their abilities.

One team was instructed to practice making baskets on a daily basis. The second team was instructed not to practice during the period and not to even think about basketball.

The third team was also instructed not to practice during the period, but instead the members were told to spend their daily practice time visualizing over and over in their minds every detail in the process of shooting perfect baskets.

At the end of the experiment, the teams were again tested. The team that rested showed a decrease in ability. The team that practiced showed a marked increase in ability. And the team that didn't practice but visualized making baskets showed an increase in ability almost equal to those who had practiced daily.

You can "deceive" your subconscious through autosuggestion. If you convincingly plant an idea in your subconscious, your subconscious will accept and work with the idea as though it were a fact.

But the key word is *convincingly.* If you try to send a message to your subconscious, but in the back of your mind you have doubts whether it will work, your subconscious will pick up the doubts too. As a result, you will have sent mixed messages that cancel each other out.

That is why Hill stresses the importance of emotionalizing your desire. Your subconscious will not judge if it is true or false, positive or negative, but it does respond to the power of the input (how emotionalized the thought is), which, as noted above, is the subject of the next chapter.

To close this chapter, on the following page we offer a review of the basic concepts of autosuggestion and the subconscious as a way to set the stage for the following chapters that build on the foundation of a Definite Chief Aim.

AUTOSUGGESTION AND THE SUBCONSCIOUS

The Method for Influencing Your Mind: First, you must choose to change the thoughts that dominate your actions by fixing your Definite Chief Aim in your conscious mind. Then you must reinforce your Definite Chief Aim in your subconscious mind through auto-suggestion.

The Conscious Mind: Your conscious mind receives information through the five senses of sight, smell, taste, hearing, and touch. Your conscious mind keeps track of what you need for thinking and operating, and it filters out what you don't need. Your conscious mind (and what your memory retains) is the intelligence with which you normally think, reason, and plan.

The Subconscious Mind: Your subconscious has access to all the same information your conscious receives, but it doesn't reason the way your conscious mind does. It takes everything literally. It doesn't make value judgments, it doesn't filter, and it doesn't forget. It doesn't draw a distinction between good and bad, positive and negative. The only thing your subconscious responds to is the intensity with which the idea is planted. The stronger the emotion attached to an idea when planted in your subconscious, the more prominent that idea will be.

Self-Suggestion: This is a suggestion that you give to yourself by thinking it, envisioning it in your imagination, saying it to yourself, or writing it down. If you wish to change some aspect of yourself, you can do so by creating a self-suggestion that tells your "self" that you want to make the change. By repeating your self-suggestion over and over, you will not only fix your desire to change in your conscious mind, but it will also become embedded in your subconscious mind.

Autosuggestion: This is a suggestion that has become planted in your subconscious and is now your automatic response. It is any outside suggestion or self-suggestion that has become so deeply fixed in your subconscious that it is the response which automatically flashes into your mind. It becomes your habit, your natural reaction.

The Key Motivation Theory: The subconscious mind cannot distinguish between what is real and what is vividly imagined.

Chapter Three

SELF-CONFIDENCE AND FAITH IN YOUR ABILITIES

WHAT WOULD NAPOLEON HILL DO?

Faith in yourself is a state of mind. You can change your state of mind through autosuggestion.

To enhance his faith in himself, Napoleon Hill would first confirm that his Definite Chief Aim is a realistic possibility that could be accomplished by an individual such as he.

Then he would focus every ounce of emotion he could muster into convincing his subconscious that he believes, without question, that he is capable of doing what needs to be done to achieve his desire.

Napoleon Hill was famous for writing aphorisms and maxims, and among the most famous was his statement that "whatever the mind of man can conceive and believe, man can achieve." The preceding chapter was about conceiving; this chapter is about believing.

As is made very clear in the previous chapter, when you are faced with making a major decision in your life, or you have a burning desire to achieve some major objective, you must first define in your own mind exactly what you want, then focus in on the part of that desire which is right at the center of it. That is your Definite Chief Aim. Once you have identified your Definite Chief Aim, and you can create a vision of that Definite Chief Aim in your mind, you must now emotionalize that desire. Emotionalizing your Definite Chief Aim is what this chapter is about.

As you learn the techniques for injecting emotion into your Definite Chief Aim, it is most important to keep in mind what was said at the end of the preceding chapter about the subconscious mind not being able to distinguish between what is real and what is vividly imagined. Your subconscious will not judge if it is true or false, positive or negative, but it does respond to how emotionalized your desire is.

The following section explains how, by infusing your desire with emotion, it will come back to you as faith in yourself and in your abilities. This excerpt is adapted from *Think and Grow Rich*, Chapter 3: Faith.

FAITH IS A STATE OF MIND

Faith is a state of mind that may be induced, or created, by affirmation or repeated instructions to the subconscious mind, through the principle of autosuggestion.

As an illustration, consider the purpose for which you are reading this book. The object is to acquire the ability to transmute the intangible thought impulse of desire into its physical counterpart: money. By following the instructions on autosuggestion and the subconscious mind, you may convince the subconscious mind that you believe you will receive what you ask for, and your subconscious will act upon that belief, which your subconscious mind passes back to you in the form of "faith," followed by definite plans for procuring what you desire.

Repetition of affirmation is like giving orders to your subconscious mind, and is the only known method of voluntary development of the emotion of faith.

Any impulse of thought that is repeatedly passed on to the subconscious mind is, finally, accepted and acted upon by the subconscious, which proceeds to translate that impulse into its physical equivalent by the most practical procedure available.

All thoughts that have been emotionalized (given feeling) and mixed with faith, begin immediately to translate themselves into their physical equivalent or counterpart.

The emotions, or the "feeling" portion of thoughts, are the factors that give thoughts vitality, life, and action.

NOT JUST FAITH, BUT APPLIED FAITH

In *Law of Success,* the lesson that corresponds to this chapter is titled Self-Confidence, which is synonymous with *faith* as Napoleon Hill uses the term. In *Think and Grow Rich,* the relevant chapter is actually entitled Faith.

In both books, Hill makes it very clear that the kind of faith he is referring to is not religious faith. The faith that Hill means is faith in yourself, the unquestioning belief in your abilities, and the complete, unwavering confidence that you can accomplish what you are setting out to do.

In order to make it even clearer that he was not speaking of religious faith, in Hill's later writings he chose to refer to the concept as applied faith. When the word *applied* is added to the word *faith,* you have a term that is used in the same way you talk about applied pressure or applied force: it is faith with power behind it.

If you have faith, you don't just sit around "having" it. Having faith without applying it is meaningless. Only when you *apply* your faith do you demonstrate that you really do have it. Faith is not something you get; faith is something you have within, and it is up to you to use it.

Faith applied to your Definite Chief Aim or purpose is like adding the yeast when you bake bread. Yeast is what makes bread something more than a flat mixture of flour, water, and salt, and faith is what makes your aim or purpose more than a collection of words repeated over and over.

Applied faith is what you add to your desire—your Definite Chief Aim or purpose—in order to make it work.

YOU CAN CREATE FAITH THROUGH AUTOSUGGESTION

Faith is an emotion. Having faith is beyond "knowing" in your mind that you can do something; it is "feeling certain" that you can do it. If you lack faith in your ability, you can create that faith and self-confidence by using autosuggestion to convince your inner-self (your subconscious mind) that contrary to what it has previously believed, you are in fact capable of doing what it takes to achieve your desire.

In the previous quotation from *Think and Grow Rich,* Hill makes a subtle but important point when he says, "You may convince the subconscious mind that you believe you will receive what you ask for, and your subconscious will act upon that belief, which your subconscious mind passes back to you in the form of '*faith.*'"

The way the process works is for you to convince your subconscious that you believe you are capable of doing what it takes, then your subconscious will pass it back to you as faith that you will receive what you desire. The key is that it is a two-step sequence. You don't convince your inner-self that you have faith; you convince your inner-self that you can accomplish your desire. Then, when your inner-self is convinced of that, it is your inner-self that tells you that you have faith in yourself.

Faith is not something you get by telling your inner-self that you have it. Faith is something that comes from within. In order for your inner-self to tell you that you have faith, it must believe that you have the ability to achieve your desire.

When you use autosuggestion to create faith within yourself, you don't repeat over and over to yourself, "I have faith I can do what I desire." Instead, you tell your subconscious, in the present tense, that you are *already* doing what you desire. You keep reinforcing your positive statement in the present tense, until your subconscious—which can't tell the difference between what is real and what is vividly imagined—becomes so convinced that you are capable of doing what you desire, that whenever the subject comes up, the first thought that comes to your mind is that you can do it. In short, you have faith in your ability.

Many readers will have doubts that you can convince yourself of something just by saying it over and over, but again we stress that this concept is based on a well-accepted principle of psychology and, more importantly, on the vast number of people who have bought Hill's books and have attested to the fact that Napoleon Hill's system has worked for them.

The rest of this chapter, and the three chapters that follow, deal with this theory in such great detail we are certain they will allay any concerns you have, and you will be able to use the technique with complete confidence.

But for now we return to Hill's elaboration on the concept, which is excerpted and adapted from *Think and Grow Rich,* Chapter 4: Auto-suggestion.

SEE AND FEEL MONEY IN YOUR HANDS

You were instructed, in the seven steps described in the chapter on Desire, to read aloud twice daily the statement of your desire for money, and to see and feel yourself already in possession of the money!

By following these instructions, you communicate the object of your desire directly to your subconscious mind in a spirit of absolute faith. Through repetition of this procedure, you voluntarily create thought habits that are favorable to your efforts to transmute desire into its monetary equivalent.

Remember, therefore, when reading aloud the statement of your desire, that the mere reading of the words is of no consequence unless you mix emotion, or feeling, with your words. Your subconscious mind recognizes and acts only on thoughts that have been well mixed with emotion or feeling.

This is a fact of such importance as to warrant repetition in practically every chapter, because the lack of understanding of this is the main reason the majority of people who try to apply the principle of autosuggestion get no desirable results.

Plain, unemotional words do not influence the subconscious mind. You will get no appreciable results until you learn to reach your subconscious mind with thoughts or spoken words that have been well emotionalized with belief.

Your ability to use the principle of autosuggestion will depend, very largely, on your capacity to concentrate upon a given desire until that desire becomes a burning obsession.

Do not become discouraged if you cannot control and direct your emotions the first time you try to do so. Remember, there is no such possibility as something for nothing. The price of ability to influence your subconscious mind is everlasting persistence in applying the principles described here. You cannot develop the desired ability for a lower price.

You, and you alone, must decide whether or not the reward for which you are striving (the "money-consciousness") is worth the price you must pay for it in effort.

MONEY-CONSCIOUSNESS

Napoleon Hill says that there is a vast difference between wishing and desiring. All your wishing and hoping for success accomplishes nothing. The only thing that counts is what you do to condition your mind for success, and then what you do to make it happen. And this brings us to what some consider to be the most controversial aspect of Hill's books: money-consciousness.

Money-consciousness, or prosperity-consciousness, is the term Hill uses to describe the state of mind that attracts riches.

You can grow rich spiritually, emotionally, or intellectually, and to some degree all of those things are true for the students of Hill's philosophy, but the truth is that most people who read his books do so to learn how to grow richer financially.

If you are going to adopt Hill's money-consciousness methods, you must be prepared to accept some ways of thinking and doing things that are much more demanding than most other motivational or self-help programs.

To succeed by using the Napoleon Hill method, you must first commit yourself to a Definite Chief Aim that offers the possibility to yield the riches you desire. Next, through autosuggestion, you fire up your faith in your ability until you are convinced that you can achieve that aim. Now, in order to turn that aim into money-consciousness, you must begin to see everything in your life from the point of view of how it relates to your Definite Chief Aim or purpose.

And remember, to be money-conscious, you must begin to evaluate the things that interest you in terms of whether they will help you to achieve your aim.

SUCCESS-CONSCIOUSNESS IS NOT FOR EVERYONE

What Napoleon Hill offers is a philosophy of personal achievement and a specific method that, if followed, will produce success and make you rich. But it will also change who you are, and some of the changes may not be entirely to your liking.

It is up to you to decide if you are prepared to commit yourself to a method that is this focused on being a success and making money. Your challenge is to decide what your monetary aim or purpose is, and then to decide how persistent you will be in pursuing your desire to have that money. You will become rich in direct proportion to the degree to which you apply these principles.

So the question is whether you should choose a Definite Chief Aim and go into it with everything you've got, or whether you should play it safe as you give it a shot but while not letting yourself go too overboard.

You may be able to make an argument for either point of view, but if you decide to put less than 100 percent into it, you must accept that what you get back will be less than 100 percent of what you could have achieved.

MOTIVES AND MOTIVATION

Throughout *Law of Success* and *Think and Grow Rich,* Hill says that you must emotionalize your Definite Chief Aim or purpose; you must mix emotion with it in order to burn it into your subconscious. To find the most effective way to emotionalize your desire, you must look inward and identify what gets you going, what stirs your emotions, what motivates you to want it.

Hill says there are nine doors through which the human mind can be entered and influenced. These nine doors are the emotions by which all people are motivated. Learn to work with these nine emotions and you will not only know how to motivate others, but you will also know how to motivate yourself.

Your challenge is to find the connection between your desire and each of these motives identified by Hill. Use the emotion that it stirs in you to help burn your Definite Chief Aim or purpose into your subconscious mind.

On the following pages you will find Hill's motives listed in the approximate order of their importance and their greatest usefulness.

1. **The motive of self-preservation:** The more you believe that your future depends on achieving your aim, the more powerfully emotionalized your desire will be. If you really are putting everything you have into your aim, your future well-being will truly be in jeopardy and you will be motivated to do anything you can to keep from failing.

2. **The motive of financial gain:** For many people, money is the barometer of success and, quite simply, the more money that is at stake, the more powerful the motivation. The degree to which this is true for you will affect how strongly money will emotionalize your desire and motivate you to achieve your aim.

3. **The motive of love:** This is probably the easiest motive to understand. Our history is full of stories of people motivated to great achievement for the love of another person or for love of country or cause. If you have a true heartfelt love for your aim or purpose, nothing could be a stronger motivator.

4. **The motive of sexuality:** Love is psychology, but sex is biology and there is an innate biological drive that motivates men and women to seek sexual satisfaction. You have heard it a million times: "sex sells." You will powerfully motivate yourself to achieve your aim if you can convince yourself that achieving it will make you more attractive to the opposite sex.

5. **The motive of desire for power and fame:** Why people desire power or fame is a complicated sociological question, but there is no doubt that modern society tells us both are valuable, so they have become powerful motivators. As with money, love, and sex, if you convince yourself that achieving your aim will give you more power or fame, you can greatly increase your drive to succeed.

6. **The motive of fear:** Napoleon Hill says there are six basic fears: fear of poverty, fear of criticism, fear of ill health, fear of the loss

of love, fear of old age, and fear of death. Here the motive is not so much to gain something as it is to overcome. If you believe the achievement of your aim or purpose will lessen any of those fears, the boost it will give your desire is obvious.

7. **The motive of revenge:** Although the desire for revenge may not be the most admirable quality, it is not hard to understand how it can be a powerful motivator if succeeding at your aim or purpose also means that you prove to your detractors you were right. If succeeding at your aim or purpose can be tied to the idea that you will get your just desserts, it can add mighty impetus to your effort.

8. **The motive of freedom (of body and mind):** Although not true everywhere in the world, in America the concepts of individual rights and freedom are integral parts of the fabric of our society. If your aim or desire is linked to your personal freedom, you will have tapped into the very principle upon which this country was founded.

9. **The motive of a desire to create or to build in thought or in material:** Probably the best-known theory of human motivation is Abraham Maslow's Hierarchy of Needs, a theory in psychology contending that once humans have met their "basic needs," they seek to satisfy successively "higher needs." Very near the top of the pyramid of needs, second only to spiritual transcendence, appears the desire to create or build. This is a motive that is more for the inner you. It is a desire for personal satisfaction, and if you can feel pride and satisfaction by achieving your aim or goal, you will increase your motivation manifold.

Do you want to succeed because succeeding will give you the confidence to do something? Or do you want to succeed because you are overflowing with the desire to share your good fortune? Or maybe the real reason you want to succeed is so you can show up your competitors or get even with your detractors.

Whatever your reasons, the end result is that you must want to succeed so badly you can almost taste it. Take that passion, love, anger, fear, or whatever it is, and use it to emotionalize your Definite Chief Aim or purpose.

The following excerpt is adapted from *Law of Success,* Lesson Three: Self-Confidence.

THE MAN IN THE MIRROR

No one knows what hidden forces lie dormant within you. You, yourself, do not know your capacity for achievement, and you never will know until you come in contact with the particular stimulus that arouses you to greater action and extends your vision, develops your self-confidence, and moves you with a deeper desire to achieve.

I have in mind a typical example of this, and of what a person can accomplish when he or she awakens to a full understanding of the value of self-confidence. The incident to which I refer happened in the city of Chicago, while I was engaged in the work of character analysis.

One day a homeless man presented himself at my office and asked for an interview. As I looked up from my work and greeted him, he said, "I have come to see the man who wrote this little book," and he removed from his pocket a copy of a book entitled *Self-Confidence,* which I had written many years previously. "It must have been the hand of fate," he continued, "that slipped this book into my pocket yesterday afternoon, because I was about ready to go out there and punch a hole in Lake Michigan. I had about come to the conclusion that everything and everybody, including God, had it in for me, until I read this book and it gave me a new viewpoint and brought me the courage and the hope that sustained me through the night.

"I made up my mind that if I could see the man who wrote this book, he could help me get on my feet again. Now I am here and I would like to know what you can do for a man like me."

While he was speaking I had been studying him from head to foot and I am frank to admit that down deep in my heart I did not believe there was anything I could do for him, but I did not wish to tell him so. The glassy stare in his eyes, the lines of discouragement in his face, the posture of his body, the ten days' growth of beard on his face, the nervous manner about this man all conveyed to me the impression that he was hopeless, but I did not have the heart to tell him.

So I asked him to sit down and tell me his whole story. I asked him to be perfectly frank and tell me, as nearly as possible, just what had brought him down to the ragged edge of life. I promised him that after I heard his entire story, I would then tell him whether or not I could be of service to him.

He related his story, in lengthy detail, the sum and substance of which was this: He had invested his entire fortune in a small manufacturing business. When the world war began in 1914, it was impossible for him to get the raw materials necessary for the operation of his factory, and he therefore failed. The loss of his money broke his heart and so disturbed his mind that he left his wife and children and went to live on the streets. He had brooded over his loss until he reached the point at which he was actually contemplating suicide.

After he had finished his story, I said to him: "I have listened to you with a great deal of interest, and I wish that there was something I could do to help you. But there is absolutely nothing."

He became as pale as he will be when he is laid away in a coffin. He settled back in his chair and dropped his chin on his chest, as much as to say, "That settles it." I waited for a few seconds, then said:

"While there is nothing that I can do for you, there is a man in this building to whom I will introduce you, if you wish, who can help you regain your lost fortune and put you back on your feet again." These words had barely fallen from my lips when he jumped up, grabbed me by the hands, and said, "For God's sake lead me to this man."

It was encouraging to note that he had asked this "for God's sake." This indicated that there was still a spark of hope within him. So I took him by the arm and led him out into the laboratory where my psychological tests in character analysis were conducted, and stood with him in front of what looked to be a curtain over a door. I pulled the curtain aside and uncovered a tall mirror in which he saw himself from head to foot. Pointing my finger at the glass, I said:

"There is the man to whom I promised to introduce you. He is the only man in this world who can put you back on your feet again. And unless you sit down and become acquainted with that man, as you never became acquainted with him before, you might just as well go on over and 'punch a hole' in Lake Michigan, because you will be of no value to yourself or to the world until you know this man better."

He stepped over to the glass, rubbed his hands over his bearded face, studied himself from head to foot for a few moments, then he stepped back, dropped his head, and began to weep. I knew that the lesson had been driven home, so I led him back to the elevator and sent him on his way. I never expected to see him again, and I doubted that the lesson would be sufficient to help him regain his place in the world, because he seemed too far gone for redemption. He seemed to be not only down, but almost out.

A few days later I met this man on the street. His transformation had been so complete that I hardly recognized him. He was walking briskly, with his head tilted back. That old, shifting, nervous posture of his body was gone. He was dressed in new clothes from head to foot. He looked prosperous and he felt prosperous. He stopped me and related what had happened to bring about his rapid transformation from a state of abject failure to one of hope and promise.

"I was just on my way to your office," he explained, "to bring you the good news. I went out the very day that I was in your office, a down-and-out tramp, and despite my appearance I sold myself at a salary of $3,000 a year [which amounts to around $50,000 or $60,000 in contemporary terms].

"Think of it, man, $3,000 a year! And my employer advanced me money enough to buy some new clothes, as you can see for yourself. He also advanced me some money to send home to my family, and I am once more on the road to success.

"It seems like a dream when I think that only a few days ago I had lost hope and faith and courage, and was actually contemplating suicide.

"I was coming to tell you that one of these days, when you are least expecting me, I will pay you another visit, and when I do I will be a successful man. I will bring with me a blank check, signed and made payable to you, and you may fill in the amount, because you have saved me from myself by introducing me to myself—that self I never knew until you stood me in front of that mirror and pointed out the real me."

As he turned and departed into the crowded streets of Chicago, I saw, for the first time in my life, what strength and power and possibility lie hidden in the mind of the person who has never discovered the value of self-reliance. Then and there I made up my mind that I, too, would stand in front of that same mirror and point an accusing finger at myself for not having discovered the lesson that I had helped another to learn. I did stand before that same mirror. And as I did, I then and there fixed in my mind, as my definite purpose in life, the determination to help men and women discover the forces that lie sleeping within them. The book you hold in your hands is evidence that my definite purpose is being carried out.

The man whose story I have related here is now the president of one of the largest and most successful concerns of its kind in America, with a business that extends from coast to coast and from Canada to Mexico.

Where fear controls, noteworthy achievement becomes an impossibility. You are condemning yourself to poverty, misery, and failure, or you are driving yourself on toward the heights of great achievement, solely by the thoughts you think. If you demand success of yourself, and also back up this demand with intelligent action, you are sure to win. Bear in mind, though, that there is a difference between demanding success and just merely wishing for it. You should find out what this difference is and take advantage of it.

Never mind "what they will say," because you might as well know that "they" will be of little aid to you in your climb up the mountainside of life toward the object of your definite purpose.

You have within you all the power necessary to get whatever you want or need in this world, and about the best way to avail yourself of this power is to believe in yourself.

The following commentary is excerpted and adapted from *Think and Grow Rich: The Workbook,* Chapter 4: Faith in Your Ability.

IS IT JUST A WISH—OR A DEFINITE AIM?

Repetition of your Definite Chief Aim or purpose is the primary method of planting it in your subconscious. However, don't make the mistake of thinking that it is the saying of the words over and over that somehow makes what you want magically happen. There are no magic words that will suddenly make your desires appear. This is psychology, not hocus-pocus. The repetition is simply an effective method of planting an idea in your subconscious so that it will become your habit to think that way.

As Hill stresses often, you may wish for something to happen, but with a Definite Chief Aim or purpose you must do more than wish; you must *believe* it will happen. If, deep down, you don't truly believe it is something that is logically within your reach, you won't really have the faith that you can do it.

YOU HAVE TO BELIEVE IT

If you are a forty-year-old who has spent your adult life in sales, it is not reasonable to set a Definite Chief Aim of being the astronaut pilot of the space shuttle—that is a wish or a dream, not a Definite Chief Aim or purpose. And not because the aim is too fanciful, but for purely practical reasons. At forty your age is against you and so are the entrance requirements. To qualify you would need to spend years learning advanced physics and aeronautics, not to mention the difficulty of qualifying to fly jets, the physical fitness requirements, and the fact that there are only a limited number of shuttle flights and many qualified astronauts ahead of you.

The point is that although you may want something to happen, and you may follow the Hill formula by repeating over and over that it *is* happening, unless there is a reasonable possibility, all the repetition in the world will not make it happen. Furthermore, by selecting an unrealistic aim and failing at it, you will have undermined your faith in yourself and created doubts in your mind about the method.

There is a fine balance between choosing a Definite Chief Aim that is challenging and choosing one that is unrealistic. But that does not mean you should choose easy-to-accomplish goals. In fact, Hill suggests choosing aims that cause you to stretch yourself.

In choosing a Definite Chief Aim or purpose, you should start from the assumption that if there is nothing mental or physical preventing you from learning the skills or the knowledge needed, there is almost nothing that can't be accomplished if you have enough time to perfect the needed skills or ability.

The only thing that should restrict your choice of a Definite Chief Aim is if it requires educational degrees or minimum entrance requirements that you have not yet achieved, or if it requires some specialized talent or physical or mental capacity that you do not possess. In many cases even that should not stop you if what you want can be learned within a reasonable amount of time.

It is true that all the faith in the world won't get you a job that requires a PhD when you only have a high school diploma, but all that means is that you've selected the wrong Definite Chief Aim. Your aim shouldn't be the job; it should be getting your PhD. Once you've done that, your *next* aim can be getting the job.

FEAR IS THE OPPOSITE OF FAITH

Faith is the art of believing by doing—and fear is the opposite of faith.

First, let us clarify that there is a difference between fear, as Hill uses it in this chapter, and the defense mechanism that is hardwired into your brain. The reaction to real danger, pain, or evil is called the fight-or-flight response, and it describes the instant reaction of your body and mind as you prepare to either attack or escape.

The fear that prompts the fight-or-flight response is both real and immediate: something happens, you respond. But there is another kind of imagined or anticipatory fear. These are the "what-if" fears. They are not real. Nothing has actually happened to you, but you become agitated by imagining what *might* happen.

The following is excerpted and adapted from *Think and Grow Rich*, Chapter 15: How to Outwit The Six Ghosts of Fear.

THE SIX BASIC FEARS

The purpose of this chapter is to turn the spotlight of attention on the cause and the cure of the six basic fears. Before you can master an enemy, you must know its name, its habits, and its place of abode. As you read, analyze yourself carefully and determine which, if any, of the six common fears have attached themselves to you.

At one time or another every person suffers from some combination of these fears. Most people are fortunate if they do not suffer from the entire six. Here these fears are named in their order of most common appearance:

The Six Basic Fears of Mankind

1. The fear of poverty
2. The fear of old age
3. The fear of criticism
4. The fear of loss of love of someone
5. The fear of ill health
6. The fear of death

As the first step in the elimination of these six evils, let us examine the sources from which we inherited them.

Napoleon Hill says that because such fears are only in your imagination, and because you can control the thoughts that you think, you can and must control this kind of what-if fear.

You cannot be positive that you will succeed and at the same time be fearful that you will fail. It is impossible to hold both a positive and a negative in your mind at the same time.

As Hill has stressed over and over, your mind will attract anything it dwells upon. If your mind dwells on a negative such as fear, you will become full of fear and worry.

As simplistic as it may sound, the only solution to rid yourself of fear is to stop thinking about what you fear. You either believe that you will achieve your aim or purpose, or you fear that you will not achieve it. It is up to you to stop dwelling on the fear of what might happen and to stay focused on accomplishing your aim or purpose.

The following is also excerpted and adapted from *Think and Grow Rich*, Chapter 15: How to Outwit The Six Ghosts of Fear.

You can create nothing that you do not first conceive in the form of an impulse of thought. The following statement is of even greater importance: Thought impulses begin immediately to translate themselves into their physical equivalent, whether those thoughts are voluntary or involuntary. Even thought impulses that are picked up by mere chance (thoughts that have been released by other minds) may determine your financial, business, professional, or social destiny just as surely as the thoughts that you create by intent and design.

This circumstance also explains why some people seem to be lucky, while others of equal or greater ability, training, experience, and brain capacity seem destined to have misfortune. The explanation is that you have the ability to completely control your own mind. With this control, you may open your mind to the thought impulses that are being released by other brains, or you can close the doors tightly and admit only thought impulses of your own choice.

Nature has endowed human beings with absolute control over only one thing, and that one thing is thought. This fact, coupled with the additional fact that everything we create begins in the form of a thought, leads us very near to the principle by which fear may be mastered.

If it is true that all thought has a tendency to clothe itself in its physical equivalent, it is equally true that thought impulses of fear and poverty cannot be translated into terms of courage and financial gain.

THE DISASTER OF WORRY
AND DESTRUCTIVE THINKING

Worry is a state of mind based upon fear. It works slowly but persistently. It is insidious and subtle. Step by step it digs itself in until it paralyzes the reasoning faculty and destroys self-confidence and initiative. Worry is a form of sustained fear caused by indecision. Therefore it is a state of mind that can be controlled.

An unsettled mind is helpless. Indecision makes an unsettled mind. Most individuals lack the will-power to reach decisions promptly and to stand by them after they have been made.

We do not worry over conditions once we have reached a decision to follow a definite line of action. Decision can also prevent one's acceptance of undesired circumstances.

Through indecision, the six basic fears become translated into a state of worry. Relieve yourself forever of the fear of death by reaching a decision to accept death as an inescapable event. Eliminate the fear of old age by reaching a decision to accept it not as a handicap but as a great blessing that carries with it wisdom, self-control, and understanding. Master the fear of loss of love by reaching a decision to get along without love, if that is necessary. Defeat the fear of criticism by reaching a decision not to worry about what other people think, do, or say. Overcome the fear of ill health by the decision to forget symptoms. And whip the fear of poverty by reaching a decision to get along with whatever wealth you can accumulate without worry.

If your mind is filled with fear, you not only destroy your own chances of intelligent action, but you transmit these destructive vibrations to the minds of all who come into contact with you, and you destroy their chances too.

Even a dog or a horse knows when its master lacks courage. It will pick up the vibrations of fear given off by its master, and behave accordingly. The vibrations of fear pass from one mind to another just as quickly and as surely as the sound of the human voice passes from the broadcasting station to a radio receiver.

The person who constantly speaks of negative or destructive thoughts is practically certain to experience the results of those words in the form of destructive feedback. Negative thoughts not only affect others but they also embed themselves in the subconscious mind of the person releasing them, and there become a part of that person's character.

You control your own mind; you have the power to feed it whatever thought impulses you choose. With this goes the responsibility of using your mind constructively. You are the master of your own earthly destiny just as surely as you have the power to control your own thoughts.

You may influence, direct, and eventually control your own environment, making your life what you want it to be. Or you may neglect to make your life what you want, and you will be adrift on the seas of "circumstance" where you will be tossed like a woodchip on the waves of the ocean.

FAITH CAN WORK IN REVERSE

Napoleon Hill says, "Faith is not something you get, it is something you have." He then adds, "But if you are not careful you may be using it in reverse."

It's true that your faith is something you have and it does not come from any outside source. There is nowhere you can go to get faith in yourself, and no one you can ask to give you faith in yourself. Faith is similar to intelligence or talent—it is something you have within you. But your faith can be subject to outside influences, and those outside influences can be positive or they can be negative. It is the negative influences that Hill is referring to when he speaks of using your faith "in reverse."

The following is excerpted and adapted from *Think and Grow Rich,* Chapter 3: Faith.

NO ONE IS "DOOMED" TO BAD LUCK

The subconscious mind will translate into its physical equivalent a thought impulse of a negative or destructive nature, just as readily as it will act upon thought impulses of a positive or constructive nature. This accounts for the strange phenomenon that so many millions of people experience, referred to as "misfortune," or "bad luck."

There are millions of people who believe themselves "doomed" to poverty and failure, because of some strange force over which they believe they have no control. They are the creators of their own "misfortunes," because of this negative belief, which is picked up by the subconscious mind and translated into its physical equivalent.

Your belief, or faith, is the element that determines the action of your subconscious mind. There is nothing to hinder you from "deceiving" your subconscious mind when giving it instructions through autosuggestion. (Remember, the subconscious mind cannot distinguish between what is real and what is vividly imagined.)

To make this "deceit" more realistic, conduct yourself just as you would if you were already in possession of the material thing that you are demanding when you call upon your subconscious mind.

The subconscious mind will transmute into its physical equivalent, by the most direct and practical media available, any order that is given to it in a state of belief or faith that the order will be carried out.

Surely, enough has been said to give a starting point from which you may acquire the ability to mix faith with any order given to the subconscious mind. Perfection will come through practice. It cannot come by merely reading instructions.

It is essential for you to encourage the positive emotions as the dominating forces of your mind, and to discourage—and eliminate—the negative emotions.

A mind dominated by positive emotions becomes a favorable abode for the state of mind known as faith. A mind so dominated may, at will, give the subconscious mind instructions, which it will accept and act upon immediately.

A positive attitude needs your encouragement, but with a negative attitude it is just the opposite. You don't even have to try to be negative. Negativity comes naturally, and it easily takes over without any effort on your part.

Hill often used the example of a garden to illustrate what happens when you let your guard down. By carefully planning what you plant, and by nurturing and tending the plants, you can grow a thriving and bountiful garden. However, if you leave it untended, it won't just stay fallow and do nothing. Even though you don't encourage weeds, they will soon find their way in, and before you know it they will take over the plot and destroy everything else.

There is a maxim that says if you are not part of the solution, you are part of the problem. Stated another way, if you don't actively focus your positive energy on your aim, you are not being neutral; you are in fact encouraging negativity, which erodes your faith.

In the following excerpt adapted from *Law of Success,* Lesson Three: Self-Confidence, Napoleon Hill gives two examples of people who have allowed faith to work in reverse without even realizing that they are using autosuggestion on themselves. In both cases, the subjects have accepted the negative suggestions that other people have made to them, and they have replayed those suggestions over and over in their minds until they have come to believe them.

Hill begins by commenting on the power of autosuggestion.

Perhaps none of the great forces of nature are more available for our personal growth and self-improvement than is the principle of autosuggestion. But ignorance of this force is leading the majority of people to apply it so that it acts as a hindrance and not as a help.

Following are examples that show how this misapplication of a great force of nature takes place.

Here is a man who has been well schooled and has the ability to render the world some needed service. Somewhere, sometime, he has heard it said that modesty is a great virtue and that to push himself to the front of the stage in the game of life shows egotism. He quietly slips in through the back door and takes a seat at the rear while other players in the game of life boldly step to the front. He remains in the back row because he fears "what they will say." Public opinion, or what he believes to be public opinion, has him pushed to the rear and the world hears little of him. His schooling counts for little because he is afraid to let the world know that he has had it. He is constantly suggesting to himself (thus using the great force of autosuggestion to his own detriment) that he should remain in the background lest he be criticized, as if criticism would do him any damage or defeat his purpose.

Here is a woman who was born of poor parents. Since the first day that she can remember, she has seen evidence of poverty. She has heard talk of poverty. She has felt the icy hand of poverty on her shoulders and it has so impressed her that she fixes it in her mind as a curse to which she must submit. Quite unconsciously, she permits herself to fall victim to the belief "once poor always poor" until that belief becomes the dominating thought of her mind.

Autosuggestion is rapidly relegating her to the back of the stage of life. Finally she becomes a quitter. Ambition is gone. Opportunity no longer comes her way, or if it does she hasn't the vision to see it. She has accepted her fate! It is a well-established fact that the faculties of the mind, like the limbs of the body, atrophy and wither away if not used. Self-confidence is no exception. It develops when used but disappears if not used.

Inaction leads to atrophy and this, in turn, leads to the loss of ambition and self-confidence. The person who has quit struggling because effort is no longer necessary is literally applying the principle of autosuggestion, undermining his or her own power of self-confidence and faith. Without these essential qualities, an individual will be carried through life on the wings of uncertainty, just as a dry leaf may be carried here and there in the stray winds.

The following commentary is excerpted from *Think and Grow Rich: The Workbook,* Chapter 4: Faith in Your Ability.

HOW TO INCREASE YOUR FAITH

Having faith, as Hill uses the term, means that you have belief in yourself and in your ability to succeed. People who don't believe in themselves generally have low expectations, and there is considerable research that supports the idea that your expectations have a lot to do with how successful you are. If you expect to win, you will win. If you expect to fail, you will fail.

There was a famous experiment done in 1968 by Jane Elliot with her third-grade class. First the school children were divided into two groups based on the color of their eyes, and Elliot told them that blue eyes were better.

Within very little time it was clear that the blue-eyed children were acting superior and the children in the brown-eyed group were performing more poorly than they had before.

Then she switched it around and told them that brown eyes were better. As a result, the brown-eyed children became accelerated and the blue-eyed children fell behind. Nothing had changed with the children except their expectations.

Robert Rosenthal of Harvard University came up with an interesting twist on that study. He administered an IQ test to all students in an elementary school, then he picked 20 percent of the students purely at random, but he told their teacher that the test had identified those students as "intellectual bloomers."

Eight months later he tested the entire student body again and found that in the first and second grades the children whose teachers had expected them to show gains actually gained between ten and fifteen IQ points.

Again, the only difference was expectation, and in this case it was the expectations the teachers had for the children.

Rosenthal did a similar experiment with rats. He gave twelve experimenters five rats each. Although the rats were identical, he told the experimenters that half of the rats were "maze-bright" and the other half were "maze-dull." At the end of the experiment the rats whose trainers thought they were "maze-bright" did better than the so-called "maze-dull" rats.

Although the rats were identical, somehow the expectations of the trainers were conveyed to the rats, and the rats responded accordingly. Or it could have been that the trainers unconsciously tried to live up to the expectations, and that may have affected the results.

In *How to Make Luck: 7 Secrets Lucky People Use to Succeed,* author Marc Myers tells of a research program done with a group of people who considered themselves lucky and another group who thought of themselves as unlucky. When they were each asked to call a series of coin tosses, it turned out that both groups averaged the same number of right guesses.

The lucky group wasn't really any more lucky than the unlucky group. But by interviewing each group, the researchers found that in general the so-called lucky group remembered the good things that happened to them in their lives, while the unlucky group tended to dwell on the bad things. In short, the only difference was in the lucky group's expectations.

A final example that makes the point is quoted from the September 2006 issue of *Money* magazine, in an article called Road Trip to Riches. The writer tells of an experiment developed by a British researcher, Richard Wiseman, who also worked with groups of people who considered themselves to be lucky or unlucky. He asked each to count the photographs in a newspaper.

The unluckies spent several minutes flipping through and counting the photos. The lucky people got it in a few seconds.

How?

On the second page of the newspaper Wiseman had inserted a message in giant headline type: "Stop counting—there are 43 photographs in this newspaper." The lucky people, always on the lookout for unexpected good fortune, spotted it right away. The unlucky people, whose minds are closed to such signs, missed it completely.

The following is excerpted and adapted from *Law of Success,* Lesson Three: Self-Confidence.

SELF-CONFIDENCE FORMULA

You learned in the lesson on your Definite Chief Aim that any idea that you firmly fix in your subconscious mind, by repeated affirmation, automatically becomes a plan or blueprint that an unseen power uses in directing your efforts toward the attainment of the objective named in the plan.

You have also learned that the principle through which you may fix in your mind any idea you choose is called autosuggestion, which simply means a suggestion that you give to your own mind.

We come now to the point at which you are ready to take hold of the principle of autosuggestion and make direct use of it in developing yourself into a positive, dynamic, self-reliant person. You are instructed to copy the following formula, and once you have transcribed it, sign it and commit it to memory:

1. I know that I have the ability to achieve the object of my definite purpose, therefore I demand of myself persistent, aggressive, and continuous action toward its attainment.

2. I realize that the dominating thoughts of my mind will eventually reproduce themselves in outward, bodily action and then gradually transform themselves into physical reality. Therefore, I will concentrate my mind for thirty minutes daily on the task of thinking of the person I intend to be, by creating a mental picture of this person and then transforming that picture into reality through my actions.

3. I know that through the principle of autosuggestion, any desire that I persistently hold in my mind will eventually seek expression through some practical means of realizing it. Therefore, I shall devote ten minutes daily to demanding of myself the development of the factors named in the lessons of the Law of Success course.

4. I have clearly mapped out, and written down, a description of my Definite Chief Aim in life, for the next five years. I have set a price on my services for each of these five years, a price that I intend to earn and receive through strict application of the principle of efficient, satisfactory service, which I will render in advance.

5. I fully realize that no wealth or position can long endure unless it is built on truth and justice. Therefore, I will engage in no transaction that does not benefit all whom it affects. I will succeed by attracting to me the forces I wish to use and the cooperation of other people. I will induce others to serve me because I will first serve them.

6. I will eliminate hatred, envy, jealousy, selfishness, and cynicism by developing love for all humanity, because I know that a negative attitude toward others can never bring me success. I will cause others to believe in me because I will believe in them and in myself.

I will sign my name to this formula, commit it to memory, and repeat it aloud once a day with full faith that it will gradually influence my entire life so that I will become a successful and happy worker in my chosen field of endeavor.

[signed] _____

Before you sign your name to this formula, make sure that you intend to carry out its instructions.

If you fill your mind with doubt and unbelief in your ability to achieve, then the principle of autosuggestion takes this spirit of unbelief and sets it up in your subconscious mind as your dominating thought and slowly but surely it draws you into the whirlpool of failure.

But if you fill your mind with radiant self-confidence, the principle of autosuggestion takes this belief and sets it up as your dominating thought and helps you master the obstacles that fall in your way until you reach the mountaintop of success.

THE DISASTER OF NEGATIVE THINKING

The subconscious mind makes no distinction between constructive and destructive thought impulses. It works with the material we feed it, through our thought impulses. The subconscious mind will translate into reality a thought driven by fear just as readily as it will translate into reality a thought driven by courage, or faith.

If you fill your mind with fear, doubt, and unbelief in your ability to connect with and use the forces of Infinite Intelligence, the law of autosuggestion will take this spirit of unbelief and use it as a pattern by which your subconscious mind will translate it into its physical equivalent. This law is well described in the following verse:

If you think you are beaten, you are
If you think you dare not, you don't
If you like to win, but you think you can't,
It is almost certain you won't.

If you think you'll lose, you're lost,
For out in the world we find,
Success begins with a fellow's will—
It's all in the state of mind.

If you think you are outclassed, you are;
You've got to think high to rise.
You've got to be sure of yourself before
You can ever win a prize.

Life's battles don't always go
To the stronger or faster man,
But soon or late the man who wins
Is the man WHO THINKS HE CAN!

Chapter Four

CONCENTRATION, AFFIRMATION, AND VISUALIZATION

WHAT WOULD NAPOLEON HILL DO?

Napoleon Hill would come up with a simple and memorable way to describe in words and visualize in images what it will be like to successfully achieve his Definite Chief Aim.

He would then burn the words and images into his subconscious mind by repeating the words and replaying the mental images over and over until the description and mental picture of success become the first thing that pops into his mind whenever he is prompted to think about what he desires.

Having clearly established the method for selecting a Definite Chief Aim, and having stressed the importance of emotionalizing that aim or purpose, this chapter focuses on teaching specific techniques for you to use to inject emotion into your Definite Chief Aim.

We will begin by quoting Napoleon Hill's process for using auto-suggestion as he originally explained it in *Law of Success,* and pair that with a similar explanation taken from his later bestseller, *Think and Grow Rich.* Following the compilation of Hill's writings on the subject, the remainder of the chapter is devoted to teaching specific techniques that you can use to break your negative habits of thinking, and open new mental pathways that will allow you to influence your subconscious to help you accomplish your desire.

When writing about his technique in *Law of Success,* Hill called it simply "concentration." But as he so often did with the key concepts in his books, he created his own definition for the word. The following is excerpted and adapted from *Law of Success,* Lesson Twelve: Concentration.

CONCENTRATION

Let me first define the word *concentration* as it is used in this lesson: "Concentration is the act of focusing the mind on a given desire until ways and means for its realization have been worked out and successfully put into operation."

Two important laws enter into the act of concentrating the mind on a given desire. One is the law of autosuggestion and the other is the law of habit.

Habit grows out of environment—the sum total of all sources by which you are influenced through the aid of the five senses of seeing, hearing, smelling, tasting, and feeling—and out of doing the same thing in the same way over and over again, out of repetition, out of thinking the same thoughts over and over.

The human mind draws from its surroundings the material out of which thought is created. Habit crystallizes this thought, storing it away in the subconscious mind where it becomes a vital part of our personality, influences our actions, forms our prejudices and our biases, and controls our opinions.

We begin to see, therefore, the importance of selecting our environment with the greatest of care, because environment is the mental feeding ground out of which the food that goes into our minds is extracted.

THE FORCES OF HABIT

It has been said that all people are the creatures of habit, and that habit is a cable; we weave a thread of it each day and it becomes so strong that we cannot break it.

If it is true that habit can compel us against our will, desire, and inclination, and thereby dominate our actions and character, then it can also be mastered, harnessed, and directed for our good. Thousands of people have applied this knowledge and have turned the force of habit into new channels.

A habit is a "mental path" over which our actions have traveled for some time, each passing making the path a little deeper and a little wider. If you have to walk over a field or through a forest, you know how natural it is to choose the clearest path. The line of mental action is precisely the same. It is movement along the lines of least resistance— passage over the well-worn path.

Habits are created by repetition and are formed in accordance to a natural law, observable in all animate things and some would say in inanimate things as well. For instance, a piece of paper once folded in a certain way will fold along the same lines the next time. Clothing forms into creases according to the person wearing it and these creases, once formed, will remain. All users of any kind of machinery know that as a machine is first "broken in," so it will tend to run thereafter. Rivers and streams cut their courses through the land, along the lines of least resistance. The law is in operation everywhere.

These examples will give you the idea of the nature of habit and will aid you in forming new mental paths—new mental creases. The best, and one might say the only, way that old habits may be broken is to form new habits to counteract and replace the undesirable ones. Form new mental paths over which to travel, and soon the old ones will become less distinct. Every time you travel over the path of the desirable mental habit, you make that new path deeper and wider—and so much easier to travel thereafter.

This mental path-making is very important, and I cannot urge you too strongly to start making the desirable mental paths over which you wish to travel.

The following are the rules through which you may form the habits you desire:

1. At the beginning of the formation of a new habit, put force and enthusiasm into your expression. Feel what you think. Remember that you are taking the first steps toward making your new mental paths and that it is much harder at first than it will be afterwards. At the beginning, make each path as clear and as deep as you can, so that you can readily see it the next time you wish to follow it.

2. Keep your attention firmly concentrated on your new path-building and forget all about the old paths. Concern yourself only with the new ones that you are building to order.

3. Travel over your newly made paths as often as possible. Create opportunities for doing so, without waiting for them to arise through luck or chance. The more often you go over the new paths, the sooner they will become well worn and easily traveled.

4. Resist the temptation to travel over the older, easier paths that you have been using in the past. Every time you resist a temptation, the stronger you become and the easier it will be for you to do so the next time. But every time you yield to the temptation, the easier it

becomes to yield again and the more difficult it becomes to resist the next time. This is the critical time. Prove your determination, persistency, and will-power now, at the very beginning.

5. Be sure that you have mapped out the right path as your Definite Chief Aim, and then go ahead without fear and without allowing yourself to doubt. Select your goal, then make good, deep, wide mental paths leading straight to it.

As we have already observed, there is a close relationship between habit and autosuggestion. Through habit, an act repeatedly performed in the same manner has a tendency to become permanent, and eventually we come to perform the act automatically or unconsciously. In playing a piano, for example, the artist can play a familiar piece while his or her conscious mind is on some other subject.

Autosuggestion is the tool with which we dig a mental path, concentration is the hand that holds that tool, and habit is the map or blueprint that the mental path follows.

An idea or desire, to be transformed into terms of action or physical reality, must be held in the conscious mind faithfully and persistently until habit begins to give it permanent form.

THE POWER OF CONCENTRATION

This brings us to an appropriate place at which to describe the method through which you may apply the principles directly and indirectly related to the subject of concentration. I call this method the Magic Key to Success.

In presenting you with this magic key, let me first explain that it is no invention or discovery of mine. It is the same key that is used, in one form or another, by all groups that are founded on the philosophy of optimism.

This magic key is—concentration.

Now let me once again define *concentration* as I use the term.

It means the ability, through fixed habit and practice, to keep your mind on one subject until you have thoroughly familiarized yourself with that subject and mastered it.

It means the ability to control your attention and focus it on a given problem until you have solved it. It means the ability to throw off the effects of habits that you wish to discard, and the power to build new habits. It means complete self-mastery.

Concentration is the ability to think as you wish to think, the ability to control your thoughts and direct them to a definite end, and the ability to organize your knowledge into a plan of action that is sound and workable.

You can readily see that in concentrating your mind on your Definite Chief Aim in life you must cover many closely related subjects that blend into each other and complete the main subject on which you are concentrating.

Nothing was ever created by a human being that was not first created in the imagination, through desire, and then transformed into reality through concentration.

Now let us put the magic key to a test through the aid of a definite formula.

First you must get rid of skepticism and doubt. No unbeliever ever enjoyed the benefits of this magic key. You must believe in the test that you are about to make.

We will assume that you have thought something about becoming a successful writer, or perhaps a powerful public speaker, or a successful business executive, or an able financier.

We will take public speaking as the subject of this test, but you can change that to your own objective. Just remember that you must follow instructions to the letter.

On a plain sheet of paper write the following:

I am going to become a powerful public speaker because this will enable me to render the world useful service that is needed—and because it will yield me a financial return that will provide me with the necessary material things of life.

I will concentrate my mind on this desire for ten minutes daily, just before retiring at night and just after arising in the morning, for the purpose of determining just how I shall proceed to transform it into reality.

I know that I can become a powerful and magnetic speaker. Therefore I will permit nothing to interfere with my doing so.

[signed]

After signing this pledge, proceed to do as you have given your word that you would do. Keep it up until the desired results have been realized.

When you come to do your concentrating, look ahead one, three, five, or even ten years, and see yourself as the most powerful speaker of your time. See, in your imagination, an appropriate income. See yourself in your own home that you have purchased with the proceeds from your efforts as a speaker or lecturer. See yourself in possession of a nice bank account for your retirement. See yourself as a person of influence, due to your great ability as a public speaker. See yourself engaged in a life-calling in which you will not fear the loss of your position.

Paint this picture clearly, through the powers of your imagination, and it will soon become transformed into a beautiful picture of deeply seated desire. Use this desire as the chief object of your concentration and observe what happens.

You can do it if you believe you can!

Hold a deeply seated desire in your consciousness, through the principle of concentration, and if you do this with full faith in its realization, that act will attract powers that the entire scientific world has failed to understand or explain.

Concentrate your mind on the attainment of the object of a deeply seated desire and very soon you will attract, through those forces that no one can explain, the material counterparts of that desire.

HOW TO VISUALIZE

Your ability to train your memory, or to develop any desired habit, is solely a matter of being able to fix your attention on a given subject until the outline of that subject has been thoroughly impressed upon your mind. Concentration itself is nothing but a matter of control of your attention.

So significant is this subject of control of attention that I must emphasize it strongly. I consider it, by far, the most important part of the lesson.

Put the hypothesis to a test of your own.

You can select no better subject than your Definite Chief Aim in life. Memorize your Definite Chief Aim so you can repeat it without looking at the written page, then make a practice of fixing your attention on it at least twice a day.

Go to a quiet place where you will not be disturbed. Sit down and completely relax your mind and your body. Then close your eyes and place your fingers in your ears, thereby blocking all light and all ordinary sound waves.

Now repeat your Definite Chief Aim, and as you do so, in your imagination see yourself in full possession of the object of that aim. If a part of your aim is the accumulation of money, as it undoubtedly is, then see yourself in possession of that money.

If a part of the object of your Definite Chief Aim is to own a home, then see a picture of that home in your imagination just as you expect to see it in reality.

If a part of your Definite Chief Aim is to become a powerful and influential public speaker, then see yourself before an enormous audience, and feel yourself playing on the emotions of that audience as a great violinist would play on the strings of a violin.

Begin now to cultivate the ability to fix attention, at will, on a given subject, with a feeling that this ability, when fully developed, would bring you the object of your Definite Chief Aim in life.

Nine years after the initial publication of *Law of Success,* Napoleon Hill combined his original findings with new research and interviews, and published the results in a new book that offered a tighter, more focused version of his theories. The following explanation of concentration is excerpted and adapted from that revised version—*Think and Grow Rich,* Chapter 4: Autosuggestion.

HOW TO STRENGTHEN YOUR POWERS OF CONCENTRATION

When you begin to carry out the instructions in the seven-step process described in the chapter on your Definite Chief Aim, it will be necessary for you to make use of the principle of concentration. Let us here offer suggestions for the effective use of concentration.

When you begin to carry out the first of the steps, which instructs you to "fix in your own mind the exact amount of money you desire," hold your thoughts on that amount of money by concentration, or fixation of attention, with your eyes closed, until you can actually see the physical appearance of the money. Do this at least once each day. As you go through these exercises, follow the instructions given in the chapter on faith, and see yourself actually in possession of the money!

Here is a most significant fact: The subconscious takes any orders given it in a spirit of absolute faith, and acts upon those orders, although the orders often have to be presented over and over again, through repetition, before they are interpreted by the subconscious.

Following the preceding statement, consider the possibility of playing a perfectly legitimate "trick" on your subconscious mind, by making it believe—because you believe it—that you must have the amount of money which you are visualizing, that this money is already awaiting your claim, that the subconscious mind must hand over to you practical plans for acquiring the money that is yours. [Remember, your subconscious mind cannot distinguish between what is real and what is vividly imagined.]

Hand over the thought suggested in the preceding paragraph to your imagination, and see what your imagination can, or will, do to create practical plans for the accumulation of money through transmutation of your desire.

Do not wait for a definite plan, through which you intend to exchange services or merchandise in return for the money you are visualizing, but begin at once to see yourself in possession of the money, demanding and expecting, meanwhile, that your subconscious mind will hand over the plan, or plans, you need.

Be on the alert for these plans, and when they appear, put them into action immediately. When the plans appear, they will probably "flash" into your mind through the sixth sense, in the form of an "inspiration." Treat it with respect, and act upon it as soon as you receive it.

Do not trust to your "reason" when creating your plan for accumulating money through the transmutation of desire. Your reasoning faculty may be lazy, and if you depend entirely upon it to serve you, it may disappoint you.

When visualizing the money you intend to accumulate (with closed eyes), see yourself rendering the service, or delivering the merchandise you intend to give in return for this money. This is important!

HOW TO STIMULATE YOUR SUBCONSCIOUS MIND

The instructions given in the chapter Definite Chief Aim will now be summarized and blended with the principles covered by this chapter, as follows:

Go into some quiet spot (preferably in bed at night) where you will not be disturbed or interrupted, close your eyes, and repeat aloud (so you may hear your own words) the written statement of the amount of money you intend to accumulate, the time limit for its accumulation, and a description of the service or merchandise you intend to give in return for the money. As you carry out these instructions, see yourself already in possession of the money.

For example: Suppose that you intend to accumulate $50,000 by the first of January, five years hence; that you intend to give personal services in return for the money, in the capacity of a salesman. Your written statement of your purpose should be similar to the following:

By the first day of January _____, I will have in my possession $50,000, which will come to me in various amounts from time to time during the interim.

In return for this money I will give the most efficient service of which I am capable, rendering the fullest possible quantity, and the best possible quality of service as salesman of _____
[describe the service or merchandise you intend to sell].

I believe that I will have this money in my possession. My faith is so strong that I can now see this money before my eyes. I can touch it with my hands. It is now awaiting transfer to me at the time and in the proportion that I deliver the service I intend to render in return for it. I am awaiting a plan by which to accumulate this money, and I will follow that plan when it is received.

Repeat this program night and morning until you can see (in your imagination) the money you intend to accumulate.

Place a written copy of your statement where you can see it at those times, and read it just before retiring, and upon arising, until it has been memorized.

Remember, as you carry out these instructions, that you are applying the principle of autosuggestion for the purpose of giving orders to your subconscious mind. Remember also that your subconscious mind will act only upon instructions that are emotionalized and handed over to it with "feeling." Faith is the strongest, and most productive, of the emotions. Follow the instructions given in the chapter on faith.

These instructions may, at first, seem abstract. Do not let this disturb you. Follow the instructions, no matter how abstract or impractical they may, at first, appear to be. The time will soon come, if you do as you have been instructed, in spirit as well as in act, when a whole new universe of power will unfold to you.

THE SECRET OF MENTAL POWER

Skepticism, in connection with all new ideas, is characteristic of all human beings. But if you follow the instructions outlined, your skepticism will soon be replaced by belief, and this, in turn, will soon become crystallized into absolute faith.

Many philosophers have made the statement that man is the master of his own earthly destiny, but most of them have failed to say why he is the master. The reason that man may become the master of himself, and of his environment, is because he has the power to influence his own subconscious mind.

The actual performance of transmuting desire into money involves the use of autosuggestion as an agency by which one may reach, and influence, the subconscious mind. The other principles are simply tools with which to apply autosuggestion.

Keep this thought in mind, and you will, at all times, be conscious of the important part the principle of autosuggestion is to play in your efforts to accumulate money through the methods described in this book.

Follow the foregoing instructions to the letter, and it will open the way for a complete understanding and mastery of the Principles of Success.

The following section is excerpted from *Think and Grow Rich: The Workbook,* Chapter 5: Autosuggestion.

This technique that Hill dubbed *concentration* is actually an amalgam of two separate but interrelated techniques which today are most often called positive affirmation and creative visualization.

Positive affirmations rely on the idea of summing up your desire in a short phrase that you repeat over and over to yourself. It is the repetition that wears away at your old thinking until it makes a new mental pathway.

Creative visualizations rely on creating such a vivid mental image of your desire that you can experience it just as if it were reality. By making it so real in your mind, you are adding emotion that, as was stressed in the previous chapter, is what is needed to burn it into your subconscious, creating a new mental pathway.

The way in which you create affirmations and visualizations is virtually identical. The only difference is that one is verbal and the other is visual, but it is completely natural and easy to do both at the same time. In fact, it is not only natural to do them simultaneously, but it may also be easier for you to create a mental image while saying a phrase that describes it.

Or, to state the obverse, keeping a vivid mental image in your mind may give more passion and meaning to the words you use to articulate your desire.

We will examine each technique separately so that you can focus on certain aspects of each that deserve special attention. We will begin with affirmations.

POSITIVE AFFIRMATIONS

A positive affirmation is a short phrase that clearly states the change you want to make in yourself. If you emotionalize that phrase with total faith and belief that you are capable of changing yourself, and if you repeat the phrase over and over to yourself until thinking that way becomes your natural habit, then you will make the change you desire.

When French psychologist Emile Coué devised the positive affirmation "Every day, in every way, I am getting better and better," his intent was to create an affirmation that could be used by many different patients suffering from a wide range of psychosomatic disorders. This general, nonspecific phrase was designed to give the subconscious a positive instruction, but was still open enough that it did not tell the subconscious a specific problem to deal with, nor did it try to tell the subconscious how to do it.

Although Coué's affirmation may indeed make you "better and better" in general, the downside is that because it is so general and does not define what "better and better" means, it leaves the interpretation up to your subconscious, which is exactly the kind of thing that the nonjudgmental subconscious mind does not do very well. Most affirmations are directed at improving a more focused aspect of your character.

Here is a list of affirmations that deals much more directly with specific issues related to self-motivation and personal achievement:

- Whatever I can conceive and believe in my mind, I can achieve in reality, as long as it does not go against the laws of nature.

- I do it now. Whenever I set a definite goal, I take immediate action to get it done. I do it now.

- I am a powerful and charismatic leader. My thoughts are creative. My decisions are fair. I lead with confidence and certainty.

- What I desire is more important than the difficulties along the way. I overcome them to reach my goals.

- I am like a mental and financial magnet, attracting to myself all that I need to prosper.

- I maintain my enthusiasm and motivation throughout today's ups and downs.

- I am a person who thrives on challenges. Every setback gives me new opportunities for success.

- My conscious mind is wide open to my subconscious mind, which sends me hunches, premonitions, and flashes of insight.

- When I speak to others I look them straight in the eye and my voice sends a message of strength and confidence.

It may be that in the preceding list you found one or more affirmations that you might like to use to deal with certain issues. But we suggest that you will have greater success if you use the following proven techniques to create your own tailor-made affirmations to deal with your life and the specific issues you want to improve.

DECIDE WHAT YOU WANT TO CHANGE

The first step in creating a personalized affirmation is to clearly identify what it is that you desire. In the earlier part of this chapter we quoted Napoleon Hill's formula for defining and writing out a statement of your aim or purpose. Hill's version is once again reprinted here so that you may compare it with today's style of affirmations:

Go into some quiet spot (preferably in bed at night) where you will not be disturbed or interrupted, close your eyes, and repeat aloud (so you may hear your own words) the written statement of the amount of money you intend to accumulate, the time limit for its accumulation, and a description of the service or merchandise you intend to give in return for the money. As you carry out these instructions, see yourself already in possession of the money.

For example: Suppose that you intend to accumulate $50,000 by the first of January, five years hence; that you intend to give personal services in return for the money, in the capacity of a salesman. Your written statement of your purpose should be similar to the following:

By the first day of January _____, I will have in my possession $50,000, which will come to me in various amounts from time to time during the interim.

In return for this money I will give the most efficient service of which I am capable, rendering the fullest possible quantity, and the best possible quality of service as salesman of _____ *[describe the service or merchandise you intend to sell]*.

I believe that I will have this money in my possession. My faith is so strong that I can now see this money before my eyes. I can touch it with my hands. It is now awaiting transfer to me at the time and in the proportion that I deliver the service I intend to render in return for it. I am awaiting a plan by which to accumulate this money, and I will follow that plan when it is received.

Repeat this program night and morning until you can see (in your imagination) the money you intend to accumulate.

Place a written copy of your statement where you can see it at those times, and read it just before retiring, and upon arising, until it has been memorized.

In the reprint of Napoleon Hill's version that is provided above, the resulting written statement is quite long and uses a formal style of language that few people would feel comfortable using today.

However, you should bear in mind that when Hill instructs his readers to memorize their written statement, he was giving that instruction at a time when school students were regularly called upon to stand up and declaim long heroic poems from memory, and stem-winding public lectures were considered popular entertainment. Times were very different then and it would not have been unusual for Hill's readers to follow his instructions and learn the statement by heart.

Today, the intent in creating your affirmation is not quite so all-encompassing. Now the challenge is to take just one aspect of your aim or purpose and use that one idea to create a short, easily remembered phrase that sums up what you desire. By narrowing the focus, it is quite likely you will find that it will require more than one affirmation to properly address each issue.

Because of these changes, the editors of this book now view the creation of an affirmation as a three-step process:

1. Identify your desire.

2. Follow Hill's template to create your own version of a formal written statement.

3. Use information from your statement, along with the techniques explained below, to create a short, memorable affirmation.

You may choose to create one overarching affirmation that you feel encapsulates your major purpose or aim, or you may create a group of different affirmations that deal with the individual goals and objectives which must be accomplished in order to achieve your overarching purpose or aim.

You might also create other affirmations that are not directly related to your chief aim or purpose, but which deal with general improvements such as overcoming procrastination or eliminating the fear of criticism. Chances are that as you work with them you will find reason to create affirmations for all of these purposes.

When you start working with your completed affirmation(s), you will read your written statement at least twice each day and repeat your memorized affirmation(s) many times a day. Your formal written statement should be read once every night, and you should follow the reading by repeating the affirmation(s) derived from the statement at least ten times. Every morning you should again read your formal statement as the introduction to the repetition of your affirmation(s). And again, you should repeat your affirmation(s) at least ten times.

SEE IT IN YOUR MIND'S EYE

Once you are completely satisfied that you clearly know your desire, you must visualize a simple but vivid image that represents things as they are now and as they will be when the aim is accomplished or the change has taken place. It's like mental before-and-after snapshots.

WRITE DOWN THE WORDS

When you can clearly see in your mind's eye the manifestation of your desire, you then create a short, simple, easy-to-remember phrase that is like a verbal accompaniment to what you feel when you bring the before-and-after images to your mind. Following are some rules of thumb that are important when formulating affirmations.

Affirmations should always be stated as a positive. Affirm what you do want, not what you don't want.

Affirmations work best when they are about a single goal. Take the time to rewrite and polish your affirmation until you can express your desire in a short statement of precise and well-chosen words.

Make the words memorable and make it feel right for you. Use powerful and inspirational words that stimulate your mind. Make up your own catch phrases or rhymes that make it easy to say. Remember, your affirmation is not just a statement; it should be an expression of your inner desire that gets you psyched up no matter how many times you've said it.

Keep your affirmation in the present, even if saying it does not represent your reality as it is right now. You are training your subconscious mind to make your aim or purpose your new habit. By repeating an affirmation that states something is true now, your mind will begin to search for ways to make it happen.

Affirmations should be specific about the desired goal, but not about how to accomplish it. Infinite Intelligence, working with your subconscious, knows better than you what it can do and how it can do it.

Do not make unreasonable time demands. Your subconscious can't make anything happen "suddenly" or "immediately."

SAYING IT WITH FEELING

Just saying the words will have little effect. When you affirm your desire you must do it with such faith and conviction that your subconscious becomes convinced of how important it is to you. As you affirm your desire to yourself, visualize it so that in your mind's eye it is as big as a billboard. Make it big, powerful, and memorable. More will be said about this in the section on visualization.

SAYING IT OVER AND OVER

Repetition of your emotionalized affirmation is crucial. At this time it is your habit to think one way, but by repeating your affirmation often every day, your new way of thinking will begin to be your automatic response.

Keep reinforcing it until it becomes second nature to you, and your habit will become to think the new way—the way you want to think.

If you have reservations about the value of repeating affirmations, we suggest that you consider the billions of dollars spent to run the same commercials over and over and to place the same print ads day after day. Or give some thought to the reasons why astronauts and athletes train over and over, why pianists and golfers practice over and over, and actors rehearse over and over. It is why Pavlov's dog salivated when the bell rang and why Skinner's rats learned to navigate the maze.

It has been scientifically proven in the laboratory, every motivational expert acknowledges it, and you prove it to yourself every time you hum a familiar jingle or reach for a familiar brand when you are shopping. Repetition makes things stick in your mind. Things that stick in your mind change the way you think. Change the way you think and you change your habits.

SAYING IT OUT LOUD

Although the most common method of using an affirmation is to silently repeat the phrase over and over to yourself a number of times each day, Hill advises that it is most effective when you say the words out loud.

Speaking it aloud sets into motion the vibration through which the thought behind your words reaches and embeds itself in your subconscious mind.

This is why you are instructed to write it out, then commit it to memory and repeat it out loud, day after day, until these vibrations of sound have reached your subconscious mind. There it takes root and grows until it becomes a great moving force in your outward, physical activities, leading to the transformation of the thought into reality.

Speaking an affirmation out loud while looking at yourself in a mirror can be especially effective. You can either look yourself in the eye and talk directly to "you," or, as Andrew Carnegie advised Hill, you can use the mirror to observe how convincing you appear making the statement.

Carnegie told Hill to look into his mirror every morning and declare: "Andrew Carnegie, I am not only going to equal your achievements in life, but I am going to challenge you at the post and pass you at the grandstand."

This is a very well-conceived affirmation. It is a clear statement of the goal, and it is short enough to easily memorize and say with feeling. It also creates a clear and colorful image that is easy to visualize.

It is worth noting that at speaking engagements Napoleon Hill often told his audiences about that affirmation and he said that it had a profound impact on him and did just what it was supposed to do. In 1962, at a lecture in Chicago, Hill said this about Carnegie's affirmation:

The first few times I said it, I felt like a fool. But you know, eventually I commenced to believe it, and then, after I started to believe it, I knew I was going to succeed. And modestly, may I state that I have reached the place in life where, in terms of the number of people I have influenced to become millionaires, my achievements far excel those of Andrew Carnegie.

Experts on visualization techniques, including Shakti Gawain, author of *Creative Visualization,* and Marilee Zdenek, author of *The Right-Brain Experience,* suggest using a variation on a technique that you might try from time to time. They suggest that as you repeat your affirmation, you change from saying it in the first person to saying it in the second person, and then to saying it in the third person.

The following illustrates the technique using the affirmation "In every failure I can find and use the seed of an equal or greater success."

First you would say: "In every failure I, *[insert your name],* can find and use the seed of an equal or greater success.

Then you would restate it as: "In every failure you, *[insert your name],* can find and use the seed of an equal or greater success." As you say this, think of it as being said by someone close to you who is encouraging you.

The third time you would say: "In every failure he/she, *[insert your name],* can find and use the seed of an equal or greater success." This time, as you say it, think of it as being said by someone in authority whom you admire, and they're praising you.

SAYING IT WHENEVER YOU CAN

Another technique that will help to fix your goal or desire in your subconscious is to make it a part of your daily vocabulary. Look for ways to include your affirmation in your normal everyday activities. The opportunity may not come up often, but by keeping the possibility in mind and looking for the chance to use a variation of your affirmation in conversation, you also keep it forefront in your mind.

WRITING IT WITH FEELING

You will have already written a version of your affirmation when you followed Hill's directions to create a formal written statement, and again when you refined and polished the words that you used in creating your affirmations. The suggestion here is simply that occasionally, in addition to repeating your statement and affirmations out loud, you sit down and *write* the words over and over.

Although this could be done at the computer, taking pen in hand and writing out your affirmation over and over makes a different kind of impression on your subconscious. In some way, the act of actually writing your thoughts compels you to turn the words over in your mind. And anything that helps to distinguish the words makes them more memorable, and therefore plants them more firmly in your subconscious.

Just as saying your affirmation in the first, second, and third person can be very effective, writing these three versions over and over can make an even stronger impact. As you now know, your subconscious mind does not question or evaluate any information that it receives.

By presenting your subconscious with a written version, you have reached your subconscious through another sense. And seeing your own name written out and repeated as second- and third-person statements is a powerful way to reinforce the message.

WRITING IT TO BE SEEN

Another value in writing out your affirmations is that you can place the written versions where they will act as reminders. Write your affirmations on cards or Post-its and put them in your wallet, on your desktop, or stick them on your mirror, the refrigerator door, or anywhere else where they will catch your eye.

A variation on this idea is to surround yourself with books, pictures, mottoes, and other things that symbolize and reinforce the idea of you succeeding at your goal.

Hill suggests that you constantly add to your collection of visual motivators, and move your pictures and reminders to new places where you can see them in a different light and in association with different things.

Some people clip pictures of the cities they want to visit on vacation, the dream car they want to be able to afford to buy, or clothes they want to be slim enough to wear. We know of people who compile magazine clippings illustrating an idea, put them into book form, and regularly flip through it as a visual version of an affirmation. And some use computer programs such as PhotoShop to insert their likeness into the pictures.

Bestselling motivational authors Mark Victor Hansen and Jack Canfield are perfect examples of how well visual affirmations can work. They tell the true story about the unique way they kept focused while working together to write a book. After they came up with a title they liked, they had it typed out in the same font as is used for the *New York Times* bestsellers list. Then they pasted their mock-up of the title into the number-one spot, and hung copies of their version of the list in their office where they could see it as they worked on their new book.

Incidentally, the book they were writing was *Chicken Soup for the Soul,* and as the whole world must know by now, it wasn't long before they were able to replace their visual affirmation with the real thing.

Can you really make something happen just by focusing on it in your mind and repeating your affirmation over and over? Well, as we have already said, the saying it over and over doesn't make it happen, but saying it over and over does make it a part of you and your personality.

When your affirmation becomes a part of you and the way you think, your subconscious will begin to pull together bits and pieces of information that you otherwise might have missed, and you will find that you are coming up with more and better plans and ideas to accomplish your desires.

CREATIVE VISUALIZATION

The following description of the process of visualization is excerpted and adapted from the directions for writing a formal statement of your desire, a version of which was quoted earlier from *Law of Success.*

To begin the visualization process, write a clear, concise statement of the amount of money you intend to acquire. Fix in your mind the exact amount of money you desire. It is not sufficient merely to say "I want plenty of money." Be definite about the amount. As you read, see and feel and believe yourself already in possession of the money.

When you concentrate on your aim or desire, visualize yourself as you will be. Look ahead one, three, five, or even ten years. See yourself as a person of influence, due to your great ability. See yourself engaged in a life-calling in which you will not fear the loss of your position. See yourself in your own home that you have purchased with the proceeds from your efforts as the success you wish to be. See yourself in possession of a nice bank account for your retirement. See yourself, in your imagination, in possession of the money you wish to receive.

When you begin to "fix in your own mind the exact amount of money you desire," close your eyes and hold your thoughts on that amount until you can actually see the physical appearance of the money. When visualizing the money you intend to accumulate, see yourself rendering the service or delivering the merchandise you intend to give in return for this money.

Make your subconscious believe that this money is already waiting for you to claim it, so your subconscious mind must hand over to you practical plans for acquiring the money that is yours. When the plans appear, they will probably "flash" into your mind in the form of an inspiration or intuition.

CAN VISUALIZING SUCCESS REALLY MAKE IT HAPPEN?

Napoleon Hill is a convincing advocate for the theory, but is there any proof that by holding a mental image in your mind it will subconsciously change the way you think?

A dramatic illustration that most readers will be able to relate to is what would happen if you were walking along a garden path and you suddenly catch a glimpse of something coiled in the grass at your feet. Or what would happen if someone frantically points at your shoulder and shouts, "Ohmygawd, it's huge and hairy!" Fear messages race to your hypothalamus, your heart rate increases, your breathing speeds up, your endocrine system pumps adrenaline into your blood, and in a split second you are prepared for flight or fight.

It doesn't matter that what you saw was a garden hose, or that the person pointing at you was just joking. In your mind's eye you saw a snake in the grass or a spider on your shoulder, and that thought, that visualization was enough to cause your whole body to change.

The reason you react so strongly to the snake or spider is that you have attached a strong emotional charge to those images. If the vision in your mind is vivid and real, then the meaning of that image will be burned into your subconscious.

The more often you visualize that image, the deeper it will penetrate, until it becomes your natural habit to respond that way. Your subconscious reacts to what is vividly imagined as if it actually happened. So if your visualization of yourself succeeding is as real to you as your mental image of the snake, then the new mental pathways will come as quickly and naturally as your flight-or-fight response.

CREATING THE MENTAL IMAGE

Visualization is like seeing in reverse. In real life, when you look at something, "seeing" it is an interaction that takes place between your eyes and your brain. If you see a real image in the real world and then close your eyes, you can still see the picture of it inside your mind as a mental image of what you saw. That is visualization.

However, what we refer to as *creative visualization* is like taking the process of seeing and reversing it.

Instead of seeing an image outside of you and re-creating it in your mind, creative visualization is seeing something inside your mind and re-creating it in reality. Obviously that does not mean you can visualize something physical, such as a book or a Rolls-Royce, and suddenly make it appear in the real world. However, what you can do is visualize something such as success, courage, confidence, or leadership and have it appear within yourself.

Can you really make something happen just by focusing on it over and over in your mind?

As we have said previously, visualizing it over and over doesn't make it happen, but it's the visualizing that makes it a part of you and your personality. Then it's up to you to take the visualization of your desire—and your faith that you can accomplish it—and turn that visualization into reality.

There are two areas in modern life where changing the way you think about yourself is crucial, and in both of those areas you will find that visualization is widely used and accepted.

In medicine it can literally mean life or death. In sports it can mean fame and wealth. Because of the long and successful history of using visualization in both sports and medicine, these two areas also have the best documentation and the most convincing statistics.

In the time since Napoleon Hill wrote about what he called concentration, his technique for visualizing yourself succeeding has become an accepted part of athletic and sports training. In fact, if you read any book by a winning coach, sports star, or Olympic medalist written since the 1970s, you will find that they almost always mention the use of some form of visualization.

When you consider how much the skill levels have improved for individual competitors in every sport, and how much of that improvement is attributed to visualization, it is only logical that creative visualization applied to other nonathletic areas should have similar results.

Most athletes use this technique like a mental dress rehearsal of a skill or talent that they have already developed. But as persuasive as the athletic achievements are, even more impressive is what has been achieved in medical science. It is especially true of the work that is being done with the autoimmune system, the treatment of cancer, and the field of pain control, where the most stunning advances are not in improving performance but in *changing* performance by actually altering the way the mind thinks and the body operates.

Although Napoleon Hill and a few others were writing about the connection between the brain and the body at the beginning of the twentieth century, it wasn't until the 1960s and 1970s that the concept began to have a serious impact on the way medicine was practiced in America. Two of the medical professionals who were instrumental in introducing the technique were oncologist Dr. O. Carl Simonton, who was teaching the technique to cancer patients, and Dr. David Bresler, who was heading up the research at the UCLA Pain Control Unit.

At that time, Dr. Simonton was beginning to document the success he was having teaching cancer patients to visualize their cancer and imagine an army of healthy white blood cells swarming over it like white knights riding to the rescue and carrying off the malignant cells. When used in conjunction with regular cancer treatments, Dr. Simonton's spontaneous remission rate far exceeded normal. Dr. Bresler was having similar success using visualization to help patients manage the pain of backache, migraine headaches, and arthritis.

The books and academic papers written by Dr. Carl Simonton, Dr. David Bresler, and a growing group of other pioneers in the field began to attract the interest of not only the medical establishment but also the media. This idea of self-healing was just the kind of thing that appealed to the personal-growth movement that was becoming influential in America. The media picked up on it, and terms such as holistic medicine and body-mind connection became more and more common in their reporting. The concept of the body-mind connection was soon a part of the popular vocabulary, and by the 1990s various visualization techniques had found their way into mainstream medical practice.

Today there are hundreds of books citing thousands of case histories where patients learned to manage an acute medical condition, went into long remission, and in some cases were even cured through the use of visualization.

The method has become so accepted in the medical field that it is no longer categorized as alternative medicine; it is now a part of what is called integrative medicine.

If there are any lingering doubts in your mind that visualization works, the editors urge you to investigate the books written about the medical use of visualization. The authors are irrefutable, and their stories will convince you beyond question that visualization can have a powerful impact on how you succeed in life.

THE FIRST STEP IS TO RELAX

The first step in the process of visualization is to allow your body and mind to relax into a calm, open, and receptive state of mind. So the first thing to do is to select a time and a place where you can let yourself relax and you won't be disturbed.

Choose a comfortable place to sit where you can rest your feet flat on the floor.

Loosen any clothing that you find binding or constricting and let your arms hang loosely with your hands resting in your lap.

Now close your eyes, place one hand lightly on your abdomen, and take a deep breath, breathing the air in through your nose and letting it out through your mouth.

As you breathe in, do not try to fill your chest. Instead, as you take each breath, think of the air filling your whole body so that both your chest and abdomen expand.

If you are breathing as you should, each time you breathe in, the hand you placed on your abdomen will be lifted out as your abdomen expands along with your lungs.

Continue to breathe deeply as you let your breathing settle into a slow, relaxed rhythm and you slowly count down from ten to one, releasing all stress and tension in your body. As you count each number, envision yourself on an escalator; with each number, the escalator takes you down to a deeper level of relaxed receptivity.

That simple exercise, which shouldn't take more than a few minutes, will put you in a state of relaxed but receptive attention.

WHAT PICTURES DO YOU SEE?

Although there is no one right way to use the technique of creative visualization, most people find that the method works best if you can hold the images in your mind and show your subconscious what you want it to learn by moving from scene to scene.

Some people find that their visualizations are like movies, while others don't see "pictures" at all. Instead, they see in visual symbols that represent the idea behind their goal.

Napoleon Hill said that nothing has ever been created that did not start as a thought. You cannot bake a cake or build a skyscraper without first thinking about it. When you have a goal, you automatically form a picture in your mind. Research indicates that about 70 percent of people say they can easily create mental images, while the remaining 30 percent feel that although they may have some trouble, they can strengthen their ability with practice. The difference may be that what they visualized was not what they expected.

What each person actually "sees" when they visualize can vary greatly. Some people find that their visualizations come in full-color mental movies, while others say that what they see is more like a single scene that dissolves or morphs into something else. Others report that they can create pictures but the scenes won't stay on subject. It is also not uncommon for people who see pictures and scenes to be concerned that their visualizations are more like something they have made up or constructed, rather than a picture of reality.

And some people don't see "pictures" at all. Instead, their mind's eye presents them with images or visual symbols that are metaphors for the idea behind their goal. Some people report that their visualizations are more like having a thought or an idea, rather than what it is like when they see something.

If you are concerned that you won't be able to use the visualization technique because you don't think you can create clear mental pictures, you can set your mind at ease.

All of these examples, and practically any other variation you can think of, can be worked with and intensified by practice. It is a matter of taking whatever comes to your mind's eye—whether it is a full-blown movie; a shifting, flickering snapshot; or a symbolic image —and visualizing it often enough that it will naturally start to come into clearer, cleaner, sharper focus.

What if you fall asleep, or your mind wanders, or you can't make heads or tails out of what you see, or you get so many images so fast that it doesn't make sense and you can't control it? The answer to all of those questions is just give it time. Your pictures are there. You just have to find them and give yourself a chance to understand them.

Professionals who teach visualization courses say that even if your first attempts produce only vague images or flashes, in time virtually everyone can learn to visualize in mental images. Many who see in symbols to begin with, find that as they work with their visualizations the symbols just naturally make the transformation into realistic mental pictures. The same is true for those who initially see only flashes of indistinct single images. If you practice consistently, you will find that the images last longer and become clearer each time you repeat the visualization. It is a matter of practice and familiarity.

MAKING MOVIES IN YOUR MIND

One technique that many professionals suggest is to visualize your mental images as though they are literally the scenes in a film that is appearing on a movie screen. Some believe it works best when you treat it as a very personal experience in which you envision it as your own private screening and you imagine the screen as though it is just behind your eyelids. Others take exactly the opposite approach and suggest that you visualize it as though you are seated in a movie theatre, watching on a huge, towering screen that fills your entire mental field of vision.

Whether your visualizations are something that just happen inside your head, or whether you turn them into a widescreen spectacular, you will likely find that your visualization allows you to use movie techniques such as zooming in when you want to add details to your mental image, or creating a mental match-dissolve when you want to impress upon your subconscious the difference between the way things are now and how they will be when you have achieved your desire. Another especially helpful film technique is the use of slow motion to slow things down so that you can study every frame and make sure it is captured and imprinted on your subconscious.

Changing the point of view is another technique that will help burn the message of your visualization into your subconscious. Many people naturally visualize in wide shots. Even if they zoom in when they are filling out details, their master shot is to stand back and look at the complete picture of themselves having accomplished their desire.

The most effective visualizations are those that focus on vivid mental pictures that resonate with you on a personal and emotional level. Some people create visualizations that focus on the process and play like a plot that takes time to advance to the point where the aim has been realized. Others focus on the goal and create a single panoramic scene that illustrates their concept of having achieved success, and they zoom in or cut to specific areas to focus on the details.

If your visualization is like a movie that moves from scene to scene, see yourself in the scenes acting exactly as you would want to be if you were overcoming obstacles and succeeding at your goal. Project yourself and your personality so that you are acting as if you already are the person you want to become.

If your style of visualization is to create a symbolic panoramic scene, visualize your aim or desire in the present tense, as already existing the way you want it to be. Use your imagination to form the picture as if it were already a fact, and see yourself as an integral part of your vision, feeling as though you have already accomplished your desire.

As you create the visualization of your desire, fill in every detail that you can think of. If your visualization involves going somewhere or doing something, create images of your actions right down to the last detail. Where do the scenes take place? Is it outside or indoors? Is it hot or cold? Is it bright or dark? If it's inside, how are the rooms furnished? If it's outside, are there trees or pavement? Can you hear traffic or birds? Do the sounds annoy you or soothe you? Keep building up your visualization and giving meaning to every detail until it is so complete that it looks like reality and feels like a real experience.

The more real and complete the visualized experience, the more power your visualization will have to influence your subconscious.

One technique that can strengthen the impression is to talk to your mind when you visualize the images—as though you are talking to another person. Whether you do it mentally or out loud, if you use words to accompany the images, it will help impress upon your subconscious the picture you are visualizing and the idea behind it.

To keep your visualizations fresh and interesting, you should change your point of view from time to time—similar to the affirmation technique of saying your affirmation in the first, second, and third persons. If your natural style is to create a broad picture of your success, you might switch to seeing the entire success scenario in close-up. Or you could get a sense of what it feels like to succeed by making yourself the central figure in the scenario and looking out through those eyes to see it from that point of view. Then see it from someone else's point of view, as though you are standing beside someone you respect and that person is watching the scene and cheering you on.

Jack Canfield, co-author of the *Chicken Soup* series of books, whom we mentioned earlier, teaches another three-step variation on the movie-theatre technique that covers all the bases. He suggests that first you view your visualization as though you are watching a movie playing on a theatre screen. Then you walk up to the screen, open a door, and step inside the movie, which plays again, but now you are in the movie and seeing it from that point of view. And as a final step, you walk out of the screen, shrink the screen down until it is like a cookie that you break into pieces and swallow, making the whole visualization literally a part of you.

WHAT VISUALIZATION CAN OR CAN'T DO

As we emphasized in earlier chapters and we will repeat here, visualizing your desire can't put actual dollars in your bank or park a Rolls-Royce in your driveway any more than it can make a cup and saucer suddenly materialize on the desk in front of you. When you visualize yourself acquiring money, a car, or any other real object, what you are really doing is confirming to yourself the belief that you are capable of making it happen.

The vivid images that you create of your desire are burned into your subconscious where they connect and interact with other bits of information so that you automatically start coming up with more and better ideas of how you can earn the money to put in your bank so you can buy the Rolls-Royce.

Visualization doesn't create concrete objects; it creates attitudes and ideas. When you change your attitudes and ideas, you go from living inside your head to making things happen in the real world, and then it is you, not your visualization, who takes action and makes the concrete things come true.

VISUALIZATION AND NEGATIVE SELF-TALK

You are who you are because of what you keep in your mind and what you tell yourself about yourself. And we all are talking to ourselves all the time. Our minds are filled with mental chatter as we constantly flip through our memory banks of thoughts and ideas—some are important, some nonsense—and a great many of which are remembrances of past failures, embarrassments, criticisms, humiliations, doubts, and fears. This negative self-talk, which some motivational experts refer to as "rerunning old tapes," has a powerful effect on your self-confidence and your faith in your abilities.

Visualization is one of the most effective ways to counteract the effect of negative self-talk and feelings of failure, and it does so by tapping into your positive self-talk. Just as recalling past embarrassments will cause you to cringe even now, recalling past successes and triumphs will do the same in reverse.

No one ever forgets what it felt like when they were on top of the world. It's a rush of confidence, enthusiasm, and pride that is almost as much physical as it is mental and emotional. Recapturing that winning feeling is one of the greatest motivators you can tap into, and that is what visualization can do.

By mentally reexamining in detail the thoughts and emotions going through your mind when you were exhilarated with success, you can take those feelings and use them to overcome the sabotaging negative self-talk. In effect, you can remake the way you are feeling now by infusing it with the confidence and faith you felt when you were a winner.

IMPROVE YOUR PERFORMANCE

Earlier we commented on the extensive use of visualization in the medical profession, and we noted the ways it has been used by Olympic athletes and sports stars, but two of the most influential pioneers in using the technique were associated with the space program. Charles Garfield, PhD, who wrote the bestseller *Peak Performance,* and Denis Waitley, author of *The Winner's Edge,* were consultants to NASA.

The intention of the program they worked on was to rehearse the astronauts in every possible way so that they would be totally familiar with everything they were to do while in space and every possible disaster that might happen. This program included using leisure time to visualize coping with emergencies. When tested, it was found that those who had visualized the tasks handled their simulated disasters most effectively. The astronauts were not just mentally convincing themselves they could do something, they were actually rehearsing the doing of it, and by rehearsing they were also improving their skills.

Because visualization allows you to zoom in for close-ups or slow down the action, it is ideally suited to doing mental practice-runs or dress rehearsals to polish almost any kind of skill or talent. In addition to motivating success and inspiring personal achievement, visualization can change behavior and improve performance in a wide range of areas, including reducing anxiety about public speaking; getting rid of the fear of flying; improving reading speed and comprehension; tackling weight control; eliminating bad habits such as substance abuse; improving any skill, talent, or ability; and improving your interpersonal skills and your relationships with others.

Chapter Five

ACCURATE THINKING AND INFINITE INTELLIGENCE

WHAT WOULD NAPOLEON HILL DO?

Whether deciding on a Definite Chief Aim, or making any other choice of consequence, Napoleon Hill would first make sure that all information he received from other people was confirmed to be fact, regardless of whether the material supported his own personal predisposition and prejudices.

Once his logical conscious mind was satisfied, he would intentionally open the way for his subconscious mind and Infinite Intelligence to come up with flashes of insight, hunches, and intuitions.

In *Law of Success,* the section that corresponds with the material presented in this chapter is Lesson Eleven: Accurate Thinking, which deals with three aspects of the thinking process: deductive reasoning, creative thought, and Infinite Intelligence.

Napoleon Hill's explanation of the first of the three aspects, deductive reasoning, is a fairly straightforward warning about the importance of making sure that your decisions are based on verifiable facts.

Hill warns against the pitfall of basing decisions on information that other people claim is fact but in reality is just their opinion, and, equally dangerous, making your decisions based on information you chose to believe because it happens to agree with your particular predisposition and prejudices.

Although Hill's approach to deductive reasoning requires no further comment here, the materials on the subjects of creative thought and Infinite Intelligence are of particular interest to the readers of this book because they are so directly connected to the process of selecting, emotionalizing, and visualizing your Definite Chief Aim.

The following is excerpted and adapted from *Law of Success,* Lesson Eleven: Accurate Thinking, and in it Hill explains that Infinite Intelligence is the actual process or system by which the human mind turns something you think in your mind into something that exists in reality. As was stated in the first chapter, Cosmic Habit Force is *why* autosuggestion works, and Infinite Intelligence is *how* it works.

INFINITE INTELLIGENCE

Accurate Thinking is thinking that makes intelligent use of all the powers of the human mind, and does not stop with the mere examination, classification, and arranging of ideas. Accurate Thinking creates ideas and it may be made to transform these ideas into their most profitable, constructive form.

The average person is totally lost the moment they get beyond what they can comprehend with the aid of their five physical senses of seeing, hearing, feeling, smelling, and tasting. Infinite Intelligence works through none of these.

The only way to use the power of Infinite Intelligence is through creative thought. Autosuggestion is the way in which you may register in your subconscious mind a description or plan of what you wish to create or acquire in physical form.

The subconscious mind is the intermediary between the conscious thinking mind and Infinite Intelligence, and you can invoke the aid of Infinite Intelligence only through the medium of the subconscious mind, by giving it clear instructions as to what you want. The subconscious mind records the suggestions that you send it through autosuggestion and it invokes the aid of Infinite Intelligence in translating these suggestions into their natural physical form.

The subconscious mind may be likened to the sensitive plate of a camera on which the picture of any object placed before the camera will be recorded. The plate does not choose the sort of picture to be recorded on it; it records anything that reaches it through the lens.

The part that you must play is clear. You select the picture to be recorded (your Definite Chief Aim). Then, through autosuggestion, you fix your conscious mind on your Definite Chief Aim with such intensity that it communicates with the subconscious mind and registers that picture. You then begin to watch for and to expect manifestations of physical realization of the subject of that picture.

Bear in mind that you do not sit down and wait, nor do you go to bed and sleep, with the expectation of awaking to find that Infinite Intelligence has showered you with the object of your Definite Chief Aim. You must work to make it happen, with full faith and confidence that natural ways for the attainment of the object of your definite purpose will open to you at the proper time and in a suitable manner.

The preceding paragraph is very important in understanding the difference between the Napoleon Hill method and other success systems that are often criticized for being unrealistic because they promise that by "mentally sending out the message" of what you want, the universe will answer you by "manifesting" what you visualize.

As Hill makes clear in the preceding paragraph, when using his method you don't just focus in your mind on what you want, and then expect that it is going to suddenly show up. According to Hill, what "manifests itself" are plans, methods, and procedures, and they show up as ideas in your imagination that you can put to use to help you achieve what you desire. It is up to you to take the plans and ideas and do the work to turn them into the reality you desire.

The following text resumes from *Law of Success,* Lesson Eleven: Accurate Thinking.

Infinite Intelligence will not build you a home and deliver that home to you, ready to enter, but Infinite Intelligence will open the way and provide the necessary means with which you may build your own house.

Infinite Intelligence will not command your bank to place a definite sum of money in your account, just because you suggested this to your subconscious mind, but Infinite Intelligence will open to you the way in which you may earn or borrow that money and place it in your account yourself.

Infinite Intelligence will not throw out the present incumbent of the White House and make you president instead, but Infinite Intelligence would most likely, under the proper circumstances, influence you to prepare yourself to fill that position and then help you to attain it through regular methods of procedure.

Do not rely on miracles for the attainment of the object of your Definite Chief Aim; rely on the power of Infinite Intelligence to guide you, through natural channels and with the aid of natural laws, toward its attainment. Do not expect Infinite Intelligence to bring to you the object of your Definite Chief Aim; instead, expect Infinite Intelligence to direct you toward that object.

The way may not open suddenly, from the first step to the last. Often it opens only one step at a time. Therefore, when you are conscious of an opportunity to take the first step, take it without hesitation. And do the same when the second, and the third, and all subsequent steps essential for the attainment of the object of your Definite Chief Aim are manifested to you.

As a beginner, do not expect Infinite Intelligence to move quickly in your behalf. But as you become more adept in the use of the principle of autosuggestion, and as your faith and understanding grow, you will see the realization of your Definite Chief Aim and its translation into physical reality.

Remember, it is in your subconscious mind that the seed of your Definite Chief Aim is planted, and it is with creative thought that you awaken that seed into growth and maturity. Your subconscious mind will not germinate the seed of your Definite Chief Aim, nor will Infinite Intelligence translate that purpose into physical reality, if you fill your mind with hatred, envy, jealousy, selfishness, and greed. These negative or destructive thoughts will choke out the seed of your definite purpose.

Creative thought presupposes that you will keep your mind in a state of expectancy of attainment of the object of your Definite Chief Aim; that you will have full faith and confidence in its attainment in due course and in due order.

INFINITE INTELLIGENCE FROM *THINK AND GROW RICH*

As noted in the introduction, Infinite Intelligence is very closely related to Hill's concept of Cosmic Habit Force. The following excerpt explains Infinite Intelligence in greater detail. It is taken from the editorial comments in *Think and Grow Rich: The Workbook*, Chapter 4: Faith in Your Ability.

Infinite Intelligence is one of Napoleon Hill's most important conceptions and it is also one of the most difficult to get a handle on. At times Hill refers to Infinite Intelligence as if it were an actual thing; at other times he seems to be discussing a location, as though it is a compartment inside the brain; and in some instances he speaks of passing an idea on to Infinite Intelligence as though it is some sort of god-like figure who sits in judgment.

Infinite Intelligence is probably best described as a process or a system, in the same way that we think of a broadcasting system or a telephone system. There are three aspects to Infinite Intelligence:

1. It is a part of your thinking process that takes bits of information and ideas which your conscious mind has filtered out or forgotten, and connects them with each other on a subconscious level to create new solutions and creative ideas.

2. It is the part of your thinking process that, through the laws of nature and science, connects you to all other things, and makes you part of all other things.

3. It is the part of your thinking process through which outside information such as hunches, intuitions, and premonitions come into your subconscious mind.

WHAT DOES IT DO?

Sometimes it is easier to understand something by what it does, rather than trying to define what it is.

What Infinite Intelligence does is give you access to ideas that wouldn't normally occur to you. It does this by taking bits of information stored in your subconscious, and mixing those bits of information and ideas with other ideas that it is able to pull from outside of your experience or knowledge.

The result is that you find yourself coming up with flashes of insight, and intuitions that can't be explained in any other way.

WHY IS IT CALLED INFINITE INTELLIGENCE?

Infinite Intelligence is a term created by Napoleon Hill to account for the fact that our world follows a set of laws of nature and laws of science that make things happen consistently and predictably. He came up with the term in order to avoid using terms such as "the creator" or "the unseen hand," which Andrew Carnegie advised against because he wanted Hill to avoid giving any particular religious connotation to the success system. However, the name has still resulted in some confusion.

Some people take the words *Infinite Intelligence* to mean that there is some sort of omniscient overseer. That was not Hill's intention, and he never suggests that Infinite Intelligence is something that meddles in human affairs. Infinite Intelligence does not make things happen *to* you, but Infinite Intelligence is something *you* can use to make things happen *for* you.

IT REALLY IS JUST NATURAL LAW

Napoleon Hill would often use his pocket watch to illustrate the concept of natural law and explain why he was so certain that our world is not just the result of some cosmic coincidence. First he would remind his audience of how well-designed our world is for the nurturing of humankind, and how perfectly we fit into the grand balancing act that keeps the celestial scheme of things humming along with precision and harmony. Then he would hold up his pocket watch and point out that it was made up of wheels and gears and cogs that were clearly designed to fit together and work in a very specific way to do a very specific thing.

If you were to take apart the watch and put the pieces into a hat and shake it, you could keep on shaking it for a million years and the pieces would never reassemble themselves into a pocket watch that keeps time. It is not an accident that a watch works. It works because it is designed and assembled according to a specific plan. And it is not an accident that life works either.

Hill believed that each of us exists in a time and place, in a world, in a solar system, in a universe that, like the pieces of a watch, all fit together and operate with precision. The world works according to natural laws that are part of an overall plan. Because you, too, are an integral part of the plan, what you do has an effect on other things that are part of the plan.

If you can understand that, you can control the thoughts you think in such a way that, working through natural law, they will produce the effect you desire.

YOU DON'T ALWAYS HAVE TO KNOW WHY

If you throw a ball up into the air you don't doubt that it will fall back down. And you believe this because of the law of gravity. But do you actually understand what gravity is or how it works?

The fact is that no one really knows how gravity works. Or exactly why electricity does what it does either. And, as Hill often liked to point out, we don't even know why a kernel of wheat knows how to extract the correct combination of things from the earth, water, and sunlight to turn itself into a stalk of wheat.

But the fact that we don't know precisely why these things work does not keep us from growing food, or making use of gravity, electricity, and all the other laws of nature. The reason we can make use of them is because we have faith that they will work, even though we cannot intellectually prove how they work.

All science is based on the faith that there is universal order. However, the same regularity and predictability that gives us faith also raises another issue: What causes the world to operate with such regularity? Why is it so orderly?

Although for some people this line of thinking leads straight to religion, Hill takes the position that in order to use this philosophy to become successful, it does not matter. Things work according to the laws of nature whether we know why or not.

Rather than be diverted into a rationalization of religion, Hill opted for a practical approach that does not involve any particular religious belief. Hill says that from a purely practical point of view, religion does not affect your ability to utilize the natural laws. Gravity works equally well for Protestants and Buddhists. It doesn't matter if you are Catholic, Muslim, or agnostic, the sun still rises in the east and sets in the west.

In the following excerpt Napoleon Hill expands upon the point. He begins by reminding us that there are many forces at work in the world that we are aware of only because we observe the results of their power, but we do not know how they do what they do. These are the kind of forces mentioned above, such as gravity, or electricity, which Hill calls the "intangible forces."

He then goes on to make the point that we would be foolish to reject electricity simply because it is intangible and we don't know why it does what it does. Is it not just as foolish for us to reject an explanation that relies on an intangible power such as Infinite Intelligence simply because we do not understand how the power works?

This excerpt is adapted from *Think and Grow Rich,* Chapter 14: The Brain.

THE GREATEST FORCES ARE INTANGIBLE

Through the ages that have passed, man has depended too much upon his physical senses, and has limited his knowledge to physical things, which he could see, touch, weigh, and measure.

Sometimes men speak lightly of the intangibles—the things that they cannot perceive through any of their five senses—and when we hear them, it should remind us that all of us are controlled by forces that are unseen and intangible.

The whole of mankind has not the power to cope with, nor to control, the intangible force wrapped up in the rolling waves of the oceans. Man has not the capacity to understand the intangible force of gravity, which keeps this little earth suspended in space, and keeps man from falling from it, much less the power to control that force. Man is entirely subservient to the intangible force that comes with a thunder storm, and he is just as helpless in the presence of the intangible force of electricity.

Nor is this by any means the end of man's ignorance in connection with things unseen and intangible. He does not understand the intangible force (and intelligence) wrapped up in the soil of the earth —the force that provides him with every morsel of food he eats, every article of clothing he wears, every dollar he carries in his pockets.

Last but not least, man, with all of his boasted culture and education, understands little or nothing of the intangible force (the greatest of all the intangibles) of thought. He knows but little concerning the physical brain and its vast network of intricate machinery through which the power of thought is translated into its material equivalent.

It is inconceivable that such a network of intricate machinery should be in existence for the sole purpose of carrying on the physical functions incidental to growth and maintenance of the physical body.

Is it not likely that the same system that gives billions of brain cells the media for communication, one with another, provides also the means of communication with other intangible forces?

In the time since Hill wrote the above comments, we have learned a great deal more about the chemistry of the brain; we can measure the energies it releases; we know which areas control the various functions of the body and which areas affect memory, emotions, reasoning, and many other subtleties related to the thinking process.

But with all of our advanced knowledge we still do not know how intuition works, why we feel instant mistrust for some people and love at first sight for others, or how we could have an intuition or hunch made up from information that we don't know and were never exposed to.

Neither modern medicine nor psychiatry nor technology can tell us why or how, but the fact remains that we have all had a hunch about somebody and it turns out to be right, a premonition that something will happen and it does, or a feeling that something isn't right with someone who is not there with you and it turns out to be true. How does this information come to us?

Psychologist Carl Jung called this intangible connection the Universal Subconscious. Others call it the Totally Unified Theory, the Great First Cause, the Universal Mind, or Spirit, and some see it as another way of describing God.

Napoleon Hill calls it Infinite Intelligence and offers a common-sense explanation that allows you to work with the phenomenon even if it is not completely understood. And that, after all, is what Hill was aiming for: to give you a way to access intangible forces that will help you turn your desire into reality.

The following returns to the commentary excerpted from the chapter on Faith, from *Think and Grow Rich: The Workbook.*

PUTTING INFINITE INTELLIGENCE TO WORK FOR YOU

For the purpose of applying the Hill method to achieving success, just the fact that there is consistency is enough for you to utilize its power.

All you have to do is look at the world around you to know that everywhere in nature there is order. Who or what created the order may be debatable, but the result is not. If you use your own experiences and reason things through, you will easily satisfy yourself that the world follows certain patterns with such regularity and predictability, it is as though the world is following an organized, definite plan.

Napoleon Hill states, without equivocation, that he is certain there is a set of natural laws that comprises a plan. He is certain that there is such a plan because the success of his method relies on it. Hill's method would only work if there is a plan, and since it has worked for literally millions of people, there must be a plan.

To make Hill's method work for you, you too must start from the assumption that the world works according to natural laws that are part of an overall plan, and that you are a part of that plan. If you make the choice to assume it is a plan, and you treat it like a plan, it will work like a plan. If it works like a plan, you can make the plan work for you.

To recap the main points:

- Hill's philosophy of success is based on the premise that there is an Infinite Intelligence that underlies the way nature operates.

- It is this intelligent plan that makes the laws of nature predictable, consistent, and reliable.

- Because the laws of nature follow predictable patterns, we can have faith in them even though we do not really understand why they do what they do.

- You must have complete faith and confidence that the possibility for you to succeed at your aim is a natural part of the plan of things.

- Just as you have no doubt that the sun will rise in the east, you must have no doubt that if you follow the Hill formula your aim or purpose is achievable.

- You must have complete faith and confidence that, by burning your desire into your subconscious, it will, as a part of the natural plan of things, connect you with ideas and concepts that can help you realize your desire.

You will need practice to acquire this art of conditioning your mind to be receptive, and the first step is to relax your natural tendency to question everything. If you don't, your sense of reason will constantly get in the way by challenging you to prove it to yourself.

But you can't prove it. The only proof is when it works and you come up with a creative solution or a new and unique idea.

In practical terms, you start by assuming that if you follow principles that have worked for others, those principles will also work for you. Then you temporarily relax your own reason and will-power, set aside your usual questioning, and open your mind to the inflow of Infinite Intelligence.

The following section is excerpted from *The Secret Law of Attraction as explained by Napoleon Hill,* with inclusions from *Law of Success* and *Think and Grow Rich.*

NAPOLEON HILL, THE CARNEGIE SECRET, AND THE NEW THOUGHT MOVEMENT

At this point we will take a brief detour to make sure that readers understand the climate of the times when Hill was formulating the Law of Success. In the early years of the twentieth century, the New Thought Movement and its ideas about the power of positive thinking and the Law of Attraction were extremely popular throughout America. Because these ideas were so much a part of the popular culture of the day, it was only natural that certain of the New Thought ideas would influence some of Andrew Carnegie's thinking, which in turn meant that some of these concepts made their way into Hill's interpretation of the Carnegie secret and the *Law of Success.*

Here is how Napoleon Hill wrote about it in *Law of Success,* Lesson Two: A Definite Chief Aim.

The subconscious mind may be likened to a magnet; when it has been vitalized and thoroughly saturated with any definite purpose, it has a decided tendency to attract all that is necessary for the fulfillment of that purpose.

Like attracts like, and you may see evidence of this law in every blade of grass and every tree. The acorn attracts from the soil and the air the necessary materials out of which to grow an oak tree. It never grows a tree that is part oak and part poplar. Every grain of wheat that is planted in the soil attracts the materials out of which to grow a stalk of wheat. It never makes a mistake and grows both oats and wheat on the same stalk.

LIKE ATTRACTS LIKE

The phrase "like attracts like" and the explanation that the mind is like a magnet, which appear in the preceding excerpt from Napoleon Hill's book, are also found throughout New Thought literature as a kind of shorthand for the Law of Attraction. In essence it means that what you focus on and hold in your mind will draw unto itself thoughts and ideas of a similar nature.

"Thoughts are things"—another phrase common among New Thought writers—takes it a step further, conveying the idea that not only will the *thoughts* you think attract similar thoughts to your mind, but the *things* you think about will attract similar things that will come to you as real things in the real world.

In short, the Law of Attraction states that whatever you focus on in your mind acts like a magnet, attracting other like-natured ideas and concepts. If the thought you focus on is of a specific thing, that thought will manifest itself as the physical embodiment of the thought, and that thought will have become a thing.

Detractors say the idea that thoughts can alter reality, by attracting the things you think about, suggests that the universe is like some mail-order catalog in the sky that will deliver all the goodies you wish for if you just think the right thoughts. They say that at the least this kind of something-for-nothing thinking creates unrealistic expectations in those naïve enough to believe it, and at its worst it cruelly holds out false hope to those who are desperate for real help.

Could this be true? Was Andrew Carnegie really so naïve? Did Napoleon Hill really get taken in for thirty years?

Not likely.

In their effort to belittle the Law of Attraction, its critics portray it as far more simplistic than the way in which it was interpreted by Andrew Carnegie.

Clearly, the man who knew more than anyone else of his generation about the achievement of success and the creation of wealth was not proposing that all you have to do is think about something and it will suddenly deposit itself in your bank account or park itself in your driveway.

There is a vast difference between the critics' implication that the Law of Attraction means that what you wish for will just materialize and the concept that a thought can become manifest as a reality.

The critics are ignoring a whole host of actions that might transpire between the time a thought is first conceived and the time when it is finally realized. It is the difference between wanting something so much that you are constantly daydreaming about how nice it would be to have it, and wanting something so much that you are constantly thinking about what you can do to make it happen.

One is hopeless, wishful thinking; the other is hopeful, willful planning!

The following explanation by Napoleon Hill, adapted from *Law of Success,* was excerpted in chapter 1 and is repeated here as a reminder.

Everyone wishes for the better things in life, such as money, a good position, fame, and recognition, but most people never go far beyond the wishing stage. Men who know exactly what they want of life and are determined to get it, do not stop with wishing. They intensify their wishes into a burning desire, and back that desire with continuous effort based on a sound plan.

All riches and all material things that anyone acquires through self-effort begin in the form of a clear, concise mental picture of the thing one seeks. When that picture grows, or it has been forced to the proportions of an obsession, it is taken over by the subconscious mind. From that point on, you are attracted in the direction of the physical equivalent of the mental picture.

Another aspect of Infinite Intelligence is the phenomenon often called *synchronicity.* The commentary that follows is taken from *Think and Grow Rich: The Workbook,* Chapter 6: Specialized Knowledge.

KNOWLEDGE ATTRACTS MORE KNOWLEDGE

As you focus in on your Definite Chief Aim, you will, as a natural matter of course, begin to seek out specialized knowledge about that aim or purpose. Whether you enroll in school or university, get a job that will give you experience in the area, or just do some reading on the subject, the more you focus on your aim, the more you will find that related material starts to show up in all aspects of your life.

It's one of those strange and inexplicable mysteries that doesn't seem to make logical sense, but almost everyone has had it happen to them. It seems that just by thinking about a particular thing, that thing begins to occur in your life.

Hill came across this theory so often as he interviewed successful entrepreneurs, inventors, industrialists, and political leaders to whom Andrew Carnegie had introduced him, that he included the concept as a part of his philosophy of personal achievement, calling it the Law of Attraction. This is how he wrote about it in his masterwork, *Law of Success,* published in 1928.

THE LAW OF HARMONIOUS ATTRACTION

Every seed has within it a perfect plant. This means that forces and things that are suited to the needs of one another have a natural tendency to come together, just as the acorn attracts from the soil and the air the necessary materials out of which to grow an oak. It never grows a Christmas tree.

As soon as you set an aim or purpose, things related to the aim you have set start to occur in your life. It's almost as if your mind is like a magnet that attracts the object of your desire.

In the same way, you will attract to you people who harmonize with your own philosophy. The mind feeds upon what we feed it. Therefore, give it an environment with suitable material out of which to carry on its work.

Fill your mind with an aim that will attract people, and circumstances that will be of help to you, not a hindrance. Associate with people who inspire you with enthusiasm, self-confidence, determination, and ambition.

Millions of people go through life in poverty and want because they have made destructive use of the Law of Attraction through which "like attracts like." Through the operation of this law, they are constantly attracting trouble and grief and hatred and opposition from others by their unguarded words and destructive acts. Those who remain in poverty seldom realize that they are where they are as the result of their own acts.

DOES LIKE REALLY ATTRACT LIKE?

Some skeptics explain away the phenomenon as nothing more than a natural response to your heightened awareness. They say that because you have increased your interest in a certain subject you are now more aware of it, and because of your heightened awareness, you recognize it in instances that in the past you would not have noticed.

Suppose the doubters are right, and it is just a heightened sense of awareness.

What does it matter?

What's important is that it works. Whether your mind really does act like a magnet and draw things to you that help you achieve your aim, or if you just think it does, the bottom line is that when you expect it to happen, it happens. It doesn't matter if it is Infinite Intelligence and the Law of Attraction, or just coincidence, it would still be foolish of you not to keep yourself open to the possibility.

WHY AND HOW DOES LIKE ATTRACT LIKE?

The following is adapted from the way Hill explains it in the opening chapter of *Law of Success*.

As far as science has been able to determine, the entire universe consists of but four things: time, space, matter, and energy. Moreover—and this statement is of stupendous importance—this earth, every one of the billions of individual cells of your body, and every subatomic particle of matter, began as an intangible form of energy. Through the combination of energy and matter has been created everything perceptible, from the largest star in the heavens down to and including man himself.

Desire is a thought impulse. Thought impulses are forms of energy. Therefore, when you begin the process of acquiring money by using the thought impulse of desire, you are drafting into your service the same "stuff" that nature used in creating this earth, as well as every material form in the universe including your body and your brain in which the thought impulses function.

One way to visualize this interrelationship of everything to everything else is to imagine a tablecloth spread out before you. There are folds and bumps in the fabric that are all different from each other, but each fold or bump is still made up of the same stuff: tablecloth. Like the folds and bumps in the tablecloth, energy and matter are made up of the same thing, just in different forms.

When you focus intently on what you want to attract into your life, you visualize it so realistically that it burns into your subconscious and becomes a part of every thought you have and everything you do. It is there in your subconscious at all times, putting together bits and pieces of every thing or thought you come into contact with, trying to come up with ideas to help you achieve your desire.

How the Law of Attraction comes into play is that when you burn your desire into your subconscious, it is like sending an SOS to the universe asking for answers. Infinite Intelligence is like the broadcasting system that you use to send out the message to your subconscious mind, and it is also your "receiver" that brings back to you the answers you are seeking. These ideas usually come to you as flashes of insight, and occasionally as intuition or foreknowledge.

Because Infinite Intelligence is not only the interconnection with the subconscious but is also the interconnection between all things, it is Infinite Intelligence that accounts for the unusual anomalies in our thinking process referred to as hunches, gut feelings, intuition, premonitions, instant dislike, and love at first sight. The following excerpt from the opening chapter of *Law of Success* further explains the science that underlies Hill's interpretation of this phenomenon.

THE STRUCTURE OF THE UNIVERSE

In the past few centuries, scientists have discovered and catalogued the physical elements of which all material forms in the universe consist.

By study and analysis and accurate measurements, humans have discovered the "bigness" of the material side of the universe as represented by planets, suns, and stars, some of which are known to be over ten million times as large as the little earth on which we live.

On the other hand, man has discovered the "littleness" of the physical forms that constitute the universe by reducing the physical elements to molecules which consist of atoms—little invisible particles of matter revolving continuously with the speed of lightning on exactly the same principle that the earth revolves around the sun. These atoms are themselves made up of even smaller particles rotating around even smaller centers of energy.

Thus, in a grain of sand or a drop of water the entire principle upon which the whole universe operates is duplicated.

How marvelous! How stupendous! You may gather some slight idea of the magnitude of it all the next time you eat a meal, by remembering that every piece of food you eat, the plate on which you eat it, the tableware, and the table itself are, in final analysis, but an organized collection of molecules, atoms, and electrons revolving around one another at inconceivable speed.

Nothing is ever still, although nearly all physical matter may appear, to the physical eye, to be motionless. There is no solid physical matter. The hardest piece of steel is but an organized mass of revolving particles.

VIBRATING MATTER

In every particle of matter is an invisible force that causes the atoms to circle around one another at an inconceivable rate of speed. All matter is in a constant state of vibration or motion.

One rate of vibration causes what is known as sound.

As the rate of cycles per second increases, they begin to manifest themselves in the form of heat.

Higher up, the vibrations register in the form of light.

Still higher, are ultraviolet rays which are invisible.

And even higher up the scale, the vibrations or cycles create the power, I believe, with which humans think.

It is my belief that all vibrations which produce energy are simply varying forms of the same thing; the difference is in the rate of vibration. The difference between sound, heat, and light is only the rate of vibration. Thoughts, too, are energy. Therefore, the only difference between sound, heat, light, and thought is the number of vibrations per second.

More times than I can enumerate, I have proven to my own satisfaction at least, that every human brain is both a broadcasting and a receiving station for vibrations of thought frequency.

This is how Hill wrote about it in *Think and Grow Rich*, Chapter 13: The Brain.

More than forty years ago, working in conjunction with the late Dr. Alexander Graham Bell and Dr. Elmer R. Gates, I observed that every human brain is both a broadcasting and receiving station for the vibration of thought.

In a fashion similar to that employed by the radio broadcasting principle, every human brain is capable of picking up vibrations of thought that are being released by other brains.

The subconscious mind is the "sending station" of the brain, through which vibrations of thought are broadcast. The creative imagination is the "receiving set," through which the energies of thought are picked up.

Autosuggestion is the medium by which you may put into operation your "broadcasting" station.

The following explanation is excerpted from *Think and Grow Rich: The Workbook,* Chapter 14: The Brain.

ENERGY, MATTER AND SENDING IDEAS

When Napoleon Hill developed his theories about the similarity between radio waves and human thought, he did so in consultation with three of the most brilliant minds in the field: Thomas Edison, who, in addition to inventing the electric light bulb, was also the inventor of the phonograph, the motion picture camera, and the movie projector; Dr. Alexander Graham Bell, the inventor of the telephone and numerous other hearing-related devices; and Dr. Elmer Gates, who was renowned for the extraordinary thinking process he created, and who had also invented numerous acoustic and electronic devices.

It is no coincidence that many of the inventions perfected by these three men involved the use and manipulation of sound waves and electricity. It was because of their deep understanding of these areas of scientific research that Hill sought their advice and counsel. He was hoping they could develop experiments that would confirm his theory that the brain operates like a radio sending and receiving station.

Although they were not able to provide Hill with conclusive scientific evidence to back up his theory, all three men held views similar to Hill's, as is clear from the books and materials they published about their work.

WAVES OF ENERGY

In the human brain there are approximately 100 billion neurons or nerve cells. When neurons communicate through the nervous system, they send pulses of electrical energy. It is these electrical impulses that are measured by EEG, PET, and MEG scans.

Each time a pulse is sent, it also creates energy that radiates outward in waves. That is how radio waves radiate out from the antenna of a radio station broadcasting sound. That is also how thought waves might radiate out from the mind of a person thinking a thought.

Hill's concept of how we might receive a hunch or an intuitive thought is essentially the same thing:

1. Your thoughts and everyone else's thoughts are energy that sends out waves.

2. Your brain and everyone else's brain is both a receiver and a transmitter of thoughts.

3. Under certain circumstances, when the receiving part of your brain is receptive to a particular frequency (like a radio that is tuned to the frequency of a particular station) your brain catches thoughts that are vibrating at that particular frequency.

Here is how Napoleon Hill explained it in the opening chapter of *Law of Success.*

It is a scientific fact that sound waves are floating around us at all times, but these waves cannot be detected, beyond a short distance from their source, except by the aid of a properly tuned radio receiver.

Now, it seems reasonable to suppose that thought, being the most highly organized form of energy known, is also constantly sending waves, but these waves, like those of sound, can only be detected and correctly interpreted by a properly attuned mind.

It is my belief that the mind is made up of the same universal energy as that which fills the universe. It is a fact as well known to the layman as to the scientist, that some minds clash the moment they come in contact with each other, while other minds show a natural affinity for each other. Between the two extremes of natural antagonism and natural affinity, there is a wide range of possibility for varying reactions of mind upon mind.

Some minds are so naturally adapted to each other that love at first sight is the inevitable outcome of the contact. In other cases, minds are so antagonistic that violent mutual dislike shows itself at first meeting. These results occur without a word being spoken, and without the slightest signs of any of the usual causes for love and hate acting as a stimulus.

It is quite probable that the mind is made up of energy, and when two minds come close enough to form a contact, the mixing of the units of this mind-stuff sets up a chemical reaction and starts vibrations that affect the two individuals pleasantly or unpleasantly.

The effect of the meeting of two minds is obvious to even the most casual observer. Every effect must have a cause! What could be more reasonable than to suspect the cause of the change in attitude between two minds that have just come in close contact is none other than the disturbance of the electrons or units of each mind in the process of rearranging themselves in the new field created by the contact?

To this day, science has not been able to produce any other theory that better explains intuition than this one developed by Napoleon Hill, Alexander Graham Bell, Elmer Gates, and Thomas A. Edison.

The following commentary is excerpted from *Think and Grow Rich: The Workbook,* Chapter 15: The Sixth Sense.

There are five senses through which you perceive things:
1. sight
2. touch
3. hearing
4. smell
5. taste

The term *sixth sense* refers to yet another way of perceiving or knowing that we have all experienced but which cannot be attributed to the usual senses. This so-called sixth sense includes all of the forms of intuition and insight, such as hunches, gut feelings, instincts, mother's intuition, premonitions, first impressions, the eureka response, sudden inspiration, empathy, instant dislikes, suspicions, mistrust, and even love at first sight.

IT'S NOT YOUR SIXTH SENSE, IT'S CREATIVE IMAGINATION

It is Napoleon Hill's position that this way of knowing is not an additional "sixth" sense; he says it is just your creative imagination doing exactly what it is supposed to do. The following will walk you through the steps that led to Hill's conclusion:

Where do the ideas come from that appear in your creative imagination?

The ideas come from your subconscious, and you are not consciously aware of them until they appear in your creative imagination.

Where does your subconscious information come from?

- From everything you ever learned through your five senses, which stays in your subconscious as unfiltered data.

- From information that your conscious mind has forgotten or had set aside as not applicable at the time.

- From the ideas you have intentionally burned into your subconscious through self-suggestion.

- From bits of information that have come to you through Infinite Intelligence from outside sources.

How do you get information from Infinite Intelligence?

- Pulses of energy are generated when other people think thoughts and create ideas.

- The pulses of energy created by an idea send waves radiating outward from the thinker, similar to broadcasting radio waves radiating from an antenna.

- Like the radio waves that are part of the electromagnetic spectrum which is traveling around us and within us at all times, thought waves are part of the Infinite Intelligence that is also around us and within us at all times.

- Sometimes your mind-brain becomes attuned to pick up certain frequencies.

- If another thinker's idea is sending pulses of energy at the same frequency that your mind-brain is attuned to, it receives that idea from Infinite Intelligence. When your physical brain intercepts these waves, the information the waves are carrying becomes a part of your subconscious.

- Ideas and information received from Infinite Intelligence become a part of the store of ideas in your subconscious mind.

How does your subconscious come up with the creative ideas?

- When you try to come up with an idea, you flip through your memory, you collect new data, and you try to fit the pieces together into something that seems right to you.

- At the subconscious level, all the bits and pieces of forgotten ideas and information are constantly interconnecting with each other, sometimes fitting together in new ways to create ideas that weren't there before.

- Also at the subconscious level, the new data from your conscious mind is interacting with the forgotten information plus the new ideas that just put themselves together out of bits and pieces of other old ideas, all combining to produce yet another level of new creative ideas.

- A more specialized kind of creative idea is produced when you have burned an aim or purpose into your subconscious and it influences only the bits and pieces of information that are related to your aim or purpose, bringing them together into new ideas that specifically support your desire.

What is the role that Infinite Intelligence plays in creative imagination?

When any of the above-listed kinds of ideas come to you in your creative imagination, you may experience a charge of excitement and satisfaction, but in those cases it always feels like it was perfectly logical that you should come up with the idea or solution. It always feels like it is the natural result of the thinking you put into it.

However, when the information that enters your subconscious mind from Infinite Intelligence appears in your creative imagination, it feels unusual and you don't know why you thought of it. It doesn't feel like it is the logical result of what you know.

Whether you call it a gut feeling, an instinct, or any of the other terms just mentioned relative to the sixth sense, Hill says the reason you don't know "where on earth that idea came from" is very simply that it doesn't come from your experience. It's not your idea. It's a random thought wave rippling through Infinite Intelligence, which happened to be of the right frequency to become part of your subconscious. When your conscious mind turned to thoughts of a similar nature, the idea naturally popped into your creative imagination, and because it doesn't feel familiar you call it a hunch, a premonition, or one of the other terms for an intuitive feeling.

What if it isn't unusual after all?

Most people tend to view intuitive events as unusual phenomena. However, Napoleon Hill has suggested that you consider an alternative approach.

What if these aren't just wild ideas that sometimes show up in your imagination? What if it's no accident that you get hunches about some person or some thing and it turns out to be true? What if it isn't some strange sixth sense, but just one of the laws of nature working exactly the way it's supposed to?

But if it is a law of nature, why is it so hit and miss?

Hill's response to that is to question the assumption that intuition is hit and miss.

What if these intuitive ideas are only supposed to happen to you some of the time and only under certain circumstances? After all, you don't always recall the right answer, you don't always get the joke, and you don't always know exactly what you want to say. If those parts of your thinking process don't always work perfectly, why should you expect these intuitive ideas to be any more regular or controllable?

So what does it matter if it is part of natural law?
Intuitive thinking has often been unfairly lumped in with such things as fortune-telling or communing with spirits. But by developing a straightforward, observation-based theory, Napoleon Hill has gotten rid of all the hocus-pocus and the New Age-y psychobabble.

First, based on science, he found a reasonable explanation of how intuitive thoughts get into your mind. It's no more mysterious than the way that radio works.

Next he came up with a reasonable explanation as to why these ideas seem to come at random times. It's simply that your mind isn't always 100 percent right 100 percent of the time.

The most important aspect of Hill's theory is that if these intuitive ideas are working according to natural law, then you can work with that law of nature just as you work with any other laws of science or nature, and through them you can better accomplish your aim.

CAN YOU REALLY RELY ON IT?

The key to making your intuition and insight a part of your thinking process is to treat your hunches and gut reactions just as you would any other information that you use to make decisions.

First you must realize it is a fact that many successes have come from flashes of insight or intuition. Then you must acknowledge to yourself that you are prepared to believe it is possible that you too may receive valuable ideas in this way.

If you do believe it is possible, then you have at least opened the door. Now you must encourage it to happen. That does not mean you immediately accept everything that pops into your mind, but it does mean that you treat everything that pops into your mind as a possibility.

You evaluate it, you give it serious consideration, and you weigh the consequences of acting on it.

Sometimes you will have a hunch that turns out to be brilliant. The next time it could be dead wrong. It doesn't always work the way you want it to, and it doesn't always work *when* you want it to either. But you can increase the likelihood of creating more and better ideas by the simple act of acknowledging to yourself that you believe your creative imagination can help you solve problems.

As you work to improve your ability with this technique, it will help to keep in mind that your intuition isn't something outside trying to get your attention. Your intuition is really just you making yourself known. Your intuition is what you know that is buried just below your consciousness. So your intuition is really you telling yourself something. When you pay attention to your intuition, it is you trusting yourself, and who knows you better than yourself?

The key is to keep an open mind and approach each intuition or insight with an attitude of open expectation. It cannot hurt to begin with a positive point of view. If it doesn't work, you can always be sensible later.

But if you don't even give it chance, if you start out negative and reject all those crazy off-the-wall ideas, you will never know if it might have been the big winner you were hoping for.

Chapter Six

IMAGINATION AND INFINITE INTELLIGENCE

WHAT WOULD NAPOLEON HILL DO?

After exploring the scientific basis for the concept of the Law of Attraction, and having established a common-sense explanation for how "like attracts like" might actually work in the real world, Napoleon Hill would focus on improving the way Infinite Intelligence is accessed through the imagination.

He would create methods to unlock the ideas hidden in the storehouse of his subconscious, and he would develop others that allow for the possibility that ideas might also be attracted from outside sources.

If Cosmic Habit Force is *why* Napoleon Hill's method works, and Infinite Intelligence is *how* it works, then it would be reasonable to say that the imagination is *where* it works.

Hill said that mankind cannot create anything in reality that isn't first created in the imagination. He often compared the chapters on imagination in his books to the hub of a wheel where all of the spokes come together, or a telephone switchboard where all of the lines converge. In his books, the central idea of each of the other chapters is connected in a way that leads both to and from imagination. Everything that mankind creates begins in the form of a thought impulse, and it is only by coming together in the imagination that thought impulses are turned into plans.

As you might suspect from reading the preceding, Hill's concept of what your imagination is capable is a little different from most other people's definition. As Hill sees it, at its basic level, imagination is just like what most people think it is: It's where you go in your mind when you want to "be creative" and "come up with good ideas."

But that's just the beginning. Beyond that, it is through your imagination that you are able to inject the needed faith into your desire so that it will burn your Definite Chief Aim into your subconscious and, in reverse, it is through your imagination that your subconscious is able to send you its responses to your Definite Chief Aim.

Hill says that imagination is an integral part of his conception of Infinite Intelligence and, as you will learn in this chapter, it is the connection to imagination that offers a perfectly logical explanation for some of the seemingly illogical mental anomalies such as hunches, intuitions, and flashes of insight that are often attributed to some sort of sixth sense.

Before going into detail about the interconnection between imagination and Infinite Intelligence, Napoleon Hill sets out the basics, beginning with the following introduction excerpted and adapted from *Law of Success,* Lesson Six: Imagination.

IMAGINATION CAN BE DEVELOPED

Imagination is the workshop of the human mind wherein old ideas and established facts may be reassembled into new combinations and put to new uses.

If you have mastered and thoroughly understood the preceding lessons of this course, you know that the materials out of which you built your Definite Chief Aim were assembled and combined in your imagination. It is in the workshop of your imagination that you will put the principle of autosuggestion into operation in creating such qualities.

You will never have a definite purpose in life, you will never have self-confidence, you will never have initiative and leadership unless you first create these qualities in your imagination and see yourself in possession of them.

First comes the thought; then organization of that thought into ideas and plans; then transformation of those plans into reality. The beginning, as you will observe, is in your imagination.

The imagination is both interpretative and creative in nature. It can examine facts, concepts, and ideas, and it can create new combinations and plans out of these.

The preceding shows how Napoleon Hill explained the imagination in *Law of Success,* and the following is how he set up the same concept when he was writing *Think and Grow Rich.* It is excerpted and adapted from *Think and Grow Rich,* Chapter 6: Imagination.

The imagination is literally the workshop of the mind where all plans are created. It is where the impulse, the desire, is given shape, form, and action through the aid of the imaginative faculty of the mind.

TWO FORMS OF IMAGINATION

The imaginative faculty functions in two forms. One is known as "synthetic imagination," and the other as "creative imagination."

- **Synthetic imagination.** Through this faculty, one may arrange old concepts, ideas, or plans into new combinations. This faculty creates nothing. It merely works with the material of experience, education, and observation with which it is fed. It is the faculty used most by the inventor.

- **Creative imagination.** Through the faculty of creative imagination, the finite mind of man has direct communication with Infinite Intelligence. It is the faculty through which "hunches" and "inspirations" are received. It is by this faculty that all basic, or new, ideas are handed over to man. It is through this faculty that one individual may "tune in," or communicate with the subconscious minds of other men.

The creative imagination works automatically. It functions only when the conscious mind is stimulated through the emotion of a strong desire. The creative faculty becomes more alert in proportion to its development through use.

The great leaders of business, industry, finance, and the great artists, musicians, poets, and writers became great because they developed the faculty of creative imagination.

Both the synthetic and creative faculties of imagination become more alert with use, just as any muscle or organ of the body develops through use.

Synthetic imagination is the one that will be used most frequently in the process of transforming the impulse of desire into money.

The following commentary is excerpted and adapted from *Think and Grow Rich: The Workbook*, Chapter 7: Imagination.

Napoleon Hill devotes the opening sections of both *Law of Success* and *Think and Grow Rich* to explaining that human imagination is divided into two separate forms: creative imagination, and interpretive or synthetic imagination. But the names Hill has chosen to identify the forms of imagination have proven to be somewhat misleading. Generally speaking, today the word *creative* implies something better than the word *synthetic,* and most people would assume from the names that using your creative imagination is superior to using your synthetic imagination. That was not Hill's intention. One form of imagination is not better than the other.

In order to remove any stigma that might be attached to the word *synthetic,* in this book we will use the term *synthesized imagination,* which would resonate positively with modern readers and therefore better convey what Hill had in mind.

SYNTHESIZED IMAGINATION

To clarify, the most creative people in the world utilize synthesized imagination most of the time to come up with their best ideas. Your synthesized imagination is what you are using when you rack your brain and call upon everything you know to come up with an idea or a solution to a problem. Synthesizing, or putting the right things together in the right way, is the height of creativity. That's what scientists, cooks, inventors, mechanics, songwriters, salespeople, students, business managers, entrepreneurs and just about everyone else does when they are using their head and working to the best of their ability.

Nothing makes the point about synthesized imagination more clearly than the story of how Thomas Edison synthesized various bits of knowledge to create the light bulb. Edison's invention is not only an excellent example of synthesized imagination, it is also the perfect illustration of creative thought working in conjunction with the storehouse concept of the subconscious mind.

Edison clearly had a Definite Chief Aim, and that was the desire to make a workable light using electricity. He certainly had faith in his ability to accomplish his desire, and he must have strongly emotionalized his desire or it never would have sustained him through ten thousand failures.

In his conscious mind, Thomas A. Edison had a vast number of facts about electricity, scientific theory, the properties of materials, and the laws of nature. He consciously accepted or rejected the thousands of bits of information that he consciously knew, to test different combinations to see which would work.

Because his desire was so foremost in his conscious mind, it also became deeply rooted in his subconscious mind. There it came into contact with a flood of other facts and bits of information, some of which had been forgotten and others that the conscious mind had rejected as unimportant.

His subconscious mind juggled and rejuggled all of the new bits of conscious information with all of its old bits of conscious and subconscious information, looking for the right combinations.

Out of this came the imaginative, creative thoughts that resulted not only in the electric light bulb but also in parallel circuits, the dynamo, voltage regulators, fuses, insulation, light sockets, on-off switches, and hundreds of other related products that were created, developed, and patented by Edison.

But which of these creative ideas were developed by Edison deliberately pulling together what he knew in his conscious mind, and which were created from subconscious information he wasn't even aware that he knew? Nobody, not even Edison, could answer that. But either way, the imaginative ideas came about because the desire was firmly planted, and the creative process was encouraged.

Although the example of Thomas Edison inventing the light bulb involves working with scientific principles and materials with which the average person might not be familiar, we present here another story which makes it clear that you can become very successful if you are just an ordinary person who is able to see ordinary things in an extraordinary way.

The following story is excerpted and adapted from *Law of Success*, Lesson Six: Imagination.

PUT IMAGINATION TO WORK

We have stated that the imagination is both interpretative and creative in its nature. It can receive impressions or ideas and out of these it can form new combinations.

As an illustration of the power of imagination, take the case of Clarence Saunders, who organized the Piggly-Wiggly system of self-help grocery stores.

Saunders was a grocery clerk in a small southern retail store. One day he was standing in a line, with a tin tray in his hands, waiting his turn to secure food in a cafeteria. He had never earned more than twenty dollars a week before that time, and no one had ever noticed anything about him that indicated unusual ability, but something took place in his mind, as he stood in that line of waiting people, that put his imagination to work. With the aid of his imagination, he lifted that "self-help" idea out of the cafeteria in which he found it (not creating anything new, merely shifting an old idea into a new use) and set it down in a grocery store. In an instant the Piggly-Wiggly chain-store grocery plan had been created, and Clarence Saunders, the twenty-dollar-a-week grocery clerk, rapidly became the million-dollar chain-store groceryman of America.

Where in that transaction do you see the slightest indication of a performance that you could not duplicate?

Using synthesized imagination, you can become hugely successful just by taking the most common everyday thing and seeing how to put it together in a new way.

CREATIVE IMAGINATION

On the other hand, what Hill calls creative imagination involves tapping into something beyond the information and ideas you have in your mind. You are using creative imagination when you get a flash of insight or inspiration that comes to you completely out of the blue. At the most rarified level, it is what scientists and inventors tap into when they create new systems or discover laws of nature that previously were unknown. More commonly, it occurs in the same way that was referred to in the preceding chapter on Infinite Intelligence: when you get a hunch, a gut feeling, or a premonition about something that turns out to be right, but you had no way of knowing in advance that it would happen.

You will recognize that parts of this next excerpt were also in previous chapters, in reference to Infinite Intelligence. Because there is so much overlap in the concepts, it is not uncommon for Hill to use the same material—and occasionally even the same phrases—in more than one chapter. The following excerpt is compiled from selections adapted from *Think and Grow Rich,* Chapter 4: Imagination.

USING YOUR CREATIVE IMAGINATION

The great leaders of business, industry, and finance, and the great artists, musicians, poets, and writers became great because they developed the faculty of creative imagination.

You are engaged in trying to turn your desire into its physical or monetary counterpart, and there are laws of nature that can help you. By describing these principles from every conceivable angle, I hope to reveal to you the secret through which every great fortune has been accumulated. Strange and paradoxical as it may seem, the "secret" is not a secret. It is made obvious in the earth, the stars, the planets, in the elements above and around us, in every blade of grass, and every form of life within our vision.

As far as science has been able to determine, the entire universe consists of but four things: time, space, matter and energy. Moreover —and this statement is of stupendous importance— this earth, every one of the billions of individual cells of your body, and every subatomic particle of matter, began as an intangible form of energy. Through the

combination of energy and matter has been created everything perceptible, from the largest star in the heavens down to and including man
himself.

Desire is a thought impulse. Thought impulses are forms of energy.
When you begin the process of acquiring money by using the thought
impulse of desire, you are drafting into your service the same "stuff"
that nature used in creating this earth, as well as every material form in
the universe including your body and your brain in which the thought
impulses function.

It is by this faculty of creative imagination that truly new ideas
are handed over to mankind. It is through this faculty that we get
hunches, and that we pick up "vibrations" from other people, and in
that way tune in the subconscious minds of others.

The reference that Hill makes about the interconnectedness of all
things is so important to understanding creative imagination and
Infinite Intelligence, that we have assembled this simple point-form
overview:

- It is a basic scientific fact that there are only four things in the
  entire universe: time, space, energy, and matter.

- If you examine any kind of matter closely, you will see that it is
  made up of molecules, which are made up of atoms, which are
  made up of protons, neutrons, and electrons, which are not solid
  at all; they are bits of energy. In fact 99 percent of each atom is
  empty space.

- Whether something is tangible, such as a chair, or intangible,
  such as a thought, it is just energy in a different form.

- All of the actual things in the entire universe are made up of one
  common substance: energy.

- Because everything is just a different part of energy, everything
  is therefore interconnected and a part of everything else.

- And finally, because everything *is* a part of everything else, occasionally a piece of that energy from outside yourself, in the form of a thought or an idea, will connect with you on a subconscious level and appear in your imagination as a pre-monition or intuition, a flash of insight or an inspiration.

Much of what is explained in the preceding section is often referred to as the "sixth sense." More often than not, these references are made in a derogatory fashion, the implication being that such things are on a par with magic tricks and carnival mind readers. Napoleon Hill acknowledges the criticism and deals with the issue head-on in the following compilation of two short excerpts taken from *Think and Grow Rich.*

I am not a believer in, nor an advocate of, "miracles," for the simple reason that I have enough knowledge of nature to understand that nature never deviates from her established laws. However, I believe that some of nature's laws are so incomprehensible that they produce what appear to be miracles. The sixth sense comes as near to being a miracle as anything I have ever experienced.

This much I do know—that there is a power, or a First Cause, or an Intelligence, which permeates every atom of matter and embraces every unit of energy perceptible to man. I know that this Infinite Intelligence is the thing that converts acorns into oak trees, causes water to flow downhill in response to the law of gravity, follows night with day and winter with summer, each maintaining its proper place and relationship to the other.

Through the philosophy explained in this book, this Intelligence can help turn your desires into material form. I know this because I have experimented with it—and I have experienced it.

Somewhere in the cell-structure of the brain is something that receives the vibrations of thought ordinarily called hunches. So far, science has not discovered where this sixth sense is located, but this is not important. The fact remains that human beings do receive accurate knowledge through sources other than the physical senses.

This sixth sense is creative imagination. Creative imagination is the direct link between your finite mind and what I have termed Infinite Intelligence. All revelations, and all discoveries of basic or new principles in the field of invention, take place through the faculty of creative imagination.

When ideas, concepts, or hunches flash into your mind, they can only have come from one or more of the following sources:

- From the mind of some other person who has just released that thought, idea, or concept, through conscious thought

- Your subconscious mind, which stores every thought and impression that ever reached your brain through any of the five senses

- From another person's subconscious storehouse

- Infinite Intelligence

There are no other possible sources from which "inspired" ideas or "hunches" may be received.

In the following section, adapted from Lesson Six: Imagination, in *Law of Success,* Napoleon Hill provides more detail about his theory of the way in which your creative imagination acts as a "receiver." In doing so, Hill uses the term *telepathy,* but as usual, Hill's interpretation is his own, and it is quite different from the usual description of some kind of mystical or psychic phenomenon.

Hill's approach to telepathy is purely practical. The fact is that in real life we all get hunches and we all pick up "vibes" from some people. If we all have these experiences, and neither science nor psychology has yet to come up with an explanation of how these ideas get into our minds, Hill's theory of Infinite Intelligence provides a reasonable common-sense answer.

TELEPATHY

Through its interpretative capacity, the imagination has the power to register vibrations and thought waves that are put into motion from outside sources, just as the radio receiver picks up the vibrations of sound. The principle through which this interpretative capacity of the imagination functions is called telepathy—the communication of thought from one mind to another, at long or short distances, without the aid of physical or mechanical appliances.

I will devote no time to proving that telepathy is a reality. To make this description understandable, we must simply accept the principle of telepathy, in the sense that every thought we release is registering itself in the minds of other people.

You have often heard of "mob psychology," which is nothing more than some strong idea that has been created in the mind of one or more persons and registers itself in the minds of other persons through the principle of telepathy. So strong is the power of mob psychology that two men fighting in the street will often start a "free-for-all" fight in which bystanders will engage each other in battle without even knowing what they are fighting about, or with whom they are fighting.

Apply the principle in another way: Place among a group of workers one person whose personality is of the positive, optimistic type, and his influence will reflect itself in every person who works with him.

Telepathy can be an important factor to a person who is preparing to make effective use of imagination, because this telepathic capacity of the imagination is constantly picking up thought waves and vibrations of every description. So-called "snap judgments" and "hunches," which prompt you to form an opinion or decide upon a course of action that is not in harmony with logic and reason, are usually the result of stray thought waves that have registered in the imagination.

Consider what happens when a salesperson who lacks confidence walks in to see a prospective buyer. Whether or not the prospective buyer is conscious of it, his or her imagination immediately "senses" that lack of confidence in the salesperson's mind. The salesperson's own thoughts are actually undermining his or her own efforts.

The principle of telepathy and the Law of Attraction, through which like attracts like, explain many a failure. If the mind has a tendency to attract those thought vibrations which harmonize with the dominating thoughts of a given mind, you can easily understand why a negative mind that dwells on failure and lacks self-confidence would not attract a positive mind that is dominated by thoughts of success.

Imagination is the only thing in the world over which you have absolute control. Others may deprive you of your material wealth and cheat you in a thousand ways, but no one can deprive you of the control and use of your imagination. Others may deal with you unfairly, as they often do; they may deprive you of your liberty, but they cannot take from you the privilege of using your imagination as you wish.

The following commentary is excerpted from *Think and Grow Rich: The Workbook,* Chapter 7: Imagination.

CREATIVE VISION

Later in his career, when Hill wrote or spoke about imagination, he devoted less attention to the division between synthesized and creative imagination, and he began using a new term: *creative vision.* Rather than dividing imagination into two separate forms, this new term embraces the idea that the two influence one another. Creative vision is a blending of the conscious mind's imagination with the subconscious mind's intuition. What this means in a practical sense is that in addition to trying to come up with an idea by consciously attempting to fit together bits and pieces of information in your imagination, you also intentionally encourage your intuitive subconscious to influence the solution.

GATHER INFORMATION

The first step in using your creative vision is to add to the information and opinions you already have in your mind by gathering all the raw material and information you can find on the subject. It is important, when you do so, that you don't get so narrowly focused that you look only to the obvious sources. If you confine your research to the predictable and the tried-and-true, the ideas you generate will very likely be just as predictable, tried, and true. Don't lock yourself into linear, logical thinking. Cast your net wide enough that there is always the possibility you may surprise yourself and catch some off-the-wall idea that suddenly shakes everything up. Remember, the whole point is to use your imagination, so be imaginative from the very start.

INCUBATION

As you are gathering and assembling information, you will have already begun reviewing it, integrating what you have learned with what you already know, and rearranging it into new combinations. That brings us to the next aspect of the process, the germination or incubation stage, when you mull things over, try to make one concept fit with another, mentally test-drive different ideas, turn things over in your mind, try to look at it from different angles, and see it with fresh eyes.

SO WHAT'S THE DIFFERENCE?

So far, this doesn't seem any different than what Hill was describing with his earlier term, *synthesized imagination.* What makes creative vision different is the next stage, in which you use a number of techniques to open the door to your subconscious mind and allow it to influence the creative thoughts incubating in the conscious part of your imagination. This is where you make room for something to happen. This is where you intentionally put yourself in the way of the creative process in the hope that something intuitive or inspirational will come to you.

An important part of the process is learning to recognizethe creative response when it happens. Very often creative vision comes to you in a kind of shorthand, appearing as images, symbols, or dreams. Because these images that emerge from your inner-self are fleeting and easily forgotten, you will need to keep close at hand a notebook or some other way to make a record of the ideas and insights before they vanish from your consciousness.

Even though the ideas dissipate quickly, you should not para-phrase or condense too much when you record your thoughts. As much as possible, you want to be sure to capture the material just the way it comes to you, because often what is good about a good idea is lost if what you recall isn't detailed enough to restimulate your senses and punch all the same buttons it did when it first hit you.

GET YOUR IMAGINATION WORKING OUTSIDE THE BOX

In the following section you will find a number of specific techniques that you can use to stimulate your creative vision. If there is one thing that is common to these techniques, it is that they offer ways to look at things differently. We often hear people talk about taking off the blinders, breaking the mold, pushing the envelope, or think-ing outside the box. All of those statements suggest that the style of thinking you are now using is constricting you and, in order to think better, something has to break down the barriers that are holding you in.

The other common thread is most techniques that help you come up with better ideas are also designed to help you come up with more ideas. One of the biggest problems in finding new solu-tions and creative ideas is that people get so focused on solving the problem quickly, that as soon as they come up with a couple of good alternatives, they stop trying for more.

On the following pages you will find some of the most widely used thinking techniques. They all suggest that the more ideas you have to choose from, the better the chance you'll find a superior solution, and that you should suspend your critical analysis until after you have pulled together a wide range of ideas to choose from.

LATERAL THINKING

Written by Edward de Bono, the renowned psychologist, business consultant, and bestselling author of over sixty books, *Lateral Thinking* is the classic book on creative thinking. In it, de Bono explains a number of techniques to free yourself from the usual style of logical thinking, which he calls vertical thinking.

The difference between the two styles of thinking is that with vertical thinking all that matters is how *right* the answers are, and with lateral thinking your main concern is how *diverse* the answers are.

With vertical thinking you move forward one step at a time, and each step has to be correct before you advance to the next. With lateral thinking you can make leaps of logic, or jump ahead, then go back to fill in the gaps later.

The whole aim of lateral thinking is to look at things in different ways, to disrupt the normal flow, to restructure patterns and to generate alternatives. In lateral thinking you are not trying to find the best approach; you are trying to come up with as many different approaches as you can. Later you will judge which are good, better, and best.

LATERAL THINKING AND OUTSIDE STIMULI

One way to shake things up and force yourself to look at things from a different point of view is to intentionally interrupt your thinking by interjecting a non sequitur that sends your thoughts off on a tangent. This is the complete opposite of a rigid, vertical style of thinking in which you only focus on what is relevant. With this approach, you intentionally look for the irrelevant.

In some ways it is similar to the practice of looking for spiritual guidance by randomly opening the bible and seeking the answer in the first passage your eye falls on. The same principle is at work in

the ancient Chinese practice of throwing three coins and then looking up the interpretation in the I-Ching.

In the case of lateral thinking, the source of stimulating words
could be anything from a dictionary to a romance novel to an item
in your desk drawer or what you see on a walk down the street. The
idea is that you set up a system to produce random words or chance
events.

It could be that you select a book, then throw dice to come up
with a page number, paragraph, and word. Or if you wanted to use a
location or a visual as the stimulant, you could decide that the thing
to throw into the mix will be the first blue object you see, or whatever
is in the window of the fifth store with a neon sign.

One of the most interesting ways of coming up with random
words is to use a random-word generator. A random-word generator
is exactly what the name implies, and if you log on to any search
engine and type in "random-word generator," it will offer you page
after page of listings for free Web sites. Click on any of these sites,
and there on the home page you will see a word to set your mental
wheels spinning. Most of these sites also offer other possibilities,
such as random names or random phrases, and some give you the
opportunity to set certain parameters to your word search. Some
sites also offer a picture option that gives you a visual image as
your cue.

LATERAL THINKING: RANDOM-WORDS STIMULATION

You can do this on your own or you can do it as part of a group, but
there must be certain ground rules that you set about the amount
of time you will devote to following the ideas stimulated by a word,
how many words you use in any one session, and who will act as
the referee to keep everyone on track or to prompt a new direction.

Once you have decided on your method for selecting a random
word or object, you state the problem you have been wrestling with,
choose your random word, and then start throwing out whatever new

thoughts and ideas are stimulated by thinking of the random word in association with your problem.

Some ideas will be one-offs, while others will generate a whole chain of related ideas. Sometimes a chain of linked thoughts will continue on for the whole session, while at other times the chains will lead nowhere and you'll have go back to the word and start a new train of thought.

You do not want to devote more than about three to five minutes to exploring the possibilities opened by the random word you have selected. And once you have reached the predetermined time limit, you should not immediately look for another stimulus word. If you do, you will find yourself going through word after word as if you are searching for the best word. That is not the point. There are no best words, because you are not trying for anything in particular; you are just looking for ideas to stimulate your mind, so you should be satisfied with whatever you get from the exercise.

LATERAL THINKING: REVERSAL

The object of lateral thinking is to create a different arrangement of information that will provoke a different way of looking at the situation. Reversal is another mental exercise that you can do as a way of jogging your thinking into a different arrangement.

You take some actual feature of the problem you are working on and begin to modify it by envisioning its opposite. You take things as they are, then turn them around, inside out, upside down, back to front.

Here is an example of one kind of reversal thinking that de Bono uses in his book:

A man late for an important meeting is driving his car down a narrow road when he comes upon a shepherd and a large flock of sheep that block the road. There is no way the sheep can move forward any faster, and the shepherd is afraid that he can't keep his sheep from being run over if the car forces its way through the herd.

How does the car get past the sheep?

It doesn't. The shepherd reverses the situation. He tells the man to stop the car. The shepherd turns his flock around, and he herds the sheep back past the now stationary car. The sheep are then behind the car and the road in front of the car is wide open. The car speeds off.

LATERAL THINKING: THE OTHER POINT OF VIEW

A variation on reversal thinking is to look at your problem from another person's point of view. The most common version of this is when manufacturers are designing products and they say that they try to look at it from the customer's point of view.

If you were trying to come up with a revolutionary design for an office chair, it would certainly be helpful to consider the person who will buy it and sit in it. But what might produce an even more creative insight would be to look at it from the point of view of the desk it will sit in front of, or see it from the point of view of the carpet its wheels will sit on, or what about the way the office cleaning crew would see it? Or consider looking at it from the point of view of the environmentalists who are trying to shut down the junkyard where it will get dumped when it is old and broken.

With either the reversal or the other point of view, your goal is to generate as many variations as possible, so remember to avoid the obvious and the tried-and-true. You should make sure that your other points of view are not all as directly related to the subject as indicated previously in the office-chair example.

For instance, you might get even better ideas if you looked at it from a kid's point of view, from an entertainment point of view, from the point of view of a clothing manufacturer, from a historical point of view, or consider what your mother-in-law would think of it.

Once you have run through a reasonable number of viewpoints, you can magnify your results even more by challenging your team to come up with what is good about each of the ways you have looked at it. Then turn it around and come up with what's bad about what you see from each point of view.

BRAINSTORMING

Brainstorming is a term that is often misused because it is assumed that it is just a synonym for kicking around ideas. However, brainstorming is actually a very specific technique that was first defined and formalized in 1939 by advertising executive Alex F. Osborne. According to Osborne, the distinguishing features of a brainstorming session are:

- It is a group method of generating insights and ideas about a specific problem.

- There is an appointed moderator.

- There is an appointed note-taker to keep track of all the ideas generated.

- The group should be no larger than a dozen people.

- All ideas, no matter how far-fetched, are equally welcomed and considered.

- Logic cannot be allowed to deter an idea.

- No criticism of any idea is allowed during the process.

- Bosses cannot shoot down ideas or have any more control than anyone else.

- No judgment is made about any idea until after the session has been completed.

A brainstorming session starts with a specific problem, and by the end of the session you will have a list of good ideas, bad ideas, top-of-the-head concepts, and wild and crazy solutions. After the session is over, the list is analyzed and the suggestions are evaluated. It is only then that critical analysis is brought to bear and the ideas are reviewed to see which ones might yield practical solutions.

THE BRAINSTORMING MODERATOR OR LEADER

Brainstorming is a perfect way to work with a Master Mind Alliance. The moderator's job is to set the problem and guide the session without trying to control it, and probably the most important job is to make sure the participants keep moving on so that the session doesn't fall into critical analysis.

THE NOTE-TAKER OR SCRIBE

The note-taker writes on a chalkboard or large flip-chart sheets, or uses some kind of video screen, so that everyone can keep track of the ideas as they are written down. The note-taker must record every idea and must refrain from judging or filtering out "crazy ideas."

THE BRAINSTORMING SESSION

In commenting on his technique, Alex Osborne said: "Brainstorm means using the brain to storm a creative problem in commando fashion." He also advised that you should get every idea out of your head, no matter how crazy you think it is, because "it is easier to tone down a wild idea than to think up a new one."

The moderator begins the session by going around the room giving everyone a chance to throw in ideas and suggestions. After a few such rounds, it is opened up to the free exchange of ideas.

From the beginning, every idea is welcome and no one is expected to defend an idea or even to discuss any one idea for very long. Every effort should be made to encourage even the most reticent members of the group to say whatever comes into their minds. The challenge is to keep the ideas coming and to keep them building on each other, and it doesn't matter if your idea is totally original or if it is based on someone else's idea. Your idea can then get picked up by another person and another person, until it becomes a chain of ideas that keeps piggybacking on the ideas that came before them.

The session terminates at the end of a predetermined period, or when the moderator senses that creativity or enthusiasm is beginning to flag. Most brainstorming sessions last only an hour at most.

Most groups usually take at least a coffee break, and some-times as much as a few hours before they tackle the evaluation. The task is to combine and modify the raw ideas to come up with a list of the best practical ideas, to discard those that are totally impractical, and to create another list that identifies the kernel of a good idea that is at the heart of some of the wilder, off-the-wall suggestions.

MIND-MAPPING

Mind-mapping is an idea-generating method that is associated with author, educator, psychologist, and brain specialist Tony Buzan. A mind map is creative-thinking techniques designed to organize your thinking and generate creative ideas. It is used as an aid in problem-solving and decision-making. A mind map is a picture that you make to explain to yourself the ideas that you came up with. Some people can get so used to working with mind-mapping that they prefer it to note-taking.

A mind map is a diagram that shows how new ideas are spun off a central keyword or idea, and it visually illustrates the connections between bits of information. By drawing what amounts to a picture of the way ideas are generated, it encourages a brainstorming approach to any organizational task.

Unlike a list that is made from top to bottom, the mind map starts from the center, or main idea, and branches out in different directions. The relative importance of the ideas is readily apparent from how and where they appear in the map. Although there are exceptions, usually the most important ideas cluster near the center and grow less important as they spread out.

The way you write or draw an idea, and how it looks on the page, can play a large part in recalling not just the facts about the idea you wanted to capture but also the feeling you had about the information when you put it on the mind map.

Tony Buzan suggests the following for mind-mapping:

- Start in the center with a word or an image of the topic.

- Use images, symbols, and multiple colors to emphasize special words or ideas and to make certain ideas stand out.

- Don't overthink where things should go; it will restrict creativity.

- The lines must be connected, starting from the central image.

- Feel free to start a new branch whenever an idea hits, or to go back and add new details to branches you started earlier.

- Do not worry about order or organization; that will take care of itself.

A mind-mapping session ends when you feel that you have set down all the information you wish to record at a particular time, or when you feel that your creativity is losing its freshness. You can always come back at a later time and add more ideas to a mind map.

If Napoleon Hill had made a mind map to plot out the chapters for *Think and Grow Rich*:

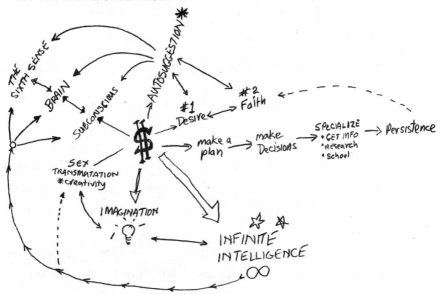

CLUSTERING

Clustering is a right-brain thinking technique devised by Gabriel Rico to break writer's block, to pull together your creative ideas and get yourself ready to start writing about your idea(s). It is a technique that jump-starts creativity and generates ideas by forcing you to break out of the linear thinking that views things in an organized, prioritized way. Clustering is more random, less restricting. It is a form of brainstorming that generates ideas, images, and feelings around a topic or stimulus word.

The editor's cluster prior to writing about Hill's childhood:

Clustering ideas is usually done by yourself with paper and pencil, although you can also adapt it to a group. It normally does not take more than a few minutes, but the session is left open-ended to allow for the "felt shift," which will be explained at the end of this description.

Begin with a blank page. In the center of the page write the word or phrase that describes your problem and draw a circle around it. This is the seed or nucleus from which you will start. Now, as quickly as possible, without censoring any ideas that may come to mind, draw a line out from the circled word at the center and write the first idea that pops into your head. Draw a circle around it, then draw a connecting line; write down the next idea, circle it, draw a line; write the next idea, circle it, draw a line, and so on and so on, until you run out of ideas to add to that chain of thoughts.

Whenever your mind shifts to a new direction, go back to the center circle, draw a new line extending out in a different direction, and start a new chain of thoughts. Keep creating clusters of circled words or ideas and starting new chains of thoughts, until you feel what Gabriel Rico calls a "felt shift." This is an odd but very descriptive term that captures something quite unique that happens when you use this technique.

When you start working outward from a central circled word, the new ideas will come quite quickly and easily. However, as you continue clustering, you will come to a point where you feel as though something about the process has changed or shifted, and that this is the time to stop because now you know what you want to do or write.

This "felt shift" is the clustering equivalent of the aha or eureka moment. It's your subconscious telling you that you've hit on something good and it's time to stop clustering and start writing it down.

One last note on clustering: Gabriel Rico is quite specific about drawing a circle or an oval around each new word or idea, as opposed to a square, rectangle, or any other shape. She does not know why, but from her many years of experience with the technique, she has found that there is something in the clusters and connections of rounded shapes that produces better results.

HILL'S INVISIBLE COUNSELORS

In both *Law of Success* and *Think and Grow Rich,* Napoleon Hill goes into detail about a mental exercise that he originally developed as a character-building device to overcome what he called the handicap of being born and raised in an environment of ignorance and superstition. He called the technique his invisible or imaginary counselors.

Each night Hill would imagine that he was conducting a meeting of the nine men in history he admired most. He would pose a question, and then each of his imaginary guests would give their answer. To prepare for this mental exercise, Hill intently studied the lives of these historical personages so that the answers they gave were completely in keeping with their character.

The answers, of course, were Hill's own thoughts and words that he was mentally putting into the mouths of his invisible counselors. But because he was coming up with the answers "in character," so to speak, those answers exhibited an intelligence and wit that Hill did not normally exhibit when he was being himself.

The following is adapted from Hill's description of his invisible counselors in the version he wrote for *Think and Grow Rich,* Chapter 14: The Sixth Sense.

LET GREAT MEN SHAPE YOUR LIFE

Long before I had ever written a line for publication, or endeavored to deliver a speech in public, I followed the habit of reshaping my own character, by trying to imitate the nine men whose lives and life-works had been most impressive to me. These nine men were Emerson, Paine, Edison, Darwin, Lincoln, Burbank, Napoleon, Ford, and Carnegie. Every night, over a long period of years, I held an imaginary council meeting with this group whom I called my "Invisible Counselors."

Just before going to sleep at night, I would shut my eyes, and see, in my imagination, this group of men seated with me around my council table. Here I had not only sat among those whom I considered to be great, but I dominated the group, by serving as the chairman.

My purpose was to rebuild my own character so it would represent a composite of the characters of my imaginary counselors.

BUILDING CHARACTER THROUGH AUTOSUGGESTION

I knew, of course, that all men have become what they are because of their dominating thoughts and desires. I knew that self-suggestion is a powerful factor in building character, that it is, in fact, the sole principle through which character is built.

With this knowledge of the principles of mind operation, I was fairly well armed with the equipment needed in rebuilding my character. In these imaginary council meetings, I called on my cabinet members for the knowledge I wished each to contribute, addressing myself to each member in audible words, as follows:

Mr. Emerson, I desire to acquire from you the marvelous understanding of nature, which distinguished your life. I ask that you impress upon my subconscious mind whatever qualities you possessed that enabled you to understand and adapt yourself to the laws of nature.

Mr. Burbank, I request that you pass on to me the knowledge that enabled you to so harmonize the laws of nature, that you caused the cactus to shed its thorns and become an edible food. Give me access to the knowledge that enabled you to make two blades of grass grow where but one grew before.

Napoleon, I desire to acquire from you, by emulation, the marvelous ability you possessed to inspire men, and to arouse them to greater and more determined spirit of action. Also to acquire the spirit of enduring faith, which enabled you to turn defeat into victory, and to surmount staggering obstacles.

Mr. Paine, I desire to acquire from you the freedom of thought and the courage and clarity with which to express convictions, which so distinguished you!

Mr. Darwin, I wish to acquire from you the marvelous patience, and the ability to study cause and effect, without bias or prejudice, so exemplified by you in the field of natural science.

Mr. Lincoln, I desire to build into my own character the keen sense of justice, the untiring spirit of patience, the sense of humor, the human understanding, and the tolerance that were your distinguishing characteristics.

Mr. Carnegie, I wish to acquire a thorough understanding of the principles of organized effort, which you used so effectively in the building of a great industrial enterprise.

Mr. Ford, I wish to acquire your spirit of persistence, the determination, poise, and self-confidence that have enabled you to master poverty, and to organize, unify, and simplify human effort, so I may help others to follow in your footsteps.

Mr. Edison, I wish to acquire from you the marvelous spirit of faith, with which you have uncovered so many of nature's secrets, the spirit of unremitting toil with which you have so often wrested victory from defeat.

THE STARTLING POWER OF IMAGINATION

I studied the records of their lives with painstaking care. After some months of this nightly procedure, I was astounded by the discovery that these imaginary figures became apparently real.

Each of these nine men developed individual characteristics that surprised me. For example, Lincoln developed the habit of always being late, then walking around in solemn parade. He always wore an expression of seriousness on his face. Rarely did I see him smile.

That was not true of the others. Burbank and Paine often indulged in witty repartee, which seemed, at times, to shock the other members of the cabinet. On one occasion Burbank was late. When he came, he was excited with enthusiasm, and explained that he had been late because of an experiment he was making, through which he hoped to be able to grow apples on any sort of tree. Paine chided him by reminding him that it was an apple that started all the trouble between man and woman. Darwin chuckled heartily as he suggested that Paine should watch out for little serpents, when he went into the forest to gather apples, as they had the habit of growing into big snakes. Emerson observed, "No serpents, no apples," and Napoleon remarked, "No apples, no state!"

This is the first time that I have had the courage to mention this. Heretofore, I have remained quiet on the subject, because I knew, from my own attitude in connection with such matters, that I would be misunderstood if I described my unusual experience.

I have been emboldened now to reduce my experience to the printed page, because I am now less concerned about what "they say" than I was in the years that have passed.

Lest I be misunderstood, I wish here to state most emphatically that I still regard my cabinet meetings as being purely imaginary, but while the members of my cabinet may be purely fictional, and the meetings existent only in my own imagination, they have led me into glorious paths of adventure, rekindled an appreciation of true greatness, encouraged creative endeavor, and emboldened the expression of honest thought.

TAPPING THE SOURCE OF INSPIRATION

Somewhere in the cell-structure of the brain is located an organ that receives vibrations of thought ordinarily called "hunches." So far, science has not discovered where this organ of the sixth sense is located, but this is not important. The fact remains that human beings do receive accurate knowledge through sources other than the physical senses.

During my meetings with the "Invisible Counselors," I find my mind most receptive to ideas, thoughts, and knowledge that reach me through the sixth sense.

Once Hill became aware of how insightful these answers could be, he switched focus from asking personal questions designed to improve his character, to posing questions about a wide range of problems that required creative solutions. It proved to be such an effective method for creating more and better ideas that he used it not only for personal purposes but also to create solutions for certain clients he advised.

The following commentary is excerpted and adapted from *Think and Grow Rich: The Workbook,* Chapter 15: The Sixth Sense.

Napoleon Hill's counselors are a variation on the use of visualization as a means of accessing knowledge stored in the subconscious and tapping into Infinite Intelligence. In effect, what Hill did was divide his mind into nine channels, each one having its own special focus and being attuned to a particular aspect of human nature. By mentally posing a question and then answering that question from those nine separate viewpoints, Hill was offering multiple opportunities for his subconscious and his creative imagination to send him intuitive solutions.

By filling his mind with so much information about each of these counselors, Hill was pumping reams of knowledge into his mind, much of which was going into the nooks and crannies of his subconscious. The probability of intuitive thoughts was greatly increased by making the nine channels so vivid and unique, and by creating each one in such detail, he was able to tap into certain ideas and information that resided in parts of his subconscious which he could not have reached in any other way. His counselors may have been imaginary, but the ideas Hill got from them provided solid solutions to real problems.

IS THERE SCIENTIFIC PROOF?

Starting in the 1930s and 1940s, the famed neurosurgeon Dr. Wilder Penfield expanded our knowledge of the brain tremendously by creating a map of the surface of the brain showing which areas governed which muscular actions and bodily responses. This was determined by applying mild electrical stimulation to various parts of the cortex while it was exposed during brain surgery. It was during this process that he also found that by stimulating the temporal lobes in the front of the brain, it would cause the patient to have vividly detailed memories and recollections.

As Penfield stimulated patients' brains and produced memories so real that the patients could smell flowers or feel textures, he was surprised to find that although these patients' brains were making them experience realistic memories, when he asked where the patients were, they knew that they were not really in the memory they were experiencing; they knew they were in the hospital.

Penfield concluded that although he could tweak the brain to make it believe hallucinations that are indistinguishable from reality, there is still a separate mind stepped back from and outside the brain that knows what is going on.

Dr. Penfield found that, separate from the kind of "knowing" that takes place in the physical brain, there is another kind of knowing that takes place in your nonphysical mind: it is a part of your mind, but also apart from your mind. In some way your mind has a part that can stand back and either observe itself or exert control over itself without the rest of itself knowing it's doing it.

This unusual part of the mind that Wilder Penfield communicated with during his open-brain surgeries was encountered in quite a different way by Ernest Hilgard, Professor Emeritus of Psychology at Stanford University and one of the most respected psychologists in America.

Ernest Hilgard and his wife, Josephine, headed the highly regarded Laboratory of Hypnosis Research at Stanford University. In 1975 they launched a scientific study into hypnosis and pain control. They developed a series of experiments to determine if a person who had been hypnotized and told not to feel pain could in fact actually feel the pain.

They began each session by confirming that the subject could indeed feel pain. They would then hypnotize the patient and instruct him or her that they would *not* feel the pain. The Hilgards would test again to ensure that it was working and that the patient was feeling no pain.

They asked the subject to give them a signal by raising one finger if there was some part of the inner self that knew they were in pain, even though the hypnotized self couldn't feel it. The subject raised a finger.

The Hilgards then asked if there was a way to communicate with the part that knew there was pain. They found that they could actually speak to that part of the subject's mind, and that it could answer by speaking through the subject. It could tell them what was really going on, even though the subject was hypnotized and not aware of the pain.

They published the results of their research in numerous papers and books in which they refer to this part of the subconscious as the "hidden observer" or the "silent witness." Their research showed that while the hidden observer knows of its own existence and the existence and experience of the patient, the hypnotized subject knows nothing of the hidden observer.

Just as Wilder Penfield found with the patient who was convinced she was at her birthday picnic but whose silent witness knew that she was in the hospital having a hallucination—and as the Hilgards' hidden observer knew the subject was having pain even though he could not feel it—Napoleon Hill's mind could send him intuitive ideas through an imaginary counselor.

When Hill would visualize his roundtable meetings, his imaginary counselors would present him with intuitive ideas that did not seem to come from anything he was aware that he knew. And although he knew in reality that the ideas originated from within his own mind, it was as though they came from someone else.

If there is a part of the mind that can observe itself and comment on itself, it is likely that it is the same part of the mind that could stand apart from Hill's normal thinking and provide him with flashes of insight or intuitive ideas through his imaginary counselors.

Following are two other examples that share some common principles with Hill's imaginary counselors. First is a thinking and problem-solving technique by Dr. Edward de Bono called Six Thinking Hats, and the other is the personal-growth therapy known as Neurolinguistic Programming.

SIX THINKING HATS

The inspiration for Dr. Edward de Bono's Six Thinking Hats is the old expression people often use when they have to solve a problem or come up with an idea, and they say that they have to put on their thinking hat. Suppose it wasn't just one thinking hat but six different thinking hats, and each hat represented a different kind of thinking. Imagine how thoroughly you would have thought about a problem or an idea if you put on the thinking hats one after the other, and each time you put on a different one of the hats, you focused on thinking about the problem just from that one point of view.

No doubt you have already recognized the similarity between using Six Thinking Hats and using nine advisers to prompt you to think more creatively.

Edward de Bono suggests that the thinking hats also help to unscramble your thinking so you can use one mode at a time instead of trying to take care of emotions, logic, information, hope, and creativity all at the same time.

Each of the thinking hats is a different color, and each color has a different style of thinking:

1. **White Hat** (think of a blank sheet—objective): Just the facts ma'am, just the facts. No opinions, no interpretations, no rationalizations, just the facts. Information, reports, facts, and figures. With white-hat thinking you focus on pulling together and reviewing all the available data. This tells you not only what you know but also helps you figure out what you don't know.

2. **Red Hat** (think of fire—subjective): The red hat represents emotional thinking and emotional intelligence. It's not what you think,

it's what you feel. It doesn't have to be logical, and you don't have to rationalize it. It's opinion, emotions, intuition, and empathy. It's also the kind of thinking you do when you try to understand the responses of others, and when you think how other people will react emotionally to your ideas.

3. **Black Hat** (think of a judge's robe—objective): The black-hat thinker looks for the faults, the errors, what is wrong and negative about the subject. This is critical and judgmental thinking. Using black-hat thinking, you look at all the bad points, the risks and dangers, and try to see why it might not work. This is important because it highlights the weak points in a plan and prompts you to prepare contingency plans.

4. **Yellow Hat** (think of the sun—objective): The yellow hat represents positive thinking, sunshine, brightness, praise, and enthusiasm. It is the optimistic viewpoint that helps you to see all the benefits of the decision, the value in it, and why it will work. However, yellow-hat thinking is not naïve. It's very constructive and it produces concrete ideas and suggestions.

5. **Green Hat** (think of plants—speculative and creative): The green hat is the hat for creative thinking. It's a freewheeling, everything-goes way of thinking in which there is little criticism of ideas. This is the kind of thinking usually referred to as thinking outside the box, or pushing the envelope, and it places the highest value on coming up with alternative ideas and new approaches.

6. **Blue Hat** (think of the sky—overview): The blue hat is the control hat or the conductor hat. The blue hat represents the big picture, looking at the overall process from all the viewpoints. It monitors all the other thinking that will be needed to explore the subject, and it is the blue hat that suggests when you should try on a different hat to get some better ideas. This is the hat worn for running things and for chairing meetings, for compiling summaries, overviews, and conclusions.

Although not as creatively vivid or as intellectually demanding as learning everything possible about nine famous people, the Six Thinking Hats technique will definitely push you to consider ideas you would not have thought of otherwise. And the more avenues you open into your thinking, the more likely the possibility of your creative imagination producing ideas from Infinite Intelligence.

NEUROLINGUISTIC PROGRAMMING

In the early 1970s, John Grinder, a professor of linguistics at the University of California at Santa Cruz, and Richard Bandler, a student leading a Gestalt therapy group there, developed a self-improvement method they called Neurolinguistic Programming.

It is a method for identifying what it is about yourself that is keeping you from being as successful as you wish to be, and then changing who you are by systematically adopting the language, beliefs, and behaviors of those people who have achieved the kind of success and excellence you want for yourself.

In short, your thoughts, gestures, and words create your world and who you are in that world. NLP can change that perception by teaching you to use new thoughts, gestures, and words that will make you successful. These new thoughts and words are guaranteed to work because they are copied from people who are proven successes.

Starting from the premise that people become successful because of the way they think, act, and speak, Bandler and Grinder set out to analyze the thoughts, actions, and speech of three people who were extremely successful communicators. They chose three highly respected therapists: Milton Erickson, the father of hypnotherapy; Fritz Perls, the founder of Gestalt therapy; and Virginia Satir, the noted family therapist. They analyzed in minute detail every aspect of the style, language, and methods used by these three individuals.

Their research revealed certain patterns from which they created "models." Their theory is that these models can be used by

anyone to remake themselves, and by remaking themselves pat-
terned after these models, they will improve their ability to communicate, which in turn will help them achieve their desires.

By studying the NLP models, you learn first what you want to
change about yourself, and second you learn specific techniques for
adopting the style and language of someone else who has already
succeeded in what you wish to accomplish.

The idea is that if someone has excelled at something, you can
learn how that person did it by observing the details of their behavior
and then copying them right down to the smallest detail. When you
are modeling another person, you must suspend your own beliefs
and adopt everything about the model.

The more realistically you act as if you are the model, the more
your brain begins to learn the model's patterns, and eventually the
patterns adapt to you so that you are no longer "acting as if"—you
have actually become your version of the pattern.

NLP has had its greatest success in the areas of motivation,
counseling, coaching, peak performance, sales training, and dealing
with personal issues ranging from changing negative beliefs to overcoming fears and phobias, depression, and addiction.

As noted earlier, Neurolinguistic Programming involves much
more than Hill's method for improving his character and coming up
with intuitive ideas, but the bloodlines are clear. The basic idea of
studying and copying someone so that you can tap into what makes
them a success is a direct line to Hill's imaginary counselors.

The amount of detail that has been provided on the Six Thinking
Hats and the Neurolinguistic Programming is enough to show the
similarities between these methods and Napoleon Hill's invisible
counselors, and perhaps even enough for readers to experiment in
a minor way with the Six Thinking Hats. However, if you are serious
about attempting the techniques, you will need much more detailed
explanations, especially for NLP.

If you wish to learn more, the editors suggest that you read *Six Thinking Hats* by Edward de Bono, which you will find available through most booksellers.

To learn more about Neurolinguistic Programming, we suggest you might start with the first book by Bandler and Grinder, *Frogs Into Princes*, or *Neurolinguistic Programming, Volume I,* by Dilts, Grinder, Bandler, and DeLozier, or just search NLP on the Internet.

The following commentary is excerpted and adapted from *Think and Grow Rich: The Workbook,* Chapter 6: Imagination.

CREATIVE VISUALIZATION

In previous chapters, creative visualization was examined as a way to burn your Definite Chief Aim or purpose into your subconscious. Visualization can also be used to stimulate your imagination and heighten your creativity. You can do this by approaching it almost as though your subconscious mind is an actual place where you can take your concept or problem, and by taking it there it will become transformed into something better and more creative.

If you have doubts that creative visualization can really work, if you feel self-conscious or uncomfortable trying, or if you feel that this kind of pretending is more silly than it is serious, just remind yourself about Thomas Edison, Alexander Graham Bell, Albert Einstein, the NASA astronauts who perform without a hitch, all the sports stars who have improved their game, and all the doctors who have saved lives by using this very technique.

You have in your mind almost endless facts and experiences that could help you make more creative and better decisions. Some of these hidden ideas and bits of knowledge have been forgotten because you learned them long ago, or they were superseded by more immediate concerns. Other bits of information didn't seem to fit anywhere when you learned them, so they were just set aside, waiting for the time you'll have need of them.

If you choose to, you can open yourself to these thoughts, ideas, and solutions by creating a mental scenario in which your subconscious believes it is right and natural for it to open the way and allow you free access to the information in the deepest regions of your mind.

Following is a method for using creative visualization to provide you with creative ideas, answers to questions, and solutions to problems.

THE FIRST THING TO DO IS RELAX . . .

Choose a time and a place where you can relax and not be disturbed. Loosen any clothing that you find binding or constricting. Choose a comfortable place to sit where you can rest your feet flat on the floor, and let your arms hang loosely with your hands resting in your lap.

Now close your eyes, place one hand lightly on your abdomen, and take a deep breath, breathing the air in through your nose and letting it out through your mouth.

As you breathe in, do not try to fill your chest. Instead, as you take each breath, think of the air filling your whole body so that both your chest and abdomen expand.

If you are breathing as you should, each time you breathe in, the hand you placed on your abdomen will be lifted out as your abdomen expands along with your lungs.

Continue to breathe deeply as you let your breathing settle into a slow, relaxed rhythm and you slowly count down from ten to one, releasing all stress and tension in your body. As you count each number, envision yourself on an escalator; with each number, the escalator takes you down to a deeper level of relaxed receptivity.

That simple exercise, which shouldn't take more than a minute or two, will put you in a state of relaxed but receptive attention—the perfect condition for creative visualization and the ideal state of mind in which to create clear, convincing, fully realized mental images.

When you are relaxed you will imagine yourself in a place that feels very calming and peaceful to you. It can be any place you want. It could be in a forest glade or in front of a cozy fireplace; it could be a vast library or an ocean cove, a castle on a hill, or any other place that gives you peace of mind. It is any place that you want it to be, and it looks and feels just exactly the way you want it to look and feel.

Take a moment or two to look around and explore this new place of yours. Notice all the details. Imagine the textures. Listen for the sounds. Feel, see, examine, and experience your chosen place.

When you have explored enough and you are satisfied that it is everything you want it to be, you will become aware of a path or passageway. Somehow you know that if you follow that path it will lead you to a place where you will find the answer you are seeking.

You lower your eyes for a moment, and when you raise them you find yourself transported and standing before a door that leads to the ideas and answers you seek. You are now entering a room, and there, almost filling one entire wall, is a large video screen. Displayed on the screen is a representation of the idea you are looking for or the problem you wish to solve.

It might be as complete as a three-dimensional scene, as simple as a symbol rotating in space, or maybe it is just the pure essence of the idea or problem and it doesn't really have a solid shape. As you watch it on the screen you are aware that there are forces at work, adjusting and molding and shaping it to complete it in the best possible way.

In your mind you know that whatever is causing the image to appear on the screen also has access to the subconscious memories of everything you have ever learned or experienced and every thought or feeling you have ever had. You also know that whatever it is that is controlling the images can draw upon that vast resource of your subconscious and it can use all of that information to transform the illustration of your problem into the solution to your problem.

In your mind, you settle on what you think is a reasonable number of ideas that you can deal with in one sitting, and you then instruct your subconscious that, one after another, the screen will begin showing you a series of creative ideas that will help you solve your problem. You will be able to help develop the solutions that appear on the screen so that each finished idea is the best combination of what you know, combined with what your subconscious knows.

VISUALIZATION: TAKE TWO

A variation on this visualization follows exactly the same procedure up to the point where you encounter the path or passageway. But this time, as you follow the path or passageway, you will encounter a person who will become your mentor or adviser.

How you picture this person is entirely up to you. You may think of your mentor as an ancient sage, a mythical oracle, or, alternatively, you might choose a hugely successful CEO, or some other kind of well-known leader. In fact, if you choose an actual living person whom you admire, it opens it up to some very interesting results, because you already know a good deal about the person and you have a feel for the kind of advice he or she would give.

Whomever you choose as your mentor, this person is everything you could ever ask for in an adviser. He or she has access to everything you have ever experienced and every thought you ever had, and is the personification of wisdom and creativity. You can ask this person to help you develop your idea or provide the answer to your problem.

WHAT TO EXPECT

Will your subconscious provide you with a set number of clear and distinct solutions to your problem, or will you get a couple of fuzzy ideas that may or may not be good? Will you see images on the screen, or will the answers come to you like ideas in your mind? Will your mentor sit you down and explain the answer, or will you just pick up a feeling for what to do? And what do you do if you don't get anything?

There is no right answer to any of these questions. What comes of working with creative visualization is completely dependent on you and how prepared you are to make it work and let it work. It is well documented that creative visualization has been the source of scientific breakthroughs and multimillion-dollar inventions. It has also been the source of a lot of fanciful ideas, numerous impractical solutions, plenty of daydreaming, and more than a few unplanned midday snoozes.

Creative visualization is a tool. It is a fact that it does work. It works better for some people than it does for others, but the more it is used the better the quality and quantity of results.

Approach your visualization sessions with faith and confidence, and have a pen and paper handy so you can quickly make notes of the thoughts and ideas that come to you. As with the other techniques, you should never try to evaluate or analyze during the process. Write down as clear a description as you can of each idea. Review what you have written later, when you can take the time to give your ideas and your solution serious consideration.

ACTING AS IF, AND RECAPTURING THAT WINNING FEELING

This acting-as-if technique is actually quite closely related to Napoleon Hill's counselors and to creative visualization, but for many this is a much more straightforward and easy-to-understand version of the concept. This technique is simply to act as if you are just as smart and intelligent and creative as you would like to be.

To restate that in a way that should make it a little clearer, you may not think you are very creative, but if you act as if you are creative, you will be surprised how creative you become.

The editors of this book assure you that this works to some degree for everyone, and if you give it a fair chance it will work for you. The next time you have to come up with a creative idea or solution, think of someone whom you believe to be as smart and creative as you would like to be.

In your mind, put yourself into that person's shoes and come up with the kind of idea you imagine that person would think of. In effect, if you pretend that you think like a creative person, you really will come up with creative ideas.

A variation on this technique would be to go back in your mind to a time when you were really on roll, when you were at the top of your game, when everything was clicking and you felt like a winner. In your mind, recall that feeling of success; vividly picture yourself full of self-confidence, clear-headed, in command, bold, and decisive.

Now, in your mind, project yourself into that winning frame of mind, and use that mind-set to solve your problem.

Chapter Seven

THE MASTER MIND ALLIANCE AND INFINITE INTELLIGENCE

WHAT WOULD NAPOLEON HILL DO?

Everything we create begins as a Definite Chief Aim forged in the workshop of the imagination, where ideas and insights are hammered into practical plans which in turn are rendered in reality.

To transform desire from abstract thought into concrete thing, Napoleon Hill would bring together in harmony two or more people to form a Master Mind Alliance. From this blending of minds would be created a third mind that generates more and better ideas which exceed the sum of its parts.

Napoleon Hill said that he thought the concept of the Master Mind Alliance was his most original and important contribution to the philosophy of personal achievement because it is the ultimate culmination of the ideas behind Cosmic Habit Force and Infinite Intelligence. However, many people, on first reading about it in *Law of Success* or *Think and Grow Rich,* don't see it as anything more than plain old cooperation or teamwork.

The fact is that although the key point that Hill wants to make is there, often his sentences have to be read two, three, or even more times for the point to emerge from the haze of words. Much of the lack of clarity is simply because the overblown writing style of Hill's day is not the plain style that the modern reader is used to.

Very often a truly striking idea is surrounded by so many other ideas that are rather ordinary, yet they are written in a blaze of capitalized words and exclamation marks that commands just as much attention as the key idea. The result is that your mind tends to tune everything down, which means that in adjusting for all of the superlatives you can undervalue what's important, such as just how different from teamwork the Master Mind really is.

THE MASTER MIND IS MUCH MORE THAN TEAMWORK

Teamwork can be achieved by any group, even if the members of the team don't like each other or have anything in common. That's because all that teamwork requires is that the members cooperate and work together. In teamwork you might work together not because you have the same goals, but simply because you like the leader, or because the team is paying you enough to buy your services. Sometimes there is good teamwork because different members have different agendas.

For instance, a board of directors may be very unfriendly and still run a business successfully. Musical groups are made up of notoriously self-centered people who work as a team if it will help them get ahead.

A Master Mind Alliance, on the other hand, is a tight-knit group of select individuals who work together because they have exactly the same agenda, a deep sense of mission, and a commitment to the same goal.

A Master Mind is the result of a conscious attempt by an individual to surround himself or herself with a group of people who are so in-tune with one another that they don't just bring out the best in each other, but the group as a whole takes on a life of its own, elevating everyone's level of thinking, and generating shared leaps of logic, insights, and flashes of intuition.

RECAPPING THE BASIC PRINCIPLES

Napoleon Hill laid the groundwork for this in the two previous chapters: Accurate Thinking and Infinite Intelligence, and Imagination and Infinite Intelligence.

- Every "thing" in the universe is one form or another of energy. The human body is made up of energy, the human mind is energy, and the thoughts and ideas that come into the mind are also energy.

- There is an undeniable similarity between radio as a burst of energy that sends out waves that can be picked up, and thought as a burst of energy that may also send out waves that can be picked up.

- When the minds of two people are working together in a spirit of harmony, the energy of each mind seems to pick up on the energy of the other mind.

- The subconscious is described as the part of the human mind where bits and pieces of information come together, and sometimes through Infinite Intelligence, tune in to the energy of outside thought waves that cause flashes of insight, hunches, and original ideas to appear in the imagination.

The concept of the Master Mind takes it a step further. If, as Napoleon Hill, Thomas Edison, and Alexander Graham Bell theorized, humans sometimes pick up external thought waves that appear in the imagination in the form of hunches or intuitions, is it not likely that the members of a group who are chosen specifically because they share the same Definite Chief Aim, are even more likely to make such connections?

- Infinite Intelligence interconnects all things in such a way that whatever you focus on in your mind acts like a magnet, attracting other like-natured ideas.

- A Master Mind is formed when two or more people come together to focus on the same thing, and it is the combination of minds that attracts the creative ideas.

- By definition, the members of a Master Mind are committed to the same philosophy, and with multiple minds focused on the same Definite Chief Aim, all members also have access to a wider, deeper, communal pool of Infinite Intelligence. The combination will produce insights and ideas that the individual minds would never have come up with independently.

The theory of the Master Mind is that two heads are not only better than one, they are better than two—because the combination is greater than the sum of its parts. No two minds ever come together without creating this third invisible, intangible force, which, in the case of a Master Mind, will produce insights and ideas that neither of the individual minds would have come up with independently.

The following is excerpted and adapted from *Think and Grow Rich,* Chapter 10: Power of The Master Mind.

GAINING POWER THROUGH THE MASTER MIND

Power is essential for success in the accumulation of money. Power may be defined as "organized and intelligently directed knowledge."

Organized effort is produced through the coordination of effort of two or more people, who work toward a definite end, in a spirit of harmony.

The Master Mind may be defined as "Coordination of knowledge and effort, in a spirit of harmony, between two or more people, for the attainment of a definite purpose."

No individual may have great power without availing himself of the Master Mind.

So you may better understand the intangible potentialities of power available to you through a properly chosen Master Mind group, I will here explain the two characteristics of the Master Mind principle, one of which is economic in nature, and the other psychic.

Economic power: The economic feature is obvious. Economic advantages may be created by any person who surrounds himself with the advice, counsel, and personal cooperation of a group of people who are willing to lend wholehearted aid, in a spirit of perfect harmony. Your understanding of this great truth may definitely determine your financial status.

Psychic power: The psychic phase of the Master Mind principle is more abstract and difficult to comprehend. You will catch a better sense of the meaning from this statement: "No two minds ever come together without creating a third, invisible, intangible force, which may be likened to a third mind." The human mind is a form of energy. When the minds of two people are coordinated in a spirit of harmony, the energy of each mind forms an affinity, and it seems that each mind picks up on the energy of the other mind, which constitutes the "psychic" phase of the Master Mind.

The previous quotation introducing the concept of the Master Mind is from *Think and Grow Rich*. The following section, expanding upon the psychic aspect of the Master Mind, is excerpted and adapted from various sections in the opening chapter of *Law of Success*.

MIND CHEMISTRY

It is my belief that the mind is made up of the same universal energy as that which fills the universe. It is a fact that some minds clash the moment they come in contact with each other, while other minds show a natural affinity for each other, the slightest signs of any of the usual causes for love and hate acting as a stimulus.

The effect of the meeting of two minds is obvious to even the most casual observer. Every effect must have a cause! What could be more reasonable than to suspect the cause of the change in attitude between two minds that have just come in close contact is none other than the disturbance of the energy of each mind in the process of re-arranging themselves in the new field created by the contact?

All master salespeople know the moment the "psychological time for closing" has arrived, not by what the prospective buyer says, but from the effect of the chemistry of the buyer's mind as interpreted or felt by that salesperson.

Every able lawyer has developed a sixth sense whereby he or she is enabled to feel their way through the most artfully selected words of the clever witness who is lying, and correctly interpret what is in the witness's mind, through the chemistry of the mind.

Enough has been said to prove that the moment two minds come within close range of each other a noticeable mental change takes place in both—sometimes registering in the nature of antagonism and at other times registering in the nature of friendliness.

Every mind has what might be termed an electric field. The nature of this field varies, depending upon the mood of the individual mind and upon the nature of the chemistry of the mind creating the field.

It is my belief that the normal or natural condition of the chemistry of any individual mind is the result of physical heredity plus the nature of thoughts which have dominated the mind. Every mind is continuously changing to the extent that the individual's philosophy and general habits of thought change the chemistry of the mind.

Any individual may voluntarily change the chemistry of his or her mind so that it will attract or repel all with whom it comes in contact. Stated in another way, any person may assume a mental attitude that will attract and please others or repel and antagonize them, and this will happen without the aid of words or facial expression or other form of bodily movement or demeanor.

MINDS MUST BE IN HARMONY

Go back now to the definition of a Master Mind—a mind which grows out of the blending and coordination of two or more minds in a spirit of perfect harmony—and you will catch the full significance of the word *harmony.* Two minds will not blend, nor can they be coordinated, unless the element of perfect harmony is present. That is the secret of success or failure of practically all business and social partnerships.

Every sales manager and every military commander and every leader in any walk of life understands the necessity of an esprit de corps—a spirit of common understanding and cooperation—in the attainment of success. This mass spirit of harmony is brought about through discipline of such a nature that the individual minds become blended into a Master Mind. That is, the chemistry of the individual minds is modified in such a manner that these minds blend and function as one.

The methods through which this blending process takes place are as numerous as the individuals engaged in all the various forms of leadership. Every leader has a method of coordinating the minds of his or her followers. One will use force; another persuasion. One will play upon the fear of penalties while another plays upon rewards.

The aim will be to reduce the individual minds of a given group of people to the point that they may be blended into a mass mind.

You will not have to search deeply into the history of statesmanship, politics, business, or finance to discover the techniques employed by the leaders in these fields in the process of blending the minds of individuals into a mass mind.

THE PSYCHOLOGY OF THE REVIVAL MEETING

The brain of a human being may be compared to an electric battery in that it will become exhausted or run down, causing the owner of that brain to feel despondent, discouraged, and lacking in energy. The human brain, when in this depleted condition, must be recharged, and the manner in which this is done is through contact with a more vital mind or minds.

The old religious orgy known as the revival meeting offers a favorable opportunity to study the principle of mind chemistry known as a Master Mind.

During revival services, the leader of the meeting has no difficulty in creating harmony in the minds of his devotees, but it is well known that this state of harmony lasts no longer than the presence of the leader, after which the Master Mind that leader has temporarily created disintegrates.

By arousing the emotional nature of his followers with the proper stage setting and music, the revivalist creates a Master Mind which becomes noticeable to all who come in contact with it. The very air becomes charged with a positive, pleasing influence that changes the entire chemistry of all minds present. The revivalist calls this energy "the Spirit of the Lord."

On several occasions I have witnessed the creation of this same positive atmosphere among a group of men and women engaged in the business of salesmanship, without calling it the Spirit of the Lord.

I once helped conduct a school of salesmanship for Harrison Parker, founder of the Cooperative Society, of Chicago, and, by the use of the principle of mind chemistry, I so transformed a group of three thousand men and women (all of whom were without former sales experience) that they sold more than $10 million worth of securities in less than nine months and earned more than $1 million for themselves. [At the beginning of the twenty-first century, that would be equal to approximately $200 million in sales and $20 million in commissions.]

The average person who joined this school would reach the zenith of his or her selling power within one week, after which it was necessary to revitalize the individual's brain through a group sales meeting. These sales meetings were conducted in the same way as modern revival meetings, with much the same stage equipment, including music and high-powered speakers which could exhort the salespeople.

Call it religion, psychology, mind chemistry, or anything you please (they are all based on the same principle), but there is nothing more certain than that wherever a group of minds are brought into contact, in a spirit of perfect harmony, each mind becomes immediately reinforced by the noticeable energy called a Master Mind.

MIND CHEMISTRY IN ACTION

When two or more people harmonize their minds and produce the effect known as a Master Mind, each person in the group becomes vested with the power to contact and gather knowledge through the subconscious minds of all the other members of the group. This power becomes immediately noticeable, having the effect of stimulating the mind to a higher rate of vibration and otherwise evidencing itself in the form of a more vivid imagination and the consciousness of what appears to be a sixth sense.

It is through this sixth sense that new ideas will flash into the mind. These ideas take on the nature and form of the subject dominating the mind of the individual. If the entire group has met for the purpose of discussing a given subject, ideas concerning that subject will come pouring into the minds of all present, almost as if an outside influence were dictating them.

The minds of those participating in the Master Mind become like magnets, attracting ideas and thoughts of the most highly organized and practical nature, from no one knows where!

Once again, the metaphor of an electric battery is apropos.

The process of mind-blending described as a Master Mind may be likened to the act of one who connects many electric batteries to a single transmission wire, thereby stepping up the power flowing over that line. Each battery added increases the power passing over the line by the amount of energy the battery carries.

It is the same with blending individual minds into a Master Mind. Each mind, through the principle of mind chemistry, stimulates all the other minds in the group, until the mind energy becomes so great that it penetrates to and connects with the universal energy, which, in turn, touches every atom of the entire universe.

The following commentary is excerpted from *Think and Grow Rich: The Workbook,* Chapter 11: Power of the Master Mind.

YOU CANNOT HAVE SUCCESS WITHOUT IT

The Master Mind is defined as "coordination of knowledge and effort, in a spirit of harmony, between two or more people for the attainment of a definite purpose. No individual may have great power without utilizing the Master Mind."

That level of commitment and cooperation among the members of a group sounds wonderful, and who wouldn't love to work in that kind of environment, but does Hill really mean that you cannot achieve success without it?

The answer is yes. As Hill defines success and power, he really does mean it. Although you may achieve some measure of success without a Master Mind Alliance, you will never have great success or the great power that comes with it. Power must be applied before it is effective. Individuals are limited as to the amount of power they can apply.

No matter how intelligent or well-informed you may be, no single individual, functioning independently, can ever possess great power. You have to get others to cooperate with you if you are going to organize your knowledge so that you can turn your plans into power. If you try to do everything yourself, it will take you longer to do things that others could have done faster and better; in the end you will waste time, money, and energy.

The following introduction to the story of Napoleon Hill's first meeting with Andrew Carnegie is excerpted from *Think and Grow Rich,* Chapter 10: Power of the Master Mind. The text of the story that follows is adapted from the version that appears in *Law of Success.*

The Master Mind principle, or rather the economic feature of it, was first called to my attention by Andrew Carnegie, almost twenty years ago. Discovery of this principle was responsible for the choice of my life's work.

Mr. Carnegie's Master Mind group consisted of a staff of approximately fifty men, with whom he surrounded himself, for the definite purpose of manufacturing and marketing steel. He attributed his entire fortune to the power he accumulated through this "Master Mind."

Analyze the record of any man who has accumulated a great fortune, and many of those who have accumulated modest fortunes, and you will find that they have either consciously or unconsciously employed the Master Mind principle.

Great power can be accumulated through no other principle!

WHAT DO YOU MEAN BY SUCCESS?

Nearly twenty years ago, I interviewed Mr. Carnegie for the purpose of writing a story about him. During the interview I asked him to what he attributed his success. With a merry little twinkle in his eyes he said:

"Young man, before I answer your question, will you please define your term 'success'?"

After waiting until he saw that I was somewhat embarrassed by this request, he continued:

"By success you make reference to my money, do you not?"

I assured him that money was the term by which most people measured success, and he then said: "Oh, well, if you wish to know how I got my money—if that is what you call success—I will answer your question by saying that we have a Master Mind here in our business, and that mind is made up of more than a score of men who constitute my personal staff of superintendents and managers and accountants and chemists and other necessary types. No one person in this group is the Master Mind of which I speak, but the sum total of all the minds in the group, coordinated, organized, and directed to a definite end in a spirit of harmonious cooperation, is the power that got my money for me. No two minds in the group are exactly alike, but each man in the group does the thing that he is supposed to do and he does it better than any other person in the world could do it."

Then and there, the seed out of which this course has since been developed was sown in my mind. But that seed did not take root or germinate until later. This interview marked the beginning of years of research which led, finally, to the discovery of the principle of psychology described in the introductory lesson as the Master Mind.

I heard all that Mr. Carnegie had said, but it took the knowledge gained from many years of subsequent contact with the business world to enable me to assimilate what he said and to clearly grasp and understand the principle behind it—which was nothing more nor less than the principle of organized effort upon which this course on the Law of Success is founded.

Carnegie's group of men constituted a Master Mind and that mind was so well-organized, so well-coordinated, so powerful, that it could have accumulated millions of dollars for Mr. Carnegie in practically any sort of endeavor of a commercial or industrial nature.

The steel business in which that mind was engaged was but an incident in connection with the accumulation of the Carnegie wealth. The same wealth could have been accumulated had the Master Mind been directed in the coal business or the banking business or the grocery business, because behind that mind was power—the sort of power that you may attain when you have organized the faculties of your own mind and allied yourself with other well-organized minds for the attainment of a Definite Chief Aim in life.

A careful checkup with several of Mr. Carnegie's former business associates, which was made after this course was begun, proves conclusively not only that there is such a law as that which has been called the Master Mind, but that this law was the chief source of Mr. Carnegie's success.

Perhaps there was never anyone associated with Mr. Carnegie who knew him better than did Mr. C. M. Schwab, who, in the following words, has very accurately described that "subtle something" in Mr. Carnegie's personality which enabled him to rise to such stupendous heights. Mr. Schwab described him as follows:

"I never knew a man with so much imagination, lively intelligence, and instinctive comprehension. You sensed that he probed your thoughts and took stock of everything that you had ever done or might do. He seemed to catch at your next word before it was spoken. The play of his mind was dazzling and his habit of close observation gave him a store of knowledge about innumerable matters.

"But his outstanding quality, from so rich an endowment, was the power to inspire other men. Confidence radiated from him. You might be doubtful about something and discuss the matter with Mr. Carnegie. In a flash he would make you see that it was right and then you would absolutely believe it; or he might settle your doubts by pointing out its weakness. This quality of attracting others, then spurring them on, arose from his own strength.

"The results of his leadership were remarkable. Never before in the history of industry, I imagine, was there a man who, without understanding his business in its working details, making no pretense of technical knowledge concerning steel or engineering, was yet able to build up such an enterprise."

In his last sentence, Mr. Schwab had conveyed a thought which corroborates the theory of the Master Mind to which I attributed the chief source of Mr. Carnegie's power.

It is obvious that his success was due to his understanding of his own mind and the minds of other men, and not to mere knowledge of the steel business itself.

This thought is most consoling to those who have not yet attained outstanding success, for it shows that success is solely a matter of correctly applying laws and principles which are available to all, and these laws are fully described in the seventeen lessons of this course.

Mr. Carnegie learned how to apply the law of the Master Mind. This enabled him to organize the faculties of his own mind and the faculties of other men's minds, and to coordinate the whole behind a Definite Chief Aim.

THE LESSON OF THE ANDREW CARNEGIE STORY

Andrew Carnegie was one of the wealthiest and most powerful men the world has ever known. He made his enormous fortune by dominating the iron and steel industry, but the fact is that he knew very little about the inner workings of that business. What he did know was people. He knew how to find the best person for each job, and he knew how to motivate them to be even better.

It was readily conceded even by Carnegie's rivals that he was a brilliant judge of character and an inspirational manager of men. And it was equally agreed that although he made his fortune in steel, he could just as easily have done the same thing in coal mining, banking, the grocery business, or anything else he set his mind to.

The secret was not that he would have learned how to dig a mine, make a loan, or harvest tomatoes. The secret was that he would have assembled a Master Mind Alliance of people who were brilliant at doing those things and he would have done so by inspiring in each of them the desire to share with him the benefit of their knowledge, talent, and ability.

Let us again stress that finding such people to join your Master Mind does not come easy or cheap. Hill often made that point in his lectures by telling about Charles Schwab, who was an integral part of Carnegie's Master Mind Alliance and the president of Carnegie's steel operations. Schwab earned a salary of $75,000 a year, which at that time would have made him one of the highest-paid employees in America. What's more, Mr. Carnegie not only paid Mr. Schwab's salary, but he gave him an annual bonus of as much as one million dollars.

When asked, Mr. Carnegie said, "I gave him his salary for the work he actually performed, and the bonus for his willingness to go the extra mile, thus setting a fine example for his fellow workers."

In the following section, excerpted and adapted from the chapter on the Master Mind in *Think and Grow Rich,* once again Napoleon Hill uses the metaphor of a battery to introduce comments on other outstanding businessmen of the day who mentored him in the science of personal achievement.

HOW TO MULTIPLY YOUR BRAIN POWER

Man's brain may be compared to an electric battery. It is a well-known fact that a group of electric batteries will provide more energy than a single battery. It is also a well-known fact that an individual battery will provide energy in proportion to the number and capacity of the cells it contains.

The brain functions in a similar fashion. This accounts for the fact that some brains are more efficient than others, and leads to this significant statement: a group of brains coordinated (or connected) in a spirit of harmony will provide more thought-energy than a single brain, just as a group of electric batteries will provide more energy than a single battery.

Through this metaphor it becomes immediately obvious that the Master Mind principle holds the secret of the power wielded by men who surround themselves with other men of brains.

There follows now another statement, which will lead still nearer to an understanding of the psychic phase of the Master Mind principle: When a group of individual brains are coordinated and function in harmony, the increased energy created through that alliance becomes available to every individual brain in the group.

It is well-known that Henry Ford began his business career under the handicap of poverty, illiteracy, and ignorance. It is equally well-known that, within the inconceivably short period of ten years, Mr. Ford mastered these three handicaps, and that within twenty-five years he made himself one of the richest men in America. Connect with this the additional knowledge that Mr. Ford's most rapid strides became noticeable from the time he became a personal friend of Thomas A. Edison's, and you will begin to understand what the influence of one mind upon another can accomplish.

Go a step further, and consider that Mr. Ford's most outstanding achievements began from the time that he formed the acquaintances of Harvey Firestone, John Burroughs, and Luther Burbank (each a man of great brain capacity), and you will have further evidence that power may be produced through the friendly alliance of minds.

Men take on the nature and the habits and the power of thought of those with whom they associate in a spirit of sympathy and harmony. Through his association with Edison, Burbank, Burroughs, and Firestone, Mr. Ford added to his own brain power the sum and substance of the intelligence, experience, knowledge, and spiritual forces of these four men. Moreover, he appropriated and made use of the Master Mind principle through the methods of procedure described in this book.

The following commentary is excerpted and adapted from *Think and Grow Rich: The Workbook,* Chapter 11: Power of the Master Mind.

THE MAKE-UP OF YOUR MASTER MIND

Napoleon Hill got his first exposure to a Master Mind when Andrew Carnegie described it to him. Hill also saw a Master Mind in action when he observed the group Henry Ford assembled, which included inventor Thomas Edison, famed botanist Luther Burbank, naturalist and essayist John Burroughs, and industrialist and founder of the rubber and tire company, Harvey Firestone.

In describing his own personal experience with the concept, Hill tells about the meetings he conducts with his staff for the purpose of blending their minds to develop creative solutions. He also mentions that his visualization technique of tapping into advice from his invisible counselors is in its own way a variation on the Master Mind.

From the above examples it is clear that Master Minds come in a variety of shapes and sizes. The most obvious is the business model, but there are other kinds that can be of great benefit to you. For instance, in the example of Henry Ford's Master Mind, his intention wasn't to have these famous men help him achieve his business goal. He was already fabulously wealthy, and he did not need their money or their advice about building cars. What Ford wanted was to learn their sensibilities.

Although Henry Ford was brilliant in vision, he was from a very poor and humble background and he had little education. It was his hope that he would improve his character and his intellect by being in association with such brilliant minds as Burbank, Burroughs, Edison, and Firestone. And apparently these educated and successful men felt it was worth it to spend time with Henry Ford, because he had just as much to offer them in the form of what today we would call his street smarts.

You can create a Master Mind in your marriage, in your family, in a partnership, in a division of a company, in a team, in a corporate board, a service club, a faith-based group, a charity, or in a thousand other ways in which two or more people get together with the idea that by being together they will come up with more and better ideas.

If you assemble a Master Mind to help you achieve your definite aim in business, there is no question about how you will keep the members motivated and loyal: you involve them in the process and you pay them from the financial rewards that come with success.

That is also how you should reward your spouse or other family members, whether they are directly involved in your business or not. Those in your immediate family are a part of everything you do, whether or not they actually go to work with you.

If you need the help you get from those at home so that you have what you need to succeed at your work, then you should reward them just as you would anyone else who helps you make it. If you rely on them, they are just as deserving of recognition and financial compensation as any of your business associates.

Assembling nonbusiness or nonfamily Master Minds can be more complicated. When your Master Mind is based on a shared interest, such as Ford's group, or with the members of amateur teams, civic associations, clubs, nonprofits, or volunteer organizations, pulling together a Master Mind can make a huge contribution to the success of the organization. The question is, if the members are not being financially rewarded for the success of the organization, how do you ensure their commitment and motivation?

If you are the one in charge of the nonbusiness Master Mind, it is your job to inspire the members to share your vision, and it is your obligation to find out what each wants to get out of it so that he or she feels properly compensated. Instead of dollars and cents, you will be giving praise, recognition, and honors, while making sure they have a sense of self-satisfaction, accomplishment, and self-expression.

WHAT'S IN IT FOR ME?

There are at least three distinctly different advantages that you gain by working with a Master Mind Alliance.

- A Master Mind increases the amount you can do. As mentioned previously, no matter how intelligent or well-informed you may be, no one person, functioning independently, can ever possess great power. If you try to do it on your own, it will take you longer to do things that others can do faster and better, and in the end you will waste time, money, and energy.

- A Master Mind improves the quality of what you can do because, in addition to more manpower, it also gives you more knowledge than any single person can have. Through your Master Mind Alliance, you combine your advice and knowledge with the advice and knowledge of others who join with you, and the others give you the use of their counsel and contacts just as if they were your own.

- A Master Mind improves your creativity. When the minds of two or more people are coordinated in a spirit of harmony, when you are working with other people and everyone is on the same wavelength, the energy of each mind seems to pick up on the energy of the other minds. This results in more and better ideas than any one person could ever come up with working alone.

HOW TO ASSEMBLE YOUR MASTER MIND ALLIANCE

The following list is compiled from comments excerpted from other lists and commentaries that appear in various chapters in both *Law of Success* and *Think and Grow Rich*.

- Clearly know your Definite Chief Aim or purpose. Your desire will tell you what kind of people you need for your Master Mind.

- Your Master Mind should be no more than a dozen people, and generally the smaller the group the better.

- Decide what financial reward or advantages and benefits you will offer the individual members of your group in return for their cooperation. If you have trouble talking about money, get over it. You *must* talk about money, and you must be absolutely honest about how you arrive at what you are offering. If you are embarrassed by your offer, either you are trying to take advantage of the member, or else you haven't arrived at a figure that you think makes sense.

- Each member must agree at the outset on the contribution each will make, and on the division of benefits and profits.

- Do not select people merely because you know them and like them.

- Choose people who not only share your vision but who will also share their ideas, information, contacts, and will let you use their knowledge as if it were your own.

- Personal ambition must be subordinate to the achievement of the purpose of the alliance. Otherwise, you will have wasted everyone's time, you will ruin friendships, and your venture will be destroyed.

- Arrange to meet with the members of your Master Mind group at least twice a week, and more often if possible.

- Don't let the meetings become so regular and formalized that they inhibit phone calls, emails, and other less formal contact.

- The members must know with certainty that you are reliable, trustworthy, and loyal. Maintain perfect harmony between yourself and every member of your Master Mind group.

- Everyone must deal with everyone else on a completely ethical basis. No member should seek unfair advantage at the expense of others.

- Create a nonthreatening environment. Explore all ideas with equal interest and concern for the originator's feelings.

- Attune yourself to every member of the group. Try to imagine how you would react in a given situation if you were in his or her shoes.

- Don't try to force the group along too quickly. Allow for those who want to test ideas by playing devil's advocate.

- Insist upon confidentiality. Some people can give away an idea simply because they love to talk. You don't need them in your group.

- You cannot succeed when surrounded by disloyal and unfriendly associates, no matter what the object of your chief aim may be. Success is built upon loyalty, faith, sincerity, and cooperation.

THE MASTER MIND AND CHANGE

In preparing the earlier chapter about selecting your Definite Chief Aim, the editors made it clear that over time you should expect your aim or purpose to change. Just as you may not get your chief aim or purpose absolutely right the first time out, you probably won't assemble the absolutely right Master Mind the first time either.

Andrew Carnegie said that practically every member of his alliance was removed and replaced with some other person who could adapt himself more loyally and enthusiastically to the spirit and objective of the alliance.

The following is excerpted and adapted from *Think and Grow Rich*, Chapter 7: Organized Planning.

IF YOUR FIRST PLAN FAILS—TRY ANOTHER!

No individual has sufficient experience, education, native ability, and knowledge to ensure the accumulation of a great fortune, without the cooperation of other people. Every plan you adopt, in your endeavor to accumulate wealth, should be the joint creation of yourself and every other member of your Master Mind group. You may originate your own plans, either in whole or in part, but see that those plans are checked, and approved, by the members of your Master Mind Alliance.

If the first plan you adopt does not work successfully, replace it with a new plan; if this new plan fails to work, replace it in turn with still another, and so on, until you find a plan that does work. Right here is the point at which the majority of men meet with failure, because of their lack of persistence in creating new plans to take the place of those that fail.

The most intelligent man living cannot succeed in accumulating money—nor in any other undertaking—without plans that are practical and workable. Just keep this fact in mind, and remember, when your plans fail, that temporary defeat is not permanent failure. It may only mean that your plans have not been sound. Build other plans. Start all over again.

Temporary defeat should mean only one thing: the certain knowledge that there is something wrong with your plan. Millions of men go through life in misery and poverty, because they lack a sound plan through which to accumulate a fortune.

Your achievement can be no greater than your plans are sound.

The following commentary resumes from *Think and Grow Rich: The Workbook,* Chapter 11: Power of the Master Mind.

More common than choosing the wrong person to join your Master Mind Alliance, is selecting someone who was right in the beginning, but whose contributions have become less relevant as your business succeeds and grows. All businesses that succeed hit a point where they have to either scale up or fail. This is when you suddenly realize that demand is too great for your manufacturing capacity. This is when you realize your business is too big to be small, but still too small to be big. This is when you have to step up and buy the new machinery, or borrow the money, or find new investors, or get a new distributor, or buy out the competitor, or take some other drastic action that could catapult you to the next level. Regardless of the particulars, there are times when you have to scale up or you will stop succeeding.

The same thing will almost surely happen to your Master Mind. There will come a point when you have to scale up your Master Mind to keep pace with your business. What you needed as a startup is not what you need as an expanding business. What helped grow a partnership may not be the same thing you need when you incorporate and take on debt. What was perfectly fine as an S-Corp is nowhere near the financial sophistication you need to launch an IPO when you decide to go public. And so it goes.

It is up to you to find the right people for your Master Mind. It is up to you to make sure they feel they are generously rewarded for their contribution. It is up to you to recognize when it is time to change the mix of the Master Mind to keep pace with your success. And it is up to you to find the way to make sure that those who leave do so feeling they succeeded at what they set out to do, and at what you had asked them to do for you.

By now it should be crystal clear why it is mandatory that your members are satisfied with the compensation arrangements when they sign on. No one should ever feel they were used up and tossed aside, or that they were undercompensated. And you should never have to feel obligated to pay to keep a member whose contribution is not living up to expectations.

The advice of the editors is that the only way to avoid anyone ever feeling that they were used or undercompensated is to be certain that everyone is completely happy with their compensation when they sign on, and that they know that changes will be made in the Master Mind as the aim evolves. They must also be told at the beginning that it will be you who decides when changes must be made.

Be honest, and be prepared to be turned down by some of the people you would love to have in your group. Any other course will only create problems down the road. Don't fool yourself into thinking it is worth the risk to convince them to join now and you'll deal with the money problems later. It's not worth the risk, and all you will do later is lose friendships and create bad feelings.

We also advise that on a very regular basis you review the progress of the project toward its stated objective, and at the same time you review the issue of compensation with all Master Mind members. That is the only way to make sure your people know if they are living up to your expectations, and it is the only way to make sure that disagreements and resentments are dealt with before they can grow into problems.

MARRIAGE AND THE MASTER MIND

Napoleon Hill says that if you are married, it is imperative to involve your husband or wife in your Master Mind. Today that advice would apply to so many other kinds of domestic relationships, we have opted to use the generic term "spouse or partner."

Hill's point is that if you are serious about following the Hill method, and you begin using his techniques to create success consciousness within yourself, it will change who you are and how you live your life. If you are going to make yourself over, it is imperative that you involve your spouse or partner in the process.

We have all been told over and over that we shouldn't bring our work home with us, and that may be true in most cases, but that advice doesn't work with Napoleon Hill's method. The change in you is going to be too great to ignore, and it is going to affect others close to you. To make it work, you should plan on setting aside time each day to involve your partner in deciding what you want to achieve and how you can work together to accomplish it. This may not be the way the average couple does things, but Napoleon Hill wasn't writing for people who wanted to be average.

On the other hand, you should know that trying to integrate input from your spouse or partner into your work is bound to be difficult because of the natural resistance of the people you work with

toward ideas from outside. Unless it is handled with tact and diplo-
macy, you will create jealousies and resentments that will negate the
value of the additional creative input. However, like it or not, you still
have to do it.

Regardless of the difficulty, Napoleon Hill's advice is that you
must build your Master Mind into your marriage from the start. It may
not be easy, but if you are going to adopt his philosophy and follow
his method, you will have to find the right way to make your spouse or
partner part of your work, and your work part of your homelife.

MASTER MIND GROUPS ARE ALL OVER THE INTERNET

In closing this chapter, it would be well to note that the basic idea
behind the concept of the Master Mind has been adopted and pop-
ularized by a number of motivational gurus and self-improvement
organizations who promote the idea that you should become a member of their Master Mind group. This is largely an extension of the
personal-growth phenomena that got started in the 1970s, gained
momentum with the infomercial boom in the 1990s, and took off with
the coming of Internet marketing.

As this is being written, when you Google the words *Master
Mind group,* it tells you that there are more than 2,290,000 Web sites
that use the term. Many of these groups are run by motivational gurus
or life coaches who charge for the leadership and guidance they
provide. There are also companies that offer membership in their
Master Mind group as a free service, usually provided by an author
or organization that promotes self-help books or other products and
services.

While such groups can be beneficial, strictly speaking, they
would not meet the criteria Napoleon Hill set forth in this chapter on
the power of the Master Mind. It is very unlikely that you can join a
phone-in or online group and find that all the members will, as Hill
suggests, ". . . not only share your vision but will also share their ideas,
information, and contacts with you. They will let you use the full

strength of their experience, training, and knowledge as if it were your own. And they will do it in a spirit of perfect harmony."

Phone-in or online groups can help you generate new ideas simply because joining one puts you in a situation with other people where the sole purpose is to come up with ideas. However, for most of these groups, the main benefit you will receive would be in encouragement and enthusiasm.

The reality is that you would be joining a group of people, all of whom want to get ahead at different things in different ways, and all of whom are hoping that by linking up with others they will pick up some ideas or contacts that will help them. And although all of these people, including you, are willing to give off-the-top-of-their-head advice to the others, if, during the give-and-take, one of the members is hit with what he or she really believes is a million-dollar idea, what are the chances that person is going to blurt it out and give it to you for free?

Would you?

Napoleon Hill's answer to that question is no. Hill advises that every time you open your mouth you either give away too much or you show how little you actually know. Either way, according to Hill it is a mistake to tell the world what you think, or what you are planning to do.

During his career Napoleon Hill was derided by his family and friends for arrogance when he told them he would write a philosophy of success, and he had his ideas stolen and his businesses ruined by jealous partners and other people who betrayed his trust in them. The result was that his personal motto became "Don't tell them; show them."

This caution does not mean that these groups don't provide some value; they can be stimulating and they can be encouraging, but you should go into them with your eyes wide open. They can offer you another way to network, and some cheerleading, but they do not provide what Hill intended for a Master Mind.

Chapter Eight

A PLEASING PERSONALITY AND CREATING CHARISMA

WHAT WOULD NAPOLEON HILL DO?

People like doing business with people they like. So, if you want to do business, make sure that you are someone whom other people like.

Napoleon Hill would begin by finding people he liked and admired, and encourage them to tell him about themselves. He would compare what he admired about them with his own personality, identify those influences that had shaped it, then he would use autosuggestion to alter those influences and create a personality that reflected the kind of person he aspired to be.

You cannot have success unless you can attract people to join you in your efforts, and you cannot attract people to help you unless you have an attractive personality.

Though obviously an important concept, in *Law of Success,* in the chapter titled A Pleasing Personality, the main thrust is so easily understood that Hill fleshes it out by devoting a large section to illustrating the key concepts by recounting personal stories and quoting a sizeable excerpt from Shakespeare's *Julius Caesar.*

Hill's anecdotes make two points. First, that you are more likely to succeed when the person you want to connect with feels that the two of you look at things in a similar way, and secondly, that the best way to establish a connection with someone is to get the other person to talk about himself or herself.

The section taken from *Julius Caesar* is quoted to demonstrate how Marc Antony turned the crowd of Romans against Brutus, who had claimed he was acting for the good of Rome and had to kill Caesar because of his ambitiousness. Antony gets the crowd to reverse itself not by arguing with Brutus, or by blatantly attacking his character, but rather by planting in the minds of the crowd the seeds of distrust about Brutus's motivations. Marc Antony won over the crowd by playing on their emotions and making them feel that he, Marc Antony, was one of them, and just like them, he too had been victimized by the imperious Brutus.

The points made by Hill's anecdotes and the excerpt from *Julius Caesar* in *Law of Success* may seem a little mundane compared with the focus of previous chapters on such challenging concepts as auto-suggestion, the subconscious, and Infinite Intelligence. However, you will learn as you read further that this lesson is clearly a successor to the previous chapters, and that there are aspects of developing a pleasing personality that draw upon all of Hill's key concepts.

In *Think and Grow Rich* the chapter most closely related to the concept of a pleasing personality is chapter 11, titled The Mystery of Sex Transmutation. As unusual as it is to encounter a chapter with that title in a book about succeeding in your career, the fact is that the lesson at the heart of the chapter explains a specific method for developing a more charismatic personality that will help you achieve success.

We begin by laying the groundwork with an excerpt adapted from *Law of Success*, Lesson Ten: Pleasing Personality.

PLEASING PERSONALITY

What is a pleasing personality? It is a personality that attracts, and in this lesson we look at what causes that attraction and how to create it.

Your personality is the sum total of your characteristics and appearances that distinguish you from all others. The clothes you wear, the lines in your face, the tone of your voice, the thoughts you think, the character you have developed by those thoughts, all constitute parts of your personality. Whether your personality is attractive or not is another matter.

By far, the most important part of your personality is that which is represented by your character. It is also the part that is not visible.

The style of your clothes and their appropriateness undoubtedly constitutes a very important part of your personality, for it is true that people form first impressions of you from your outward appearance.

Even the way you shake hands forms an important part of your personality and goes a long way toward attracting or repelling those with whom you shake hands, but this art can be cultivated.

The vitality of your body—sometimes called personal magnetism —also constitutes an important part of your personality.

The expression in your eyes also forms an important part of your personality, for there are people, and they are more numerous than one might imagine, who can look through your eyes into your heart and see the nature of your most secret thoughts.

The following section, excerpted and adapted from *Law of Success*, Lesson Twelve: Concentration, refers back to the key points in the previous chapters, pointing out the direct connection between the nature of your personality and the influences to which your subconscious mind is exposed.

ENVIRONMENT AND PERSONALITY

As we have already seen, we absorb the material for thought from our surrounding environment. The term *environment* covers a very broad field. It consists of the books we read, the people with whom we associate, the community in which we live, the nature of the work we do, the country or nation in which we reside, the clothes we wear, the songs we sing, and, most important of all, the religious and intellectual training we receive prior to the age of fourteen years.

The purpose of analyzing the subject of environment is to show its direct relationship to the personality we are developing, and how its influence will give us the materials out of which we may attain our Definite Chief Aim in life.

The mind feeds upon that which we supply it, or that which is forced upon it, through our environment. Therefore, let us select our environment, as much as possible, with the object of supplying the mind with suitable material out of which to carry on its work. If your environment is not to your liking, change it!

The first step is to create in your own mind a clear, well-defined picture of the environment in which you believe you could best attain your Definite Chief Aim. Then concentrate your mind on this picture until you transform it into reality.

Just as you learned in Lesson Two, the first step you must take in the accomplishment of any desire is to have in your mind an exact picture of what it is that you intend to accomplish. This is also the first principle to be observed in your plans for the achievement of success, and if you fail to observe it you cannot succeed, except by chance.

Your daily associates constitute one of the most important and influential parts of your environment, and may work for your progress or against it. As much as possible, you should select as your closest daily associates those who are in sympathy with your aims and ideals—especially those represented by your Definite Chief Aim. You should make it a point to associate with people whose mental attitudes inspire you with enthusiasm, self-confidence, determination, and ambition.

Remember that every word spoken within your hearing, every sight that reaches your eyes, and every sense impression that you receive through any of the five senses, influences your thoughts. This being true, can you not see the importance of controlling, as far as possible, the environment in which you live and work? Can you not see the importance of reading books which deal with subjects that are directly related to your Definite Chief Aim? Can you not see the importance of talking with people who are in sympathy with your aims, and who will encourage you and spur you on toward their attainment?

The following returns to the excerpted material from *Law of Success*, Lesson Ten, Pleasing Personality.

CHARACTER COUNTS

To study the ways and means through which one may develop a pleasing personality, I will begin with the first essential, which is character, for no one can have a pleasing personality without the foundation of a sound, positive character. Through the principle of telepathy you "telegraph" the nature of your character to those with whom you come in contact, which is also why you may have had an "intuitive" feeling that the person you had just met, but about whom you did not know very much, was not trustworthy.

You may wear the best and latest clothes, and conduct yourself in a most pleasing manner outwardly, but if there is greed and envy and hatred and jealousy and selfishness in your heart, you will never attract anyone except those who are the same. Like attracts like, and you may be sure, therefore, that those who are attracted to you are those whose inward natures parallel your own.

You may present an artificial smile and you may practice hand-shaking so that you can imitate, perfectly, the handshake of a person who is adept at this art, but if these outward manifestations of a pleasing personality lack that vital factor called earnestness of purpose, they will turn people away rather than attract them to you.

How, then, does one build character? The first step in character building is rigid self-discipline.

PRAISE OTHERS & SPEAK WELL

First, think of people whose characters are made up of the qualities you wish to build into your own character, and then proceed to take on these qualities, through the aid of autosuggestion [as is suggested in the story about Hill's imaginary advisers].

Create, in your imagination, a council table and gather your characters around it each night, first having written out a clear and concise statement of the particular qualities that you wish to assume from each. Then proceed to affirm or suggest to yourself, aloud, that you are developing the desired qualities in yourself.

As you do this, close your eyes and see, in your imagination, the figures seated around your imaginary table, in the manner described in the previous lesson.

Second, through the principles described in the lesson on self-control, focus your thoughts and keep your mind energized with thoughts of a positive nature. Let the dominating thought of your mind be a picture of the person that you intend to be: the person that you are deliberately building, through this process. At least a dozen times a day, when you have a few minutes to yourself, shut your eyes and direct your thoughts to the figures that you have selected to sit at your imaginary council table. Then feel—with a faith that knows no limitation—that you are actually growing to resemble in character those figures of your choice.

Third, find at least one person each day, and more if possible, in whom you see some good quality that is worthy of praise—and praise them for it. Remember, however, that this praise must not be in the nature of cheap, insincere flattery; it must be genuine. Speak your words of praise with such earnestness that they will impress those to whom you speak.

Then watch what happens. You will have rendered those whom you praise a decided benefit of great value to them, and you will have gone just one more step in the direction of developing the habit of looking for and finding the good qualities in others.

I cannot overemphasize the far-reaching effects of this habit of praising, openly and enthusiastically, the good qualities in others, for this habit will soon reward you with a feeling of self-respect and manifestation of gratitude from others that will modify your entire personality. Here, again, the Law of Attraction enters, and those whom you praise will see in you the qualities that you see in them. Your success in the application of this formula will be in exact proportion to your faith in its soundness.

I do not merely believe that it is sound—I know that it is. And the reason I know is that I have used it successfully and I have also taught others how to use it successfully. Therefore, I have a right to promise you that you can use it with equal success.

Furthermore, you can, with the aid of this formula, develop a pleasing personality so quickly that you will surprise all who know you. The development of such a personality is entirely within your own control, which gives you a tremendous advantage and at the same time places the responsibility on you if you fail or neglect to exercise your privilege.

I would like to point out the reason for speaking, aloud, the affirmation that you are developing the qualities that you have selected as the materials out of which to develop a pleasing personality. This procedure has two desirable effects.

First, it sets into motion the vibration through which the thought behind your words reaches and imbeds itself in your subconscious mind. There it takes root and grows until it becomes a great moving force in your outward, physical activities, leading to the transformation of the thought into reality.

Second, it helps you develop the ability to speak with force and conviction, which can lead to great ability as a public speaker. No matter what your calling in life may be, you should be able to stand on your feet and speak convincingly.

Put feeling and emotion into those words as you speak, and develop a deep, rich tone of voice. If your voice is inclined to be high-pitched, tone it down until it is soft and pleasing. You can never express an attractive personality, to best advantage, through a harsh or shrill voice. You must cultivate your voice until it becomes rhythmical and pleasing to the ear.

Remember that speech is the chief method of expressing your personality, and for this reason it is to your advantage to cultivate a style that is both forceful and pleasing.

I do not recall a single outstanding pleasing personality that was not made up, in part, of an ability to speak with force and conviction. Study the outstanding figures of the past in politics and statesmanship and observe that the most successful ones were those who were noted for their ability to speak with force and conviction. Study the prominent men and women of today, wherever you find them, and observe the significant fact that the more prominent they are the more efficient they are in speaking forcefully.

In the field of business, industry, and finance it seems significant also that the most prominent leaders are men and women who are able public speakers. In fact no one may hope to become a prominent leader in any noteworthy undertaking without developing the ability to speak with forcefulness that carries conviction. While the salesperson may never deliver a public address, they will profit, nevertheless, if they develop the ability to do so, because this ability increases his or her power to speak convincingly in ordinary conversation.

Let us now summarize the seven chief factors that enter into the development of a pleasing personality:

1. Form the habit of interesting yourself in other people, and make it your business to find their good qualities and speak of them in terms of praise.

2. Develop the ability to speak with force and conviction, both in your ordinary conversational tones and before public gatherings, where you must use more volume.

3. Dress in a style that is becoming to you and appropriate to the work in which you are engaged.

4. Develop a positive character, through the aid of the formula outlined in this lesson.

5. Learn how to shake hands so that you express warmth and enthusiasm through this form of greeting.

6. Attract other people to you by first "attracting yourself" to them.

7. Remember that your only limitation, within reason, is the one that you set up in your own mind.

These seven points cover the most important factors, although such a personality will obviously not develop of its own accord. It *will* develop, however, if you submit yourself to the discipline herein described, with a firm determination to transform yourself into the person that you would like to be.

The following commentary is excerpted from *Think and Grow Rich: The Workbook,* Chapter 12: Sexuality, Charisma, and Creativity.

THE ELEMENTS OF CHARISMA
AND A PLEASING PERSONALITY

By reviewing each of the chapters in *Think and Grow Rich* and *Law of Success,* the editors have assembled the following overview of the elements of a pleasing personality.

1. **Good showmanship.** A showman is someone who appeals to people through their imagination and keeps them interested through curiosity. A good showman is quick to recognize and to capitalize on other people's likes and dislikes at the right psychological moment.

2. **Harmony with yourself.** You cannot have a pleasing personality without first developing harmony and control within your own mind.

3. **Definiteness of purpose.** The procrastinator who drifts through life without a plan or a purpose does not have a very pleasing personality.

4. **Appropriateness of style and clothing.** First impressions are lasting. The person with a pleasing personality dresses in clothing appropriate to the situation.

5. **Posture and carriage of the body.** Everyone judges others by their body language—the way they walk and the general posture of their bodies.

6. **Voice.** The tone, volume, pitch, and general emotional coloring of a person's voice constitute important factors of a pleasing personality.

7. **Sincerity of purpose.** This quality needs little explanation, but having it is essential if you want to gain the confidence of others.

8. **Choice of language.** The person with a pleasing personality is comfortable talking in everyday language or speaking formally, and he or she knows which to use when.

9. **Poise.** Poise is a quality that comes naturally when you have self-confidence and self-control.

10. **A good sense of humor.** Perhaps no other quality is more essential than this.

11. **Unselfishness.** Selfishness and a pleasing personality are never found together.

12. **Facial expression.** This is an accurate medium for the interpretation of your moods and thoughts. You can have a big smile, a crooked grin, or it may be as subtle as a twinkle in the eye, but you can always tell if it is sincere.

13. **Positive thought.** The vibrations of your thoughts are picked up by others. To be pleasing, you must be radiating good feelings and pleasant thoughts.

14. **Enthusiasm.** People who lack enthusiasm cannot inspire others. Enthusiasm is also an essential factor in all forms of salesmanship.

15. **A sound body.** Poor health does not attract others. You are unlikely to project a pleasing personality without health and vigor.

16. **Imagination.** This is one of the most essential factors of a pleasing personality.

17. **Tact.** Lack of this quality has cost many people their positions. Lack of tact is usually expressed through insensitivity to others and loose conversation.

18. **Versatility.** A general knowledge of the important subjects of current interest, as well as of the deeper problems of life and living, is a quality conducive to a pleasing personality.

19. **The art of being a good listener.** Train yourself to listen attentively when other people are speaking.

20. **The art of forceful speech.** Forceful speech can only be acquired by practice. Have something to say worth listening to, then say it with all the enthusiasm at your command.

21. **Personal magnetism or charisma.** This is a manifestation of sexuality. It is the major asset of every great leader, and it is the factor of a pleasing personality that is the hardest to teach. You must discover your own charismatic qualities, then make the most of what you have.

THE ELEMENTS OF A NEGATIVE PERSONALITY

1. **Disloyalty.** There is no substitute for loyalty! And the person who lacks loyalty cannot possibly market personal services effectively.

2. **Dishonesty.** There is no substitute for honesty! It is the keystone to character. Without sound character, no person can market their services effectively.

3. **Greed.** A person who is cursed by greed cannot keep it under cover.

4. **Envy and hatred.** These qualities make a pleasing personality impossible. Remember that like attracts like.

5. **Jealousy.** This is a mild form of insanity. It is fatal to a pleasing personality.

6. **Anger.** Whether passive or active in form, this is a quality that arouses antagonism and makes one disliked by others.

7. **Fear.** There are six basic fears against which every person must guard. These are negative states of mind that must be eliminated before one can develop a pleasing personality.

8. **Revenge.** A vengeful person cannot be pleasing to anyone.

9. **Fault-finding.** The person who has the habit of finding fault with others might more profitably spend time looking within for faults.

10. **Gossiping.** People may listen to the scandalmonger, but they will not like the person. And you cannot trust them.

11. **Uncontrolled enthusiasm.** Too much enthusiasm is as bad as none.

12. **Excuses.** It is better to take responsibility for mistakes you did not make than to develop the habit of trying to place responsibility for these mistakes on others.

13. **Exaggeration.** It is better to understate a truth than to overstate it. Exaggeration causes loss of confidence.

14. **Egotism.** Self-confidence is one of the most desirable and necessary traits, but it must be controlled and directed to definite ends. All forms of self-praise are easily recognized as evidences of inferiority complexes. Therefore, your motto should be "Deeds, not words."

15. **Obstinacy and stubbornness.** A certain amount of determination and the ability to stand by your opinions is essential, but these qualities should not become a blanket policy.

16. **Selfishness.** A selfish person cannot be trusted.

This is the end of the excerpts from *Law of Success,* Chapter Ten: Pleasing Personality. The material that follows is from *Think and Grow Rich,* Chapter 11: The Mystery of Sex Transmutation, augmented by commentary from *Think and Grow Rich: The Workbook,* Chapter 12, Sexuality: Charisma and Creativity.

We begin with the following commentary adapted from *Think and Grow Rich: The Workbook,* Chapter 12, Sexuality: Charisma and Creativity.

The basic Principles of Success identified and explained by Napoleon Hill have not changed in the years since the first edition of *Think and Grow Rich* was published. However, the social climate and what are often called traditional values have gone through a cultural revolution during that time.

Because this chapter deals with the ways human sexuality can affect motivation, success, and achievement, and because society's attitudes toward sexuality have changed so dramatically, modern readers often find this to be the most challenging chapter in the book.

Although Hill was a very forward thinker, people's lives in the America of 1937 were vastly different from the way people live in the America of the twenty-first century. As Hill was writing *Think and Grow Rich,* America was still deep in the Great Depression, jobs were scarce, the stock market had not recovered, the middle of the country was a dustbowl, soup kitchens were still feeding the hungry, and many men were riding the rails looking for any kind of work or a handout.

As for sex, the average home was a married husband and wife with children, most mothers didn't work outside the home, people could still leave their front doors unlocked at night, children had the run of their neighborhoods, divorce was uncommon, very few people were unconventional enough to openly "live in sin," cursing or using "dirty words" in mixed company just wasn't done, sex education was usually an embarrassing conversation between mothers and daughters or fathers and sons, books that had "good parts" were banned in Boston because they offended the public's morals, love scenes in movies dissolved to skyrockets bursting in the air, and, to quote an old joke, that was back in the days when the air was clean and sex was dirty.

It was in this rather straight-laced atmosphere that Napoleon Hill became interested in the theory that sex and love were among the most powerful factors in human motivation. He was intrigued by the idea that if sex and love are such powerful forces in driving humans to action, there might be a correlation between the level of a person's sexuality and how well that person achieved material success. And if such a relationship exists, can the motivating force be intentionally channeled to this purpose?

The following is a commentarial overview of what Hill wrote in the original edition of *Think and Grow Rich,* Chapter 11: The Mystery of Sex Transmutation.

THE KEY POINTS IN THIS CHAPTER

- Sexuality is a natural and normal part of everyone's life.

- The desire for sex tops the list of the ten most powerful stimulants that prompt a person to take action.

- People who are good at influencing others do so by knowing how to transmute their sexuality into charm or charisma.

- You can learn to transmute your sexuality into charisma, which can be used to influence others.

- Most creative people have a highly sexual nature.

- You can develop your creativity by learning techniques that will increase the possibility of accessing your creative imagination and Infinite Intelligence.

- Artificial stimulants are not as good as your internal emotional stimulants.

- Many people don't hit their stride until after the age of forty or fifty because they haven't learned that they can channel their sexual drive into success.

- Love is the safety valve that can help you control your sexuality.

To explain the key points about what Hill calls sex transmutation, we have excerpted the following selections taken from *Think and Grow Rich,* Chapter 11: The Mystery of Sex Transmutation.

Before proceeding with this material, we note that some will be dubious about the basic concept, which isn't helped by the fact that Hill uses terms such as "sex emotion" and "sex energy," which modern readers may find off-putting. The answer to the issue of the unusual terminology is simply that if Hill were writing today he would likely have used the words "sexuality" or "charisma" instead.

As to any reservations readers may have about the basic concept, we encourage you to read with an open mind, and you will be surprised at the practical application offered in the final commentary.

THE MYSTERY OF SEX TRANSMUTATION

The meaning of the word "transmute" is, in simple language, "the changing, or transferring of one element, or form of energy, into another."

The emotion of sex brings into being a state of mind.

Because of ignorance on the subject, this state of mind is generally associated with the physical, and because of improper influences, to which most people have been subjected in acquiring knowledge of sex, things essentially physical have highly biased the mind.

The emotion of sex has behind it the possibility of three constructive potentialities:

1. The perpetuation of mankind

2. The maintenance of health

3. The transformation of mediocrity into genius through transmutation

Sex transmutation is simple and easily explained. It means the switching of the mind from thoughts of physical expression, to thoughts of some other nature.

Sex desire is the most powerful of human desires. When driven by this desire, men develop a keenness of imagination, courage, willpower, persistence, and creative ability unknown to them at other times. So strong and impelling is the desire for sexual contact that men freely run the risk of life and reputation to indulge it. When harnessed, and redirected along other lines, this motivating force maintains all of its attributes of keenness of imagination, courage, etc., which may be used as powerful creative forces in literature, art, or in any other profession or calling, including, of course, the accumulation of riches.

The transmutation of sex energy calls for the exercise of willpower, to be sure, but the reward is worth the effort. The desire for sexual expression is inborn and natural. The desire cannot, and should not, be submerged or eliminated. But it should be given an outlet through forms of expression that enrich the body, mind, and spirit of man. If not given this form of outlet, through transmutation, it will seek outlets through purely physical channels.

A river may be dammed, and its water controlled for a time, but eventually it will force an outlet. The same is true of the emotion of sex. It may be submerged and controlled for a time, but its very nature causes it to be ever seeking means of expression. If it is not transmuted into some creative effort, it will find a less worthy outlet.

The following is excerpted from a later section of the same chapter.

PERSONAL MAGNETISM

A teacher, who has trained and directed the efforts of more than thirty thousand salespeople, made the astounding discovery that highly sexed men are the most efficient salesmen. The explanation is that the factor of personality known as "personal magnetism" is nothing more nor less than sex energy. Highly sexed people always have a plentiful supply of magnetism. Through cultivation and understanding, this vital force may be drawn upon and used to great advantage in the relationships between people. This energy may be communicated to others through the following media:

- **The handshake.** The touch of the hand indicates, instantly, the presence of magnetism, or the lack of it.

- **The tone of voice.** Magnetism, or sex energy, is the factor with which the voice may be colored, or made musical and charming.

- **Posture and carriage of the body.** Highly sexed people move briskly and with grace and ease.

- **The vibrations of thought.** Highly sexed people mix the emotion of sex with their thoughts, or may do so at will, and in that way, may influence those around them.

- **Body adornment.** People who are highly sexed are usually very careful about their personal appearance. They usually select clothing of a style becoming to their personality, physique, complexion, etc.

When employing salesmen, the more capable sales manager looks for the quality of personal magnetism as the first requirement. People who lack sex energy will never become enthusiastic nor inspire others with enthusiasm, and enthusiasm is one of the most important requisites in salesmanship, no matter what one is selling.

The public speaker, orator, preacher, lawyer, or salesman who is lacking in sex energy is a "flop," as far as being able to influence others is concerned. Couple with this the fact that most people can be influenced only through an appeal to their emotions, and you will understand the importance of sex energy as a part of the salesman's native ability. Master salesmen attain the status of mastery in selling because they either consciously or unconsciously transmute the energy of sex into sales enthusiasm! In this statement may be found a very practical suggestion as to the actual meaning of sex transmutation.

The salesman who knows how to take his mind off the subject of sex, and direct it in sales effort with as much enthusiasm and determination as he would apply to its original purpose, has acquired the art of sex transmutation, whether he knows it or not. The majority of salesmen who transmute their sex energy do so without being in the least aware of what they are doing, or how they are doing it.

Transmutation of sex energy calls for more will-power than the average person cares to use for this purpose. Those who find it difficult to summon will-power sufficient for transmutation may gradually acquire this ability. Though this requires will-power, the reward for the practice is more than worth the effort.

The following is excerpted from *Think and Grow Rich: The Workbook*, Chapter 12, Sexuality: Charisma and Creativity.

Although Napoleon Hill stated his belief in the theory of sexual trans-mutation in a number of his books and programs, the version that he included in *Think and Grow Rich* does not explain the process in much detail. This commentary offers further interpretation and explanation based on the editors' extensive knowledge of Hill's writings and lectures.

DOES HILL REALLY MEAN WHAT I THINK HE MEANS?

Today, in an age when large segments of the population accept laissez faire sexuality and live by an as-long-as-they-are-consenting-adults moral standard, when people hear the words *sexual transmutation,* it definitely has an old-fashioned ring to it. Morality has changed so much that many people are taken aback by the notion of doing any-thing that would inhibit sexual expression. To them, the idea that you would do anything with your urges other than enjoy them is so far out of the modern mainstream, they find it difficult to relate to.

Does Hill really mean that you should repress your sexual urges so you can get ahead and make money?

It may not mesh very well with contemporary theories about sexuality, but the answer to the question is yes.

And can you really take something as visceral as the desire to have sex and turn it into a desire to do something else?

Once again, Napoleon Hill's answer may not be in line with modern thinking, but his answer is not only "yes you can" but "yes you should."

Hill had a very idealistic and romantic view of sexual relations be-tween a man and woman. To him, sex was more than an act of passion or procreation; it was the manifestation of nature's great creative force.

Sex transmutation is the ability to switch a desire for physical contact into a desire for another kind of expression. It was Napoleon Hill's belief that if you chose to, you could refocus the desire to create in one way, and turn it into a desire to create in another way.

It should be noted that the basis of this concept is by no means limited only to Hill's philosophy. Sigmund Freud also wrote about the same response, calling it sublimation, which he considered a defense mechanism that gives humans a way to let out emotions that otherwise would not be socially acceptable. Certain Hindus and Buddhists practice a technique called Tantra, which is a way to control raw, sexual energy and transform it into a higher, spiritual form of energy.

Although most explanations refer to transforming sexual desire into some more rarified form of expression, in Napoleon Hill's view the point of sexual sublimation doesn't have to be as exalted as a path to spiritual enlightenment. To Hill, turning your sexuality into success and money are also worthwhile goals. To emphasize the point, in one of Hill's books he says that channeling sexual energy applies just as much to bricklayers as it does to great painters. Hill says even bricklayers will lay more bricks faster and in straighter rows if they apply sexual energy to the process. In his own case, he was certain that there was a difference between books he had written when he was channeling sexual energy and those written without that extra intensity.

The purpose of transmuting sexual energy is to channel the energy into a dynamic drive that brings success. What is success? It could be creative success, it could be successful self-expression, it could be laying bricks successfully, or it could be transmuting your sexual energy into personal magnetism or charisma.

OKAY, BUT HOW DO YOU ACTUALLY DO IT?

Perhaps the clearest explanation of how you actually transmute sexual energy can be conveyed by the following examples:

- Anyone can sing the words to a blues song. But if the next time you sing that song you are feeling heartsick because the person you love has just left you for someone else, the words will be charged with meaning they didn't have before.

- Your attitude during a sales call you made just before the person you love agreed to meet you at your favorite restaurant is entirely different than what your attitude will be on the sales call you'll make five minutes later.

- If you are frustrated from a lack of love and physical contact, you can channel those inner yearnings into a fierce determination to overcome the roadblocks that have held you back, and you will then succeed where you failed before.

In effect, you can take the sexual emotion—whether it is frustration, loneliness, joy, satisfaction, or any other sexually charged emotion—and use the strength of your feelings to push yourself beyond what you thought was a limitation.

The preceding examples should give you a good sense of the concept of sex transmutation, but it still leaves some unanswered questions about how to use it as a practical technique:

- Do you decide one day that you will take every sexual feeling you have and transmute them all until you accomplish your aim or purpose?

- Do you start with one urge and see if transmuting that one works before you try another?

- Do you do it for a month? Or do you do it for a year?

- Do you do it just when you want something in particular? Or is it something you keep in the back of your mind all the time and use it whenever it occurs to you?

Napoleon Hill says he came to believe in this theory of sexual transmutation because of what he learned from his research into the lives of the successful men to whom he was introduced by Andrew Carnegie and by studying the great achievers throughout history. He also says he personally used sexual transmutation in his own work.

But unfortunately he does not explain the specifics of what he learned through his research, and nor does he tell us how often or under what circumstances he used the technique himself.

PUTTING THE THEORY INTO PRACTICE

Although there's not much specific detail about putting the method to use in *Think and Grow Rich,* by going through Hill's books, lectures, and other writings, the editors of this book have assembled a visualization exercise targeted at transmuting sexual energy to enhance your sex appeal or charisma.

This exercise is a variation on creative visualization, and like all autosuggestion techniques, the more often you practice it the better the results will be. However, it is unlikely that you will be in a position to go into a deep visualization every time you want to turn on your charisma, so we have included a cue that you can use to give you instant recall of what it feels like to be full of confidence. As part of your visualization, you will tell yourself that by pressing your thumb and middle finger together, it will act as a triggering device that instructs your subconscious to instantly recall what it feels like to be at your best. As simple as that sounds, it is a technique that is widely used by psychiatrists and motivational experts.

In order to educate your subconscious mind about how you want to feel, you should practice the transmutation visualization as often as you can find adequate time to be by yourself and completely relax. Once you have taught yourself this visualization, including the instant recall cue, whenever the occasion arises that you need an extra boost, you can use the cue to call up your confidence and charisma.

Begin by looking inward and going back in your mind to recall a specific time when you were at your most confident, sexually. Find in your memory one specific time when you were completely satisfied and content. Using all of your powers of recall and visualization, re-create your feelings just as you felt them then.

In your imagination, bring those feelings forward, making them so real and so vivid that you can actually experience those feelings now, and remember how it feels in every muscle and sinew of your body. It is that sense of confidence, satisfaction, and of being in control that you want to project outward in everything you do.

Let that remembered feeling flow through your body, influencing the way you stand, the way you walk, the way you talk, the way you shake hands, the way you make eye contact, the way you focus your attention, and in every way you interact with other people. It is there, just below the surface, present in everything you do.

In the future, whenever you want to recall this feeling and be at your most confident and project your most charismatic personality, all you have to do is press your thumb and your middle finger together, and you will immediately feel the confidence, satisfaction, and sense of control filling your body and mind, and radiating outward from you.

This does not mean that you try to be openly flirtatious or seductive. If you are charismatic, you do not have to "come on" to another person in order for that person to pick up on your confidence and personal magnetism. You don't even have to try. Just by knowing in the back of your mind what it feels like when you are at your most powerful and persuasive, you give off subtle signals.

Keeping the picture of yourself at your most powerful and persuasive in the back of your mind will make you *feel* powerful and persuasive. And when you feel that confidence inside, it radiates from you.

Chapter Nine

ENTHUSIASM AND SUCCESS-CONSCIOUSNESS

WHAT WOULD NAPOLEON HILL DO?

Just as your Definite Chief Aim needs to be injected with your faith and self-confidence, your faith and self-confidence needs to be injected with enthusiasm.

Napoleon Hill would boost his self-confidence by focusing on the can-do parts of every challenge, he would choose role models brimming with enthusiasm, then pattern his own attitudes after them. He would fill his mind with the good he wants to accomplish, he would always see the glass half-full, and he would find the hidden benefit in any disappointment.

The only significant disagreement Napoleon Hill ever had with his friend and co-author, W. Clement Stone, was over which was the most important concept in achieving success. Hill believed it was A Definite Chief Aim, and Stone preferred his signature phrase—A Positive Mental Attitude—which is basically a pleasing personality mixed with enthusiasm.

The answer of course is that they were both right. You can't be successful without a Definite Chief Aim to strive for, and it is equally hard to imagine how you can be successful if you don't have enthusiasm for what you are doing.

No matter who you are or what you do, you have to deal with other people, and every time you explain something, make a judgment, or give an opinion, you are putting yourself or your ideas forward. In effect, you are selling yourself. And if that is true, you better be doing it with enthusiasm.

In professional sales, one of the most commonly heard pieces of advice is, "The first sale you must make is to yourself." If you try to sell something you don't believe in, you can say all the right words but something will be missing. And people can always spot a phony.

On the other hand, everyone has had the experience of being convinced by a speaker who is passionate about an idea, or of being persuaded to try a product because the salesperson just seemed so sincere. In such instances it isn't a slick sales pitch or overwhelming logic that does the trick—it is an attitude that emanates from the person. It is enthusiasm.

If you have enthusiasm for what you are selling or explaining, it is as though you don't even have to try to sell. You simply present your story and, in doing so, your enthusiasm for it gives off a sense of confidence and faith that other people pick up on.

It should be noted that this is also true when you are trying to sell your Definite Chief Aim to yourself. Previously we have stressed the importance of using autosuggestion to inject faith into your Definite Chief Aim. However, if you aren't honestly enthusiastic about what you are telling your inner-self, you can repeat the words of your auto-suggestion over and over a thousand times, and the effect will be negligible if you aren't doing it with enthusiasm.

The following is excerpted and adapted from *Law of Success*, Lesson Seven: Enthusiasm.

ENTHUSIASM

Enthusiasm is a state of mind that inspires and arouses you to put action into the task at hand. It does more than this—it is contagious and vitally affects not only you, but all with whom you come in contact.

Enthusiasm bears the same relationship to a human being that steam does to the locomotive—it is the vital moving force that impels action. The greatest leaders are those who know how to inspire enthusiasm in their followers. Enthusiasm is the most important factor entering into salesmanship. It is, by far, the most vital factor that enters into public speaking.

HOW ENTHUSIASM WILL AFFECT YOU

Enthusiasm is not merely a figure of speech; it is a vital force that you can harness and use. Without it you would resemble an electric battery without electricity.

Enthusiasm is the vital force with which you recharge your body and develop a dynamic personality. Some people are blessed with natural enthusiasm, while others must acquire it. The procedure through which it may be developed is simple. It begins by doing work you like. If you cannot engage in the work which you like best, for the time being, then you can proceed along another line very effectively by adopting a Definite Chief Aim that contemplates your engaging in that particular work at some future time.

Lack of money and other circumstances over which you have no control may force you to engage in work that you do not like, but no one can stop you from determining in your own mind what your

Definite Chief Aim in life shall be. Nor can anyone stop you from planning ways and means for translating this aim into reality, and nor can anyone stop you from mixing enthusiasm with your plans.

Happiness, the final object of all human effort, is a state of mind that can be maintained only through the hope of future achievement. The happy person is the one who dreams of heights of achievement that are yet unattained. The home you intend to own, the money you intend to earn and place in the bank, the trip you intend to take when you can afford it, the position in life you intend to fill when you have prepared yourself, and the preparation itself—these are the things that produce happiness. Likewise, these are the materials out of which your Definite Chief Aim is formed; these are the things over which you may become enthusiastic, no matter what your present station in life may be.

More than twenty years ago I became enthusiastic over an idea. When the idea first took form in my mind, I was unprepared to take even the first step toward its transformation into reality. But I nursed it in my mind, and I became enthusiastic over it as I looked ahead, in my imagination, and saw the time when I would be prepared to make it a reality.

The idea was this: I wanted to become the editor of a magazine, based upon the Golden Rule, through which I could inspire people to keep up courage and deal with one another squarely.

Finally my chance came, and on Armistice Day 1918, I wrote the first editorial for what was to become the material realization of a hope that had lain dormant in my mind for all those years.

With enthusiasm I poured into that editorial the emotions I had been developing in my heart. My dream had come true. My editorship of a national magazine had become a reality.

As I have said, this editorial was written with enthusiasm. I took it to a man of my acquaintance, and with enthusiasm I read it to him.

The editorial ended in these words: "At last my twenty-year-old dream is about to come true. It takes money, and a lot of it, to publish a national magazine, and I haven't the slightest idea where I am going to get this essential factor, but this is worrying me not at all because I know I am going to get it somewhere!" As I wrote those lines, I mixed enthusiasm and faith with them.

I had hardly finished reading this editorial when the man to whom I read it—the first and only person to whom I had shown it—said:

"I can tell you where you are going to get the money, for I am going to supply it."

And he did!

There was no rational business reason why the man should decide on the spot to finance Napoleon Hill's magazine. In fact at that time, in that financial climate, there were many logical reasons why he shouldn't, but logic didn't count against the power of suggestion that came with Hill's enthusiasm.

HOW YOUR ENTHUSIASM AFFECTS OTHERS

We come now to one of the most important subjects of this course, namely, suggestion. Suggestion is the principle through which your words and your acts and even your state of mind influence others.

If you accept the principle of telepathy as a reality, you of course understand why enthusiasm is contagious, and why it influences all within its radius.

[As noted earlier, Hill's definition of telepathy is nonmystical and pure common sense: simply the acknowledgment that sometimes, in some way, you pick up on cues and clues about the attitude of another person or other people.]

When your own mind has been stimulated with enthusiasm, that vibration registers in the minds of all within its radius, and especially in the minds of those with whom you come in close contact. When a public speaker "senses" the feeling that his audience is "en rapport" (in harmony) with him, he is merely recognizing the fact that his own enthusiasm has influenced the minds of his listeners until their minds are vibrating in harmony with his own.

When the salesman senses that the "psychological" moment for closing a sale has arrived, he merely feels the effect of his own enthusiasm as it influences the mind of his prospective buyer and places that mind "en rapport" with his own.

The subject of suggestion constitutes so vitally an important part of this lesson, and of this entire course, that I will describe the three mediums through which it usually operates—namely, what you say, what you do, and what you think!

WHAT YOU SAY

When you are enthusiastic over the goods you are selling or the services you are offering, or the speech you are delivering, your state of mind becomes obvious to all who hear you, by the tone of your voice. Whether you have ever thought of it in this way or not, it is the tone in which you make a statement, more than it is the statement itself, that carries conviction or fails to convince. No mere combination of words can ever take the place of a deep belief in a statement that is expressed with burning enthusiasm. Words are but devitalized sounds unless colored with feeling that is born of enthusiasm.

Thus, what you say, and the way in which you say it, conveys a meaning that may be just the opposite to what is intended. This accounts for many a failure by the salesman who presents his arguments in words which seem logical enough, but lack the coloring that can come only from enthusiasm that is born of sincerity and belief in the goods he is trying to sell. His words said one thing, but the tone of his voice suggested something entirely different; therefore, no sale was made.

WHAT YOU DO

What you say is an important factor in the operation of the principle of suggestion, but not nearly so important as what you do. Your acts will count for more than your words, and woe unto you if the two fail to harmonize.

If you preach the Golden Rule as a sound rule of conduct, your words will fall upon deaf ears if you do not practice what you preach. The most effective sermon that a person can preach on the soundness of the Golden Rule is the one that is preached by suggestion, when that person applies this rule in relationships with others.

If a salesman of Ford automobiles drives up to his prospective purchaser in a Buick, all the arguments he can present in behalf of the Ford will be without effect.

WHAT YOU THINK

Your thoughts constitute the most important of the three ways in which you apply the principle of suggestion, for the reason that they control the tone of your words and, to some extent at least, your actions. If your thoughts and your actions and your words harmonize, you are bound to influence others.

CHARACTER

No one can become a master salesman if he compromises falsehood. Even though no one ever catches him red-handed in expressing what he does not believe, his words will fail in the accomplishment of their purpose because he cannot give them "flesh" if they do not come from his heart, and if they are not mixed with genuine, unadulterated enthusiasm.

You cannot afford to suggest to another person, by word of mouth or by an act of yours, that which you do not believe.

Surely, that is plain enough.

And the reason you cannot afford to do so, is this:

If you compromise with your own conscience, it will not be long before you will have no conscience; for your conscience will fail to guide you, just as an alarm clock will fail to awaken you if you do not heed it.

There is but one thing in the world that gives us real and enduring power, and that is character. Reputation, bear in mind, is not character. Reputation is what people are believed to be; character is what people are! If you would be a person of great influence, then be a person of real character.

Without character you have nothing; you are nothing; and you can be nothing. Character is something that you cannot beg or steal or buy. You can get it only by building it; and you can build it by your own thoughts and deeds, and in no other way. Through the aid of autosuggestion, any person can build a sound character, no matter what his past has been.

I do not believe that I can afford to try to deceive anyone, about anything, but I *know* that I cannot afford to try to deceive myself. To do so would destroy the power of my pen and render my words ineffective.

It is only when I write with the fire of enthusiasm burning in my heart that my writing impresses others favorably; and it is only when I speak from a heart that is bursting with belief in my message, that I can move my audience to accept that message.

RAISING THE CHAIN OF DOUBT

As we have already seen, suggestion differs from autosuggestion only in one way: We use suggestion, consciously or unconsciously, when we influence others, while we use autosuggestion as a means of influencing ourselves.

Before you can influence another person through suggestion, that person's mind must be in a state of neutrality; that is, it must be open and receptive to your method of suggestion. Right here is where most salespeople fail—they try to make a sale before the mind of the prospective buyer has been rendered receptive or neutralized.

The human mind is a marvelous piece of machinery! One of its outstanding characteristics is noticed in the fact that all impressions which reach it, either through outside suggestion or autosuggestion, are recorded together in groups which harmonize in nature. The negative impressions are stored away, all in one portion of the brain, while the positive impressions are stored in another portion. When one of these impressions (or past experiences) is called into the conscious mind, through the principle of memory, there is a tendency to recall with it all others of a similar nature, just as the raising of one link of a chain brings up other links with it.

For example, anything that causes a feeling of doubt to arise in a person's mind is sufficient to call forth all of his experiences which caused him to become doubtful. If a person is asked by a stranger to cash a check, he or she immediately remembers having cashed checks that were not good, or of having heard of others who did so. Through the law of association, all similar emotions, experiences, and sense impressions that reach the mind are filed away together, so that the recalling of one has a tendency to bring back to memory all the others.

To arouse a feeling of distrust in a person's mind has a tendency to bring to the surface every doubt-building experience that person ever had. For this reason, successful salespeople endeavor to keep away from the discussion of subjects that may arouse the buyer's "chain of doubt impressions" from previous experiences. The successful salesman quickly learns that "knocking" a competitor may result in bringing to the buyer's mind certain negative emotions which may make it impossible for the salesman to "neutralize" the buyer's mind.

This principle applies to and controls every sense impression that is lodged in the human mind. Take the feeling of fear, for example; the moment we permit a single emotion that is related to fear to reach the conscious mind, it calls with it all of its unsavory relations. A feeling of courage cannot claim the attention of the conscious mind while a feeling of fear is there. One or the other must dominate.

They make poor roommates because they do not harmonize in nature. Like attracts like. Every thought held in the conscious mind has a tendency to draw to it other thoughts of a similar nature. These feelings, thoughts, and emotions growing out of past experiences, which claim the attention of the conscious mind, are backed up by an army of supporting soldiers of a similar nature.

The following commentary expands upon the concept that the mind cannot hold a positive and negative at the same time. This excerpt is adapted from *Think and Grow Rich: The Workbook,* Chapter 2: Thoughts Are Things.

SUCCESS-CONSCIOUSNESS

Success-consciousness is Napoleon Hill's term for a particular kind of enthusiastic attitude and way of looking at things.

The classic illustration of success-consciousness is the example of a glass that contains water to the halfway point. Is the glass half-full or is it half-empty? Quite clearly it is both or either. It all depends on how you look at it.

The person who has developed an enthusiastic success-consciousness looks at the glass and immediately sees it half-full. It is Hill's contention that if you are going to succeed with the *Think and Grow Rich* program, it will only work if you decide to become a person who sees the glass as half-full.

FAILING YOUR WAY TO SUCCESS

Closely related to the concept of the half-full glass is Hill's creed that every failure or misfortune holds the seed of an equal or greater success. Once again this deals with how you see things, but here it is whether you see failure as a defeat or as an opportunity to learn a lesson that will help you succeed the next time.

Napoleon Hill's creed, "Every failure brings with it the seed of an equivalent success," was the inspiration for entrepreneur and motivational speaker Wayne Allyn Root to write his book *The Joy of Failure.* Published in the late 1990s, it not only tells Wayne's personal story of using his failures as steppingstones to success, but he also recounts stories from other successful people which prove that the rich and famous got to be that way only because of what they learned from their failures. People such as Jack Welch, the hugely successful CEO of General Electric, who, early in his career failed dramatically when a plastics plant for which he was responsible blew up. Billionaire Charles Schwab was a failure at school and university, flunking Basic English twice due to a learning disability, and then he failed on Wall Street more than once, before he thought of the idea that grew to make him very rich indeed.

Sylvester Stallone, Bruce Willis, Oprah Winfrey, Bill Clinton, Steven Jobs, Donald Trump, and a host of other equally well-known achievers all had to fail in order to learn the lessons that ultimately made them successes. Every one of them was a failure, but none of them was defeated.

Charles F. Kettering, who patented more than two hundred inventions including the automobile ignition, the spark plug, Freon for air conditioners, and the automatic transmission, said, "From the time a person is six years old until he graduates from college he has to take three or four examinations a year. If he flunks once, he is out. But an inventor is almost always failing. He tries and fails maybe a thousand times. If he succeeds once, then he's in. These two things are diametrically opposite. We often say that the biggest job we have is to teach a newly hired employee how to fail intelligently. We have to train him to experiment over and over and to keep on trying and failing until he learns what will work. Failures are just practice shots."

The important point about both the half-full glass and the failure-as-opportunity is not just that it depends on how you see it, but that how you see it is up to you. It is entirely within your power to control the way in which you respond to things.

POSITIVE MENTAL ATTITUDE

Napoleon Hill's concept of success-consciousness is the precursor of the theory behind the bestseller *Success Through a Positive Mental Attitude,* which Hill co-authored with W. Clement Stone. In their book they use the acronym PMA to refer to the state of mind that results from approaching life with a positive mental attitude. W. Clement Stone practiced that philosophy every day of his life, and he believed that this, combined with Hill's Principles of Success, was the reason he had achieved so much in life. As Stone defines it, PMA is much more than what we usually consider to be positive thinking.

Starting with only one hundred dollars and a burning desire to succeed, W. Clement Stone turned himself into a master salesman and built a multibillion-dollar insurance empire. As his success grew, he made a point of analyzing his achievements and identifying each technique that worked for him. He would then formalize it into a written theory and it would become part of his personal PMA philosophy.

W. Clement Stone was an avid reader, an inveterate memo-writer, and an inspirational motivator who loved to share the lessons he had learned as he built his empire. He made sure that every person he hired learned the PMA method, and he gave each new employee a free copy of the book that had been the greatest inspiration to him —*Think and Grow Rich.* By doing so, he changed their mind-set and helped make many of them successful and wealthy beyond their wildest dreams.

HAVING ENTHUSIASM OR BEING ENTHUSIASTIC?

Anyone who ever experienced W. Clement Stone's upbeat, larger-than-life personality has witnessed PMA in action. No moment in his presence was ordinary, no subject got less than his full attention, and every idea was approached as though it had at least the possibility to be wonderful. PMA is not just giving something the benefit of the doubt; PMA is active enthusiasm for its possibilities.

Is it really possible for you to emulate W. Clement Stone and have honest enthusiasm for everything that comes your way? According to Stone's philosophy, to do so you must first understand the difference between having enthusiasm and being enthusiastic. The difference between the two is that enthusiasm is an inward mental attitude, while acting enthusiastically is the outward expression. According to Stone, either one can create the other.

We all know that acting enthusiastic comes naturally if you have inner enthusiasm. But Stone says it can also work the other way and be just as genuine. Even if you don't feel enthusiasm for something to begin with, if you intentionally give it the benefit of the doubt and act enthusiastically anyway, your outward actions will influence your inner attitude. It is a fact, acting "as if" really does work. You cannot be positive and negative at the same time, and it is entirely within your power to control the way in which you respond to things.

Now, does everything deserve your enthusiasm?

Probably not, but isn't it better to at least start from the point of view that it does? If it proves to be less than you'd hoped, you can always change your mind. That way you are less likely to be the person who doesn't listen to F. W. Woolworth's idea about cheap prices, who turns down the script for Star Wars because sci-fi is dead, the person who fired Steven Jobs, the person who . . . well, you get the idea. It's always easier to say no than to say yes. And that brings us back to success-consciousness.

Success-consciousness means that in every way and in everything you do, you enthusiastically expect the best and look for the possibility of success. Simply stated, you consciously make the decision that you will see the glass half-full instead of half-empty. You decide for yourself that the next time you fail at something you will not see it as a defeat but as an opportunity to learn a lesson that will help you succeed the next time.

A WORD OF CAUTION

There is a certain kind of person who will belittle your glass-half-full attitude and look down on you as being naïve. We all know at least a few of those people. They are the ones who pride themselves on being realistic and facing facts. They will tell you that they don't want to burst your balloon, but by converting you to their half-empty point of view, they are doing it for your own good and to keep you from being hurt.

The next time someone tells you that, you should stop and ask yourself a few questions. What will it gain you to view life from their cynical point of view? Will cautious suspicion and guarded optimism inspire anyone you know? Does moderation and sober reserve fling open any doors for you? In what way will your chance of success be made better by filtering everything through the lens of the worst-case scenario?

The next time someone tells you to face facts or to see things as they really are, here's the fact you should face: the fact is that the glass is just as much half-full as it is half-empty. If it's a choice, why not go for the one that could make you a winner? The chances of you taking a half-full glass and making something of it are a lot better than if you are trying to build on something you see as half-empty.

As was mentioned previously, Napoleon Hill warns that you will not succeed with the *Think and Grow Rich* program unless you make enthusiasm and success-consciousness your natural habit.

The following returns to the adapted excerpt from *Law of Success*, Lesson Seven: Enthusiasm.

THE SEVEN SOURCES OF ENTHUSIASM

Enthusiasm knows no defeat! The sales manager who knows how to send out an army of enthusiastic salespeople may set his own price on his services, and what is more important even than this, he can increase the earning capacity of every person under his direction; thus, his enthusiasm benefits not only himself but perhaps hundreds of others.

Enthusiasm is never a matter of chance. There are certain stimuli which produce enthusiasm, the most important of these being:

- Occupation in work which one loves best

- An environment where one comes in contact with others who are enthusiastic and optimistic

- Financial success

- Complete mastery and application, in one's daily work, of the Seventeen Laws of Success

- Good health

- Knowledge that one has served others in some helpful manner

- Good clothes, appropriate to the needs of one's occupation

All of these seven sources of stimuli are self-explanatory, with the exception of the last. The psychology of clothes is understood by very few people, and for this reason it will be here explained in detail. Clothes constitute the most important part of the outward embellishment that every person must have in order to feel self-reliant, hopeful, and enthusiastic.

Needless to say, clothing and what is acceptable to wear in business today is a far cry from what was considered appropriate in the early part of the twentieth century. As you begin to read the following, you may wonder what Napoleon Hill, who wore celluloid collars and spats, could have to say to a world where Casual Friday is common and billion-dollar deals are signed by people dressed in blue jeans or sweats.

The editors assure you that as you read on, it will become abundantly clear that the philosophy behind the words supersedes the fashion of any particular era, and that in fact Hill's psychology of good clothes is more about self-motivation than it is about fashion.

THE PSYCHOLOGY OF GOOD CLOTHES

I got my first training in the psychology of good clothes from my friend Edwin C. Barnes, whom I mentioned earlier had ridden into West Orange on a freight train (not being able to raise sufficient money for passenger fare). What I had not elaborated upon then is that when Mr. Barnes arrived, he had announced at the Edison offices that he had come to enter into a partnership with Mr. Edison.

Nearly everybody around the Edison plant laughed at Barnes, except Edison himself. He saw something in the square jaw and determined face of young Barnes which most of the others did not see, despite the fact that the young man looked more like a tramp than he did a future partner of the greatest inventor on earth.

Barnes got his start, sweeping floors in the Edison offices. That was all he sought—just a chance to get a toehold in the Edison organization. From there on he made history.

I first became acquainted with Barnes during the early days of his association with Edison, before he had "arrived."

In those days he had the largest and most expensive collection of clothes I had ever seen or heard of one man owning. His wardrobe consisted of thirty-one suits; one for each day of the month. He never wore the same suit two days in succession.

One day, in a spirit of fun, I asked him to save some of his old suits that he did not need, for me.

He informed me that he hadn't a single suit that he did not need!

He then gave me a lesson on the psychology of clothes which is well worth remembering: "I do not wear thirty-one suits of clothes entirely for the impression they make on other people; I do it mostly for the impression they have on me."

Barnes then told me of the day when he presented himself at the Edison plant, for a position. He said he had to walk around the plant a dozen times before he worked up enough courage to announce himself, because he knew that he looked more like a tramp than he did a desirable employee.

Barnes is said to be the most able salesman ever connected with the great inventor of West Orange, New Jersey. His entire fortune was made through his ability as a salesman, but he has often said that he never could have accomplished the results which have made him both wealthy and famous had it not been for his understanding of the psychology of clothes.

For the benefit of the more "dignified" students of this philosophy, who may object to resorting to "trick clothing" as a means of achieving success, let me say that the real lesson here is that practically every successful person on earth has discovered some form of stimulus through which he can and does drive himself on to greater effort.

Times too numerous to mention, I have gone into conference with colleagues who had the appearance of worry written all over them, only to see those same colleagues straighten up their shoulders, tilt their chins at a higher angle, soften their faces with smiles of confidence, and get down to business with that sort of enthusiasm which knows no defeat.

The change took place the moment harmony of purpose was established.

If a person goes about the affairs of life devoid of enthusiasm, he is doomed to failure. Nothing can save him until he changes his attitude and learns how to stimulate his mind and body to unusual heights of enthusiasm at will!

Your business in life, you are reminded once again, is to achieve success!

With the stimulus you will experience from studying this philosophy, you should be able to create a definite plan that will lift you to great heights of achievement. However, there is no plan that can produce this desirable result without the aid of some influence that will cause you to arouse yourself, in a spirit of enthusiasm, to where you will exert greater than the ordinary effort that you put into your daily occupation.

The following, taken from the commentary in *Think and Grow Rich: The Workbook,* Chapter 10: Persistence, returns to the subject of success-consciousness, and its close cousin money-consciousness, to make the point that there are aspects of this form of enthusiasm that require special commitment.

MONEY-CONSCIOUSNESS

There is a vast difference between wishing and desiring. All your wishing and hoping for success accomplishes nothing. The only thing that counts is what you do to condition your mind for success and what you do to make it happen.

That brings us to what some consider the most controversial aspect of this book: *money-consciousness*—the term Hill uses to describe the state of mind that attracts riches.

You can grow rich spiritually, emotionally, or intellectually, and to some degree all of those things are true for students of Napoleon Hill's philosophy, but the truth is that most people who read this book do so to learn how to grow richer financially.

In these days of political correctness, you might have reservations about admitting that you want to make a lot of money, but Hill wrote *Think and Grow Rich* during the time that America was just beginning to recover from the worst depression in history, and the whole point of the book was to help people make money.

Today the Great Depression is long behind us, but no matter if it's depression, recession, boom, bubble, or bust, people want to know how to succeed and make more money, and *Think and Grow Rich* continues to be a bestseller year after year.

NOBODY SAID IT WAS EASY

If you are going to adopt Hill's money-consciousness methods, then you must be prepared to accept some ways of thinking and doing things that are much more demanding than most other motivational or self-help programs.

To succeed by using the Hill method, you must first commit yourself to a Definite Chief Aim that offers the possibility to yield the riches you desire. Next, through autosuggestion, you fire up your faith in your ability until you are convinced that you can achieve your aim. Now, in order to turn that aim into money-consciousness, you must begin to see everything in your life from the point of view of how it relates to your aim or purpose.

If you follow Hill's method, you will become a very focused and goal-directed person, and most people would agree that's a very good thing. However, there are some negatives that you must guard against.

On one hand you may become so preoccupied with your goal that it becomes all you can talk about, and other people begin to lose interest in you. On the other hand, there is the danger that by becoming so obsessed with your goal, it's you who loses interest in other people.

The editors would expect that anyone who is smart enough to succeed with Napoleon Hill's philosophy is also smart enough to know the difference between being a person with a passionate interest and being a self-obsessed bore. However, even if you don't become a bore or a recluse, if you embrace prosperity-consciousness with the commitment Hill says it requires, there are going to be some changes in you.

So the question is whether you should choose a Definite Chief Aim and go into it with everything you've got, or whether you should play it safe as you give it a shot, while not letting yourself go too overboard.

You may be able to make an argument for either point of view, but if you decide to put less than 100 percent into it, you must accept that what you get back will be less than 100 percent of what you could have achieved.

SUCCESS-CONSCIOUSNESS IS NOT FOR EVERYONE

What Napoleon Hill offers is a philosophy of personal achievement and a specific method that, if followed, will produce success and make you rich. But it will also change who you are, and some of the changes may not be entirely to your liking.

It's true that you might become successful without following Hill's principles. There are people who make huge fortunes just by being in the right place at the right time or by taking a gamble and winning or by exploiting their natural talent or ability. That may be the kind of success that you wish for, but it is not the kind of success that you can plan on. Hill's methods cannot help you have that kind of success.

It is up to you to decide if you are prepared to commit yourself to a method that is this focused on being a success and making money. Your challenge is to decide what your monetary aim or purpose is, and then to decide how persistent you will be in pursuing your desire to have that money. You will become rich in direct proportion to the degree to which you apply these principles.

POVERTY-CONSCIOUSNESS

Just as money is attracted to those who deliberately set their minds on it, poverty is attracted to those whose minds are open to it.

Money-consciousness is something you have to work hard at to achieve. Poverty-consciousness requires no work at all. It is always there, waiting for you to let down your guard. Money-consciousness is demanding, but poverty-consciousness is easy. It's easier than working hard. It's easier than taking responsibility. It's easier to blame your failure and poverty on others who don't understand you, or who don't appreciate you, or don't give you the breaks, or don't like you, or any of the other excuses that let you off the hook for your own lack of ambition and persistence.

Poverty-consciousness and poverty are not the same thing. There are people right now who are living in poverty who don't have poverty-consciousness. For them, poverty is only a temporary circumstance. They have every intention of getting themselves out of poverty and they see the possibility of success in every opportunity.

There are also people who are living in much better circumstances with much better opportunities, but they will never see an opportunity as the possibility of success. All they see is the possibility of failing, the possibility of embarrassing themselves, the possibility of being turned down, the possibility that someone else will do better than they will, the possibility they might be wrong, the possibility of losing what they have. And because they are locked into such a poverty-conscious mind-set, they will never see the upside of the possibilities and they will never rise to the top.

Money-consciousness and poverty-consciousness are not what you are—they're what you think. Both are states of mind, and you can change your mind and change your habits.

To close this chapter, we go back to *Law of Success* and offer a brief story of how one small comment, made at the right time and said with the right degree of enthusiasm, made an impression on Napoleon Hill that influenced his entire life.

ENTHUSIASM AND SUGGESTION

Deliberately place in your own mind, through the principle of autosuggestion, the ambition to succeed through the aid of a Definite Chief Aim, and notice how quickly all of your latent or undeveloped ability in the nature of past experiences will become stimulated and aroused to action in your behalf.

If you would plant a suggestion "deeply," mix it generously with enthusiasm, for enthusiasm is the fertilizer that will ensure its rapid growth as well as its permanency.

When a kind-hearted old gentleman planted in my mind the suggestion that I was a "bright boy" and that I could make my mark in the world if I would educate myself, it was not so much what he said, as it was the way in which he said it that made such a deep and lasting impression on my mind. It was the way in which he gripped my shoulders and the look of confidence in his eyes that drove his suggestion so deeply into my subconscious mind that it never gave me any peace until I commenced taking the steps that led to the fulfillment of the suggestion.

This is a point that I would stress with all the power at my command. It is not so much what you say as it is the TONE and the MANNER in which you say it that makes a lasting impression.

It naturally follows therefore, that sincerity of purpose, honesty, and earnestness must be placed behind all that you say if you would make a lasting and favorable impression.

Whatever you successfully sell to others, you must first sell to yourself!

Read over the description of your Definite Chief Aim each night, just before retiring, and as you read, see yourself (in your imagination) in full possession of the object of your aim. Do this with full faith in your ability to transform your Definite Chief Aim into reality. Read aloud, with all the enthusiasm at your command, emphasizing every word. Repeat this reading until the small still voice within you tells you that your purpose will be realized. Sometimes you will feel the effects of this voice from within the first time you read your Definite Chief Aim, while at other times you may have to read it a dozen or fifty times before the assurance comes, but do not stop until you feel it.

Chapter Ten

SELF-CONTROL
IS THOUGHT CONTROL

WHAT WOULD NAPOLEON HILL DO?

Self-control is the way to focus attention on your Definite Chief Aim and condition your subconscious mind to direct its power toward a specific end.

Napoleon Hill would intentionally close his mind to the bombardment of outside influences by focusing so enthusiastically on his Definite Chief Aim that there was no room for negatives to enter his mind. He used enthusiasm as a source of power, but it went both ways: he also refused to allow himself to become so enthusiastic that it would cloud his judgment.

This chapter on self-control and the previous one on enthusiasm are like two sides of the same coin. Just as you can't have right without left, up without down, or a valley without having mountains, you can't have self-control without having enthusiasm.

However, that is not the same as saying that self-control is the opposite of enthusiasm, or the absence of enthusiasm. In fact, it might be better described as the *result* of enthusiasm—not the lack of it.

As Napoleon Hill uses the term, self-control should not inhibit your enthusiasm, it should focus it. There is a lesson in Zen that nicely captures the Hill approach to enthusiasm: "When walking, walk. When sitting, sit. Above all, don't wobble." Meaning, if you are enthusiastic about something, don't try to tamp it down; be 100 percent enthusiastic. But the flip side is that someone who is constantly enthusing about everything not only gets tiresome but also loses credibility.

The final lesson is this: don't overreact and become so self-controlled that you are flat and boring. Keep on not wobbling in your enthusiasm, but you should be just as nonwobbling in your self-control, and only use your self-control to focus your enthusiasm when you really mean it, and where it will really count.

Enthusiasm and self-control are the two halves of the whole; the yin and yang of how you should pursue your Definite Chief Aim. Be enthusiastic, but do it with self-control.

The following explanation is excerpted and adapted from *Law of Success*, Lesson Eight: Self-Control.

SELF-CONTROL

In the preceding lesson you learned of the value of enthusiasm. You also learned how to generate enthusiasm and how to transmit its influence to others, through the principle of suggestion.

You come now to the study of self-control, through which you may direct your enthusiasm to constructive ends. Without self-control, enthusiasm resembles the unharnessed lightning of an electrical storm —it may strike anywhere; it may destroy life and property.

Enthusiasm is the vital quality that arouses you to action, while self-control is the balance wheel that directs your action so that it will build up and not tear down.

Self-control is important because those who do not exercise it suffer the loss of a great power that they need in their struggle for the achievement of their Definite Chief Aim.

If you neglect to exercise self-control, you are not only likely to injure others, but you are sure to injure yourself!

HOW DOES SELF-CONTROL HELP?

- A person with well-developed self-control does not indulge in envy, hatred, jealousy, fear, revenge, or any similar destructive emotions.

- A person with well-developed self-control does not go into ecstasies or become ungovernably enthusiastic over anything or anybody.

- Greed and selfishness and excessive self-approval indicate lack of self-control in one of its most dangerous forms.

- Self-confidence is one of the important essentials of success, but when this faculty is developed beyond the point of reason, it becomes very dangerous.

- Self-sacrifice is a commendable quality, but when it is carried to extremes, it also becomes one of the dangerous forms of a lack of self-control.

- Love is essential for happiness, but the person who loves so deeply that his or her happiness is placed entirely in the hands of another is literally out of control.

- A person with well-developed self-control will not permit himself to be influenced by the cynic or the pessimist; nor will he permit another person to do his thinking for him.

- A person with well-developed self-control will stimulate his imagination and his enthusiasm until they have produced action, but he will then control that action and not permit it to control him.

- A person with well-developed self-control will never, under any circumstances, slander another person or seek revenge for any cause whatsoever.

- A person with self-control will not hate those who do not agree with him; instead, he will endeavor to understand the reason for their disagreement, and profit by it.

- A person with self-control does not form opinions based on nothing more than the desire for a thing to be or not to be. A person with self-control studies the facts.

- A person with self-control does not spend beyond his or her means. Between the miser who hoards every penny, and the person who spends every cent, there is a "happy medium."

- One very common and very destructive form of lack of self-control is the habit of talking too much. It is nearly always more profitable to listen than it is to speak.

SELF-CONTROL IS THOUGHT CONTROL

You are the product of at least a million years of evolutionary change. For countless generations preceding you, nature has been tempering and refining the materials that have gone into your make-up. No other animal has ever been endowed with such self-control as you possess. You have been endowed with the power to use the most highly organized form of energy known—that of thought.

You have not only the power to think, but, what is a thousand times more important still, you have the power to control your thoughts and direct them to do your bidding! Your brain may be likened to a dynamo, in that it generates or sets into motion the mysterious energy called thought. The stimuli that start your brain into action are of two sorts—one is autosuggestion and the other is suggestion. You can select the material out of which your thinking is produced, and that is autosuggestion. You can permit others to select the material out of which your thinking is produced, and that is suggestion.

It is a humiliating fact that most thought is produced by the outside suggestions of others, and it is more humiliating still to have to admit that the majority of us accept this suggestion without either examining it or questioning its soundness. We read the daily papers as though every word were based upon fact. We are swayed by the gossip and idle chatter of others as though every word were true.

Thought is the only thing over which you have absolute control. Yet you permit other people to enter your mind and deposit, through suggestion, their troubles and woes, adversities and falsehoods, just as though you did not have the power to close the door and keep them out.

You have within your control the power to select the material that constitutes the dominating thoughts of your mind, and just as surely as you are reading these lines, those thoughts which dominate your mind will bring you success or failure, according to their nature.

Self-control is solely a matter of thought control!

You are studying this course because you are earnestly seeking truth and understanding sufficient to enable you to attain some high station in life.

You are searching for the magic key that will unlock the door to the source of power, and yet you have the key in your own hands and you may make use of it the moment you learn to control your thoughts.

Place in your own mind, through the principle of autosuggestion, the positive, constructive thoughts which harmonize with your Definite Chief Aim, and your mind will transform those thoughts into physical reality and hand them back to you as a finished product.

This is thought control!

When you deliberately choose the thoughts that dominate your mind and firmly refuse admittance to outside suggestion, you are exercising self-control in its highest and most efficient form. Human beings are the only animals that can do this.

YOU CAN DO IT IF YOU WANT TO

A student in one of my classes once asked how you go about controlling your thoughts when in a state of intense anger.

I replied: "In exactly the same way that you would change your manner and the tone of your voice if you were in a heated argument with a member of your family and heard the doorbell ring, warning that company was about to visit. You would control yourself because you would desire to do so."

If you have ever been in a similar predicament, where you found it necessary to cover up your real feelings and change the expression on your face quickly, you know how easily it can be done. You also know that it can be done because one wants to do it!

Behind all achievement, behind all self-control, behind all thought control, is that magic something called desire.

It is no misstatement of fact to say that you are limited only by the depth of your desires. When your desires are strong enough, you will appear to possess superhuman powers to achieve.

If you desire to acquire the art of successful negotiation, as you undoubtedly will when you understand its significance in relation to your achievement of your Definite Chief Aim, you will do so, providing your desire is intense enough.

Don't say "It can't be done," or that you are different from these and thousands of others who have achieved noteworthy success in every worthy calling. If you are "different" it is only in this respect: they desired the object of their achievement with more depth and intensity than you desire yours.

SELLING YOURSELF IS SELF-CONTROL

In the following, when I use the term *salesperson*, I mean all people who try to persuade or convince others by logical argument or appeal to self-interest. In my view we are all salespeople, or at least we should be, no matter what form of service we are rendering or what sort of goods we are offering.

If you would be a master salesperson of goods or of personal services, you must exercise sufficient self-control to shut out all adverse arguments and suggestions. Many salespeople have so little self-control that they hear the prospective purchaser say no, even before they say it. They have so little self-control that they actually suggest to themselves that their prospective purchaser will say no when asked to purchase their wares.

How different is the person of self-control! He or she not only makes the self-suggestion that the prospective purchaser will say yes, but if the desired yes is not forthcoming, he or she stays on the job until the opposition breaks down.

If the prospective purchaser says no, the person of self-control does not hear it. If the prospective purchaser says no a second, and a third, and a fourth time, he or she does not hear it, for a person of self-control permits no suggestions to reach the mind except those which are invited.

The master salesperson, whether he or she is engaged in selling merchandise or personal services or sermons or public addresses, understands how to control his or her own thoughts. Instead of being a person who accepts, with meek submission, the suggestions of others, the master salesperson is one who persuades others to accept his or her suggestions. The master salesperson becomes a dominating personality.

This, too, is self-control!

A master salesperson is one who takes the offensive, and never the defensive, side of an argument, if argument arises.

If you are a master salesperson, you know that it will be fatal to your sale if you permit the buyer to place you on the defensive and keep you there. It is your business to exercise such perfect poise and self-control that you will change places with your prospective purchasers without them noticing that you have done so.

Many salespeople sweep this aside by becoming aggressive and trying to intimidate the prospective purchaser into buying, but the master of the craft remains calm and serene, and usually comes out the winner.

SUCCESSFUL NEGOTIATION IS SELF-CONTROL

The ability to negotiate with other people without friction and argument is the outstanding quality of all successful people. Observe those nearest you and notice how few there are who understand this art of tactful negotiation.

Observe, also, how successful are the few who understand this art, despite the fact that they may have less education than those with whom they negotiate. It is a knack that you can cultivate.

The art of successful negotiation grows out of patient and painstaking self-control. Notice how easily the successful salesperson exercises self-control when handling a customer who is impatient. The salesperson may be boiling inside, but you will see no evidence of it in manner or in words.

That person has acquired the art of tactful negotiation!

A single frown of disapproval or a single word denoting impatience will often spoil a sale. Successful salespeople exercise self-control, and as a reward they set their own salary and choose their own position.

To watch those who have acquired the art of successful negotiation is an education in itself.

Watch those public speakers who have acquired this art; notice the firmness of step as they mount the platform; observe the firmness of voice as they begin to speak; study their facial expressions as they sweep the audience with the mastery of their arguments. These are people who have learned how to negotiate without friction.

Study those physicians who have acquired this art, as they walk into the sick room and greet their patients with a smile.

Watch the managers or supervisors who have acquired this art, and observe how their very presence spurs the employees to greater effort and inspires them with confidence and enthusiasm.

Watch the lawyer who has acquired this art, and observe how he or she commands the respect and attention of the court. There is something about the tone of voice, the posture, and expression, that cause opponents to suffer by comparison.

All of this is predicated upon self-control. And self-control is the result of thought control!

Deliberately place in your own mind the sort of thoughts that you desire there, and keep out of your mind those thoughts that others place there through suggestion, and you will become a person of self-control.

YOU ARE WASTING YOUR TIME TO FIGHT BACK

Very early in my public career I was shocked when I learned how many people there are who devote most of their energies to tearing down that which the builders construct. By some turn of the wheel of fate, one of these destroyers crossed my path by making it his business to try to destroy my reputation.

At first, I was inclined to "strike back" at him, but as I sat at my typewriter late one night, a thought came to me which changed my entire attitude toward this man. Removing the sheet of paper that was in my typewriter, I inserted another one on which I stated this thought, in these words:

"You have a tremendous advantage over the man who does you an injury: You have it within your power to forgive him, while he has no such advantage over you."

As I finished writing those lines, I made up my mind to decide upon a policy toward those who criticize my work or try to destroy my reputation.

Two courses of action were open to me. I could waste much of my time and energy in striking back, or I could devote this energy to furthering my life's work and let the result of that work serve as my sole answer to all who would criticize my efforts or question my motives. I decided on the latter as being the better policy and adopted it.

"By their deeds you shall know them!"

The world soon forgets its destroyers. It builds its monuments to and bestows its honors upon none but its builders. Keep this fact in mind and you will more easily reconcile yourself to the policy of refusing to waste your energies by "striking back" at those who offend you.

MASTER THE LAW OF RETALIATION

By developing self-control, you also develop other qualities that will add to your personal power. Among other laws that are available to the person who exercises self-control is the Law of Retaliation.

You know what *retaliate* means!

In the sense that we are using here, it means to "return like for like," and not merely to avenge or to seek revenge, as is commonly meant by the use of this word.

If I do you an injury, you retaliate at first opportunity. If I say unjust things about you, you will retaliate in kind, in even greater measure!

On the other hand, if I do you a favor you will reciprocate in even greater measure if possible.

Through the proper use of this law, I can get you to do whatever I wish you to do. If I wish you to dislike me, I can accomplish this result by inflicting upon you the sort of treatment that I want you to inflict upon me through retaliation.

If I wish your respect, your friendship, and your cooperation, I can get these by extending to you my friendship and cooperation.

The person who attracts you to him through his pleasing personality is merely making use of the law of harmonious attraction, or the Law of Retaliation, both of which, when analyzed, mean that "like attracts like."

When you have mastered this simple law and learned how to use it, you will have learned all that can be learned about salesmanship.

The first and probably the most important step to be taken in mastering this law is to cultivate complete self-control. You must learn to take all sorts of punishment and abuse without retaliating in kind. This self-control is a part of the price you must pay for mastery of the Law of Retaliation.

When an angry person starts in to vilify and abuse you, justly or unjustly, just remember that if you retaliate in a like manner you are being drawn down to that person's mental level, therefore that person is dominating you.

On the other hand, if you refuse to become angry, if you retain your self-composure and remain calm and serene, you take the other person by surprise. You retaliate with a weapon with which he is unfamiliar, consequently you easily dominate him.

Like attracts like! There's no denying this!

Literally speaking, every person with whom you come in contact is a mental looking-glass in which you may see a perfect reflection of your own mental attitude.

Through the principle of retaliation we can actually convert our enemies into loyal friends. If you have an enemy whom you wish to convert into a friend, you can prove the truth of this statement if you will forget that dangerous millstone hanging around your neck, which we call "pride" (stubbornness). Make a habit of speaking to this enemy with unusual cordiality. Go out of your way to favor him in every manner possible. He may seem immovable at first, but gradually he will give way to your influence and "retaliate in kind"!

The following is excerpted and adapted from *Think and Grow Rich*, Chapter 8: Decision.

MAKING YOUR OWN DECISIONS

The majority of people who fail to accumulate money sufficient for their needs are, generally, easily influenced by the opinions of others. They permit the newspapers and the gossiping neighbors to do their thinking for them. Opinions are the cheapest commodities on earth. Everyone has a flock of opinions ready to be wished upon anyone who will accept them. If you are influenced by opinions when you reach decisions, you will not succeed in any undertaking, much less in that of transmuting your own desire into money.

If you are influenced by the opinions of others, you will have no desire of your own.

Keep your own counsel, when you begin to put into practice the principles described here, by reaching your own decisions and following them. Take no one into your confidence, except the members of your Master Mind group, and be very sure in your selection of this group that you choose only those who will be in complete sympathy and harmony with your purpose.

Close friends and relatives, while not meaning to do so, often handicap one through "opinions" and sometimes through ridicule, which is meant to be humorous. Thousands of men and women carry inferiority complexes with them all through life, because some well-meaning but ignorant person destroyed their confidence through opinion or ridicule.

You have a mind of your own. Use it, and reach your own decisions. If you need facts or information from other people to enable you to reach decisions, as you probably will in many instances, acquire these facts or secure the information you need quietly, without disclosing your purpose.

It is characteristic of those people who have but a smattering or a veneer of knowledge to try to give the impression that they have much knowledge. Such people generally do far too much talking, and too little listening. Keep your eyes and ears wide open—and your mouth closed—if you wish to acquire the habit of prompt decision. Those who talk too much do little else. If you talk more than you listen, you not only deprive yourself of many opportunities to accumulate useful knowledge, but you also disclose your plans and purposes to people who will take great delight in defeating you, because they envy you.

Remember also that every time you open your mouth in the presence of a person who has an abundance of knowledge, you display to that person your exact stock of knowledge, or your lack of it! Genuine wisdom is usually conspicuous through modesty and silence.

Keep in mind that every person with whom you associate is, like yourself, seeking the opportunity to accumulate money. If you talk about your plans too freely, you may be surprised when you learn that some other person has beaten you to your goal by putting into action, ahead of you, the plans of which you talked unwisely.

Let one of your first decisions be to keep a closed mouth and open ears and eyes.

As a reminder to yourself to follow this advice, it will be helpful if you copy the following epigram in large letters and place it where you will see it daily: "Tell the world what you intend to do, but first show it."

This is the equivalent of saying that "Deeds, and not words, are what count most."

The following commentary is excerpted from *Think and Grow Rich: The Workbook,* Chapter 9: Decision.

Napoleon Hill advises that you should never let others have undue influence on how you make your decisions. It should make no difference to you what other people might decide for themselves. Hill is especially critical of the way in which family and friends can put pressure on you to do what they think is right, while insisting that they are only doing it for your own good.

As you may have deduced from the preceding excerpt, Hill's advice is based not only on his extensive research into the people who achieved outstanding success, but also on his own personal experience. Hill began his quest to assemble the philosophy of personal achievement in 1908.

Law of Success, the first version of his philosophy, was published twenty years later in 1928, and he finally published *Think and Grow Rich* nine years after that, in 1937. For almost thirty years, Hill personally paid for the research needed to write the philosophy, and practically every day of that time he had to decide to keep doing so despite constant opposition.

During those years he was severely criticized by his family and his friends. They criticized him for putting his family at risk by not taking a stable job, they made fun of him for being so naïve as to work for one of the richest men in the world at no salary, they scoffed at his business schemes, and they ridiculed him for being so full of himself as to think he could write a philosophy. The fact is, if Napoleon Hill had listened to his family and friends, the world would not have the philosophy of personal achievement of which *Law of Success* and *Think and Grow Rich* are a direct result.

Following is a series of questions that will help you to understand your own susceptibility to the influence of friends and family. This is not a questionnaire that can be graded, because there are no absolute right or wrong answers. But by taking the time to think about the questions, noting how you have dealt with friends and relatives in the past, you will gain some valuable insights into yourself and your decisions.

1. Do you give undue attention to what your friends or family say about you?

2. Have you ever not done something because you feared what your family would say?

3. Have you ever not done something because you feared what your friends would say?

4. Whose opinion do you value most?

5. Whose opinion do you fear most?

6. Is there something you would like to be doing right now that you are not doing because of your concern for what your family or friends might think or say?

7. Do you feel that you have an obligation to live up to someone's expectations? Who is that person or persons?

8. Is someone making demands on you that you do not deserve? What do they expect?

9. Do you have an idea or a plan or a concept that you would be pursuing right now if it wasn't for the opinions of others?

10. Are your family or friends more afraid to take a chance than you are?

11. Are you confident in your own ability to assess risk and act in your own best interests?

12. Do you believe that your family or friends are sincerely concerned about you when they give advice, or are they looking out for their own interests?

13. Is there someone in your family or among your friends whom you suspect may secretly want you to fail because they would be jealous if you succeeded?

TELL THE WORLD OR SHOW IT?

There are some motivation and self-help experts who suggest that the best way to make sure you stick to your decisions is to declare yourself and let the world know what you plan to do. Their theory is that if you let everyone know what you plan to do, you will be so afraid to embarrass yourself or to let people down that you will stick to your announced plan and see it through to completion.

Hill's advice is exactly the opposite. He cautions against being too outspoken about your aims and plans for the simple reason that there are too many unscrupulous people who, given the chance, will steal your ideas. Once again, Hill's advice is not only based on his research and interviews with those who achieved success, but also on his own personal experience.

In the years when Hill was starting his own businesses to support his family and fund his research, he lost at least three of them because he trusted dishonest people who he had thought were his friends. He mistook the intentions of bankers who extended him credit; his reputation was tarnished by associates who embezzled funds; and on more than one occasion, companies that he founded and built were literally stolen away from him by unscrupulous partners.

Hill's conclusion and advice was to take no one into your confidence except members of your Master Mind Alliance. Never tell others what you plan to do, and don't call attention to your plans by bragging or showing off your knowledge. In short, do not "tell" the world what you can do—show it!

The following six questions are designed to bring to mind those occasions when you allowed your ego to get the best of you. If you answer these questions honestly, you will very likely be surprised at how easily you can lose sight of what is really important.

1. Have you ever tried to impress someone in business by exaggerating your position or bragging about who you know?

2. Did it benefit you in the long run?

3. Have you ever resisted the opportunity to make yourself look important, and just listened instead of talking about yourself or your ideas?

4. What was the result?

5. Have you ever regretted having given away too much because you couldn't resist the urge to show how smart or how important you are?

6. Has the fear of embarrassment ever actually motivated you to do what you said you were going to do?

The following, excerpted from *Think and Grow Rich*, Chapter 7: Organized Planning, is the definition of the one kind of lack of self-control to which no one is immune.

DON'T PUT OFF 'TIL TOMORROW

This is one of the most common causes of failure. "Old Man Procrastination" stands within the shadow of every human being, waiting his opportunity to spoil your chances of success.

Most of us go through life as failures, because we are waiting for the "time to be right" to start doing something worthwhile. Do not wait. The time will never be "just right." Start where you stand, and work with whatever tools you may have at your command, and better tools will be found as you go along.

The following is excerpted and adapted from the "After-The-Lesson" segment which appears at the end of *Law of Success*, Lesson Sixteen: The Golden Rule.

INDECISION—AN AFTER-THE-LESSON VISIT WITH THE AUTHOR

Procrastination robs you of opportunity. You may be shocked if you kept accurate account of the time you waste in a single day. Second by second, as the clock ticks off the distance, time is running a race with you. Delay means defeat, because no one may ever make up a second of lost time. Wasted time is one of the chief causes of failure.

Time is also, however, a master worker that heals the wounds of failure and disappointment, and rights all wrongs and turns all mistakes into capital.

But it favors only those who kill off procrastination and remain in action when there are decisions to be made.

If you are one of those who makes up your mind today and changes it again tomorrow, you are doomed to failure. If you are not sure which way to move, it is better to shut your eyes and move in the dark than to remain still and make no move at all.

The world will forgive you if you make mistakes, but it will never forgive you if you make no decisions, because it will never hear of you outside the community in which you live.

No matter who you are or what may be your life's work, you are playing checkers with Time! It is always your next move. Move with quick decision, and Time will favor you. You cannot always make the right move, but if you make enough moves you may take advantage of the law of averages and pile up a creditable score before the great game of life is ended.

HOW TO ELIMINATE PROCRASTINATION

If you procrastinate you are not just wasting your time, but you are wasting the time of everyone else who is waiting for you to decide. The age-old advice is that procrastination is the thief of time.

The method through which you may eliminate procrastination is based on self-suggestion and autosuggestion. Copy the following formula and put it in a conspicuous place where you will see it often.

This formula is designed to prompt you to take the initiative and make firm decisions. As you know from the chapter on autosuggestion, every time you read the written version of the formula, it will deepen the imprint on your subconscious mind and it will help you stick with your decision. This formula is adapted from *Law of Success*, Lesson Five: Initiative and Leadership.

PROCRASTINATION

Having chosen a definite aim or purpose as my life's work, I now understand it to be my duty to transform this aim into reality. Therefore I will form the habit of taking some definite action each day that will carry me one step nearer the attainment of my definite aim or purpose.

I know that procrastination is a deadly enemy of all who would become leaders in any undertaking, and I will eliminate this habit from my make-up by:

Doing some one definite thing each day, something that ought to be done, without anyone telling me to do it.

Looking around until I find at least one thing that I can do each day that I have not been in the habit of doing, and that will be of value to others, without expectation of pay.

Telling at least one other person each day of the value of practicing this habit of deciding to do something that ought to be done without being told to do it.

I can see that the muscles of the body become strong in proportion to the extent to which they are used. Therefore I understand that the habit of initiative and decision also becomes fixed in proportion to the extent that it is practiced.

I realize the place to begin developing the habit of initiative and decision is in the small, commonplace things connected with my daily work. Therefore I will go at my work each day as if I were doing it solely for the purpose of developing this necessary habit of initiative and decision.

I understand that by practicing this habit of taking decisive action in connection with my daily work, I will be not only developing that habit but I will also be attracting the attention of those who will place greater value on my services as a result of this practice.

[signed] _____

Every day brings you a chance to render some service, outside of the course of your regular duties, that will be of value to others. You render this service not only because it is of help to others, but also because it provides you with ways of taking the initiative and making firm decisions—qualities which you must possess before you can ever become an outstanding figure in your chosen field.

The following is another variation on overcoming the temptation to procrastinate. It is excerpted and adapted from *Law of Success*, Lesson Thirteen: Cooperation.

1. Form the habit of each day doing the most distasteful tasks first. This procedure will be difficult in the beginning, but after you have formed the habit you will take pride in first dealing with the hardest and most undesirable part of your work.

2. Place this sign in front of you, where you can see it in your daily work, and put a copy where you can see it before you go to sleep and when you arise: "Do not tell them what you can do—show them!"

3. Repeat the following words, aloud, twelve times each night just before you go to sleep: "Tomorrow I will do everything that should be done, when it should be done, and as it should be done. I will perform the most difficult tasks first because this will destroy the habit of procrastination and develop the habit of action in its place."

4. Carry out these instructions with faith in their soundness and with belief that they will develop action, in body and in mind, sufficient to enable you to realize your Definite Chief Aim.

The following exercise is adapted from *Think and Grow Rich*, Chapter 7: Organized Planning.

TAKE AN ANNUAL INVENTORY OF YOURSELF

You either go ahead, stand still, or go backward in life. Your object, of course, should be to go ahead. This list of questions all pertain to things that are under your control. How well you have managed them will tell you a lot about whether you are going forward, and how well you have exercised self-control over the areas of your life that you should control.

Take this inventory by asking yourself the following questions, and by checking your answers with the aid of someone who will not permit you to deceive yourself as to their accuracy.

1. Have I attained the goal that I established as my objective for this year? (You should work with a definite yearly objective to be attained as a part of your major life objective.)

2. Have I delivered service of the best possible quality of which I was capable, or could I have improved any part of this service?

3. Have I delivered service in the greatest possible quantity of which I was capable?

4. Has the spirit of my conduct been harmonious and cooperative at all times?

5. Have I permitted the habit of procrastination to decrease my efficiency, and if so, to what extent?

6. Have I improved my personality, and if so, in what ways?

7. Have I been persistent enough in following my plans through to completion?

8. Have I reached decisions promptly and definitely on all occasions?

9. Have I permitted any one or more of the six basic fears to decrease my efficiency?

10. Have I been either overcautious or undercautious?

11. Has my relationship with my associates in work been pleasant, or unpleasant? If it has been unpleasant, has the fault been partly, or wholly, mine?

12. Have I dissipated any of my energy through lack of concentration of effort?

13. Have I been sufficiently open-minded and tolerant in connection with all subjects?

14. In what way have I improved my ability to render service?

15. Have I been intemperate in any of my habits?

16. Have I expressed, either openly or secretly, any form of egotism?

17. Has my conduct toward my associates been such that it has induced them to respect me?

18. Have my opinions and decisions been based upon guesswork, or accuracy of analysis and thought?

19. Have I followed the habit of budgeting my time, my expenses, and my income, and have I been conservative in these budgets?

20. How much time have I devoted to unprofitable effort, which I might have used to better advantage?

21. How might I rebudget my time, and change my habits so I will be more efficient during the coming year?

22. Have I been guilty of any type of conduct that was not approved by my conscience?

23. In what ways have I rendered more service and better service than I was paid to render?

24. Have I been unfair to anyone, and if so, in what way?

25. If I had been the purchaser of my own services for the year, would I be satisfied with my purchase?

26. Am I in the right vocation, and if not, why not?

27. Has the purchaser of my services been satisfied with the service I have rendered, and if not, why not?

Self-control is mind control. Mind control is the result of self-discipline and habit. You either control your mind or it controls you. There is no halfway compromise.

The most practical method for controlling your mind is the habit of keeping it busy with a definite purpose backed by a Definite Chief Aim.

Chapter Eleven

COOPERATION, TEAMWORK, AND ORGANIZED EFFORT

WHAT WOULD NAPOLEON HILL DO?

Success is the development of the power to get whatever you want in life without interfering with the rights of others. Power is organized energy or effort; cooperation and teamwork produce power.

Napoleon Hill would multiply his power by asking others for their help to do what he could not do as well or as quickly. He would stay alert to the desires of those he depended upon, and he would help them achieve their goals as they helped him achieve his.

The thirteenth principle in the original *Law of Success* is cooperation. In the lesson explaining that principle, Napoleon Hill writes about two aspects of cooperation that have some relationship to each other, but it is not immediately apparent why he has chosen to link them in this lesson. The following is how Hill explains it in the introduction to Lesson Thirteen in *Law of Success*.

COOPERATION

Cooperation is the beginning of all organized effort. As was stated in the second lesson of this course, Andrew Carnegie accumulated a gigantic fortune through the cooperative efforts of a small group of men numbering not more than twenty. You, too, can learn how to use this principle.

There are two forms of cooperation that will be discussed in this lesson.

The first is the cooperation between people who group themselves together or form alliances for the purpose of attaining a given end, under the principles known as the law of the Master Mind.

The second is the cooperation between the conscious and the subconscious minds, which is the basis upon which I have built my hypothesis that we can develop the ability to contact, communicate with, and draw upon Infinite Intelligence.

Quite clearly, when writing about the Principles of Success, there is no argument that cooperation is one of the key principles. However, as with the two previous lessons, Enthusiasm and Self-Control, the central idea of this lesson is so obvious that Hill may have concluded that it did not warrant an involved explanation, so instead he chose to use the chapter as a way to reinforce and further define his key principles—Infinite Intelligence and the Master Mind—even though they are only linked to the concept of cooperation in a general way.

In this book, *What Would Napoleon Hill Do?*, there is even less need for explanations, not only because the concept of cooperation is so self-explanatory, but also because of the extensive detail already presented in previous chapters that cover Infinite Intelligence and the Master Mind.

In the chapters on Imagination and Accurate Thinking, the concept of Infinite Intelligence is set out in great detail, starting with the basic material from *Law of Success* chapters, which is augmented with excerpts from *Think and Grow Rich,* supplemented with commentaries from *Think and Grow Rich: The Workbook,* and further elaborated upon in new original editorial notes written specifically for this book.

The same meticulous approach was taken with the chapter on the Master Mind Alliance.

Because readers are already familiar with so much of the background to this chapter, most of the material presented here focuses on the way Hill links Cooperation to Infinite Intelligence and to the Master Mind.

RECAPPING THE PHYSIOLOGY AND THE PSYCHOLOGY

Following the introduction to the lesson, Napoleon Hill quotes extensively from one of the leading New Thought books of the day, *The Edinburgh Lectures on Mental Science,* by Judge Thomas Troward. In the excerpt Hill relies upon Troward's words to explain the physiology of the human brain and the central nervous system, and in the hope of bolstering his own theory of Infinite Intelligence, he also includes Troward's speculation about the way in which the physical brain is connected to the metaphysical mind.

Troward's book was written in 1909, and his scientific knowledge, which was a little sketchy even at the time, has now been superseded by many advances in medical science. However, even though his pseudoscientific explanation of the Law of Attraction doesn't stand up to modern scrutiny, the reason why Hill mentioned it in this lesson—to support the theory of Infinite Intelligence and the Master Mind—remains unaffected. Modern science may disprove

Troward, but modern science still hasn't come up with a proven scientific theory that would explain these phenomena.

As was noted at the beginning of this book, Napoleon Hill's review of his research showed the phenomenon happening to so many individuals, so often, over so many years, that in his later work he concluded it was explained by the law of nature he called Cosmic Habit Force.

RECAPPING COOPERATION IN THE REAL WORLD

In the section on the more obvious kind of cooperation—working together to achieve an objective—Napoleon Hill seems to be stretching as he goes on about the self-evident advantages of professional associations such as doctors and lawyers, labor unions, merchant associations, and service clubs.

He also comments on the make-up of lawyers in law firms, the balance of salesmen vs. finance people in businesses, and he even elaborates on the advantages of cooperative merchandising in department stores and chain stores.

Aside from the many examples, the main theme of this part of the chapter is captured in the following collection of brief excerpts taken from throughout the section.

This course touches some phase of cooperation in practically every lesson. This was inevitable, because one object of the course is to help the student develop power, and power is developed only through organized effort.

It is a well-known fact that all who have amassed large fortunes have been known as able "organizers." This means that they possessed the ability to enlist the cooperative efforts of others who supplied talent and ability which they themselves did not possess.

Analyze power, no matter where or in what form it may be found, and you will find organization and cooperation as the chief factors behind it.

All success is based upon power, and power grows out of knowledge that has been organized and expressed in terms of action. The world pays for but one kind of knowledge—the kind that is expressed in constructive service.

A person who can induce others to cooperate and do effective teamwork, or inspire others so that they become more active, is no less a person of action than the one who renders effective service in a more direct manner.

Andrew Carnegie so ably directed the efforts of those who constituted his personal staff that he made many wealthy men of those who would never have become wealthy without the directing genius of his mind.

The following is excerpted from *Law of Success*, Lesson One: The Master Mind.

There is a story about a man who had seven sons who were always quarreling among themselves. One day he called them all together and informed them that he wished to demonstrate just what their lack of cooperative effort meant.

He had prepared a bundle of seven sticks which he had carefully tied together. One by one he asked his sons to take the bundle and break it. Each son tried, but in vain. Then he cut the strings and handed one of the sticks to each of his sons and asked each to break it over his knee.

After those sticks had all been broken with ease, he said: "When you boys work together in a spirit of harmony you resemble the bundle of sticks, and no one can defeat you; but when you quarrel among yourselves, anyone can defeat you one at a time."

There is a worthwhile lesson in this story of the man and his seven quarrelsome sons, and it may be applied to the people of a community, the employees and employers in a given place of business, or to the state and nation in which we live.

Organized effort may be made a power, but it may also be a dangerous power unless guided with intelligence. This course is devoted to describing how to direct the power of organized effort so that it will lead to success—the sort of success that is founded on truth and justice and fairness which leads to ultimate happiness.

The following returns to the material excerpted and adapted from *Law of Success,* Lesson Thirteen: Cooperation. In this section Napoleon Hill again comments on Infinite Intelligence and the body-mind connection, then extends the concept to encompass cooperation in general, and differentiates between the need for ordinary cooperation and the desirability of the special kind of cooperation that he has designated as the Master Mind Alliance.

COOPERATION OF MIND AND BODY

In Definite Chief Aim, the second lesson of this course, you learned that your chief aim in life should be supported by a burning desire for its realization. You can have no burning desire for achievement when you are in a negative state of mind, no matter what the cause may be.

"As a man thinketh in his heart, so is he."

You cannot think fear and act courageously. You cannot think hatred and act in a kindly manner toward others. And the dominating thoughts of your mind—meaning the strongest, deepest, and most frequent of your thoughts—influence the physical action of your body.

Every thought put into action by your brain reaches and influences every cell in your body. In the first lesson of this course you learned how thought travels from one mind to another, through the principle of telepathy. In this lesson you should go a step further and learn that your thoughts not only register themselves in the minds of other people through the principle of telepathy, but what is a million times more important for you to understand is that they register themselves on the cells of your own body and affect those cells in a manner that harmonizes with the nature of the thoughts.

Action, in the sense that the term is used in this lesson, is of two forms. One is physical and the other is mental. You can be very active with your mind while your body is entirely inactive, or you can be very active with both body and mind.

YOUR STATE OF MIND IS YOUR STATE OF BODY

In the lesson on Imagination you learned how to recombine old ideas into new plans. But no matter how practical your plans may be, they will be useless if they are not expressed in action. To dream dreams and see visions of the person you would like to be or the station in life you would like to obtain are admirable, provided you transform your dreams and visions into reality through intensive action.

There is a psychological as well as an economic reason why you should form the habit of intensive action. Your body is made up of billions of tiny cells that are highly sensitive to the influence of your mind. If your mind is lethargic and inactive, the cells of your body become lazy and inactive also. If you doubt this, the next time you feel lazy think about an activity of which you are fond and notice how quickly the cells of your body will respond to your enthusiasm and your lazy feeling will disappear.

The cells of the body respond to the state of mind. The same principle applies to the relationship between the mind and the body. An active, dynamic mind keeps the cells of the body in a constant state of activity.

You cannot be a person of action if you overeat and underexercise. Neither can you be a person of action if you run to the pill bottle every time you have, or imagine you have, an ache or a pain.

There is another enemy that you must conquer before you can become a person of action, and that is the habit of worry.

Worry, envy, jealousy, hatred, doubt, and fear are all states of mind that are fatal to action. These negative states of mind destroy the most essential factor in the achievement of success: the desire to achieve.

COOPERATION IS POWER; A MASTER MIND IS SUPERPOWER

Any form of group effort, where two or more people form a cooperative alliance for the purpose of accomplishing a Definite Chief Aim, becomes more powerful than mere individual effort.

But all alliances may be made more powerful and effective if based upon a foundation of perfect harmony, thus permitting the development of the supplemental power of the Master Mind.

All cooperative effort produces power, there can be no doubt about this, but cooperative effort that is based upon complete harmony of purpose develops superpower.

Let every member of any cooperative group set their hearts on the achievement of the same definite end, in a spirit of perfect harmony, and the way has been paved for the development of a Master Mind—providing all members of the group willingly subordinate their own personal interests for the attainment of the objective for which the group is aiming.

A great leader, whether in business, finance, industry, or statesmanship, is one who understands how to create a motivating objective that will be accepted with enthusiasm by every member of their group of followers.

The degree of power created by the cooperative effort of any group of people is measured, always, by the nature of the motive that the group is laboring to attain. This may be profitably kept in mind by all who organize group efforts for any purpose whatsoever. Find a motive around which people may be induced to rally in a highly emotionalized, enthusiastic spirit of perfect harmony, and you have found the starting point for the creation of a Master Mind.

Most people will work harder for the attainment of an ideal than they will for mere money. In searching for a "motive" as the basis for developing cooperative group effort, it will be profitable to bear this in mind.

Give someone a sufficiently vitalized motive and even the person of average ability, under ordinary circumstances, will suddenly develop superpower.

There are three major motivating forces to which man responds in practically all of his efforts:

- The motive of self-preservation

- The motive of sexual contact

- The motive of financial and social power

You will recall that in chapter 3, Self-Confidence and Faith in Your Abilities, Hill makes the point that in order to find the most effective way to emotionalize your desire, you must look inward and identify what gets you going, what stirs your emotions, what motivates you to want what you want. The nine motives listed as personal motivators in that chapter are in fact the logical extension of the list of three major motivating forces presented here as the keys to motivating others.

The extent to which people may be induced to cooperate, in harmony, depends on the motivating force that impels them to action. The perfect harmony that is essential for creating a Master Mind develops only when the motivating force of a group is sufficient to cause each member of the group to completely forget his or her own personal interests and work for the good of the group, or for the sake of attaining some idealistic, charitable, or philanthropic objective.

MR. HILL SEEKS COOPERATION

There was nothing Napoleon Hill liked better than telling a true story that illustrated how his Principles of Success worked. So naturally he had worked up a great personal story that he almost always told when he was lecturing on the importance of cooperation.

For your enjoyment, and because it illustrates the point so well, we are including the following version of Napoleon Hill's Lumberport story, excerpted and adapted from *Law of Success,* Lesson Five: Initiative and Leadership.

THE LUMBERPORT STORY

Some eighteen years ago I made my first trip to the little town of Lumberport, West Virginia. At that time the only means of transportation leading from Clarksburg, the largest nearby center, to Lumberport was either the Baltimore & Ohio Railroad, or an interurban electric line which ran within three miles of the town. If you chose the trolley it meant you had to arrange for someone to pick you up or you'd have to walk the three miles to town.

Upon my arrival at Clarksburg I found that the only train going to Lumberport before noon had already gone, and not wishing to wait for the later afternoon train, I made the trip by trolley, with the intention of walking the three miles. On the way down, the rain began to pour, and those three miles had to be navigated on foot, through deep yellow mud. When I arrived at Lumberport, my shoes and pants were muddy, and my disposition was none the better for the experience.

The first person I met was V. L. Hornor, who was then cashier of the Lumberport Bank. In a rather loud tone of voice I asked of him, "Why do you not get that trolley line extended from the junction over to Lumberport so your friends can get in and out of town without drowning in mud?"

"Did you see a river with high banks, at the edge of town, as you came in?" he asked. I replied that I had.

"Well," he continued, "that's the reason we have no streetcars running into town. The cost of a bridge would be about $100,000 and that is more than the company owning the trolley line is willing to invest. We have been trying for ten years to get them to build a line into town."

"Trying!" I exploded. "How hard have you tried?"

"We have offered them every inducement we could afford, such as free right of way from the junction into the town, and free use of the streets, but that bridge is the stumbling block. They simply will not pay the expense. Claim they cannot afford such an expense for the small amount of revenue they would receive from the three-mile extension."

Right then the Principles of Success began to come to my rescue. I asked Mr. Hornor if he would take a walk over to the river with me, that we might look at the spot that was causing so much inconvenience. He said he would be glad to do so.

When we got to the river I began to take inventory of everything in sight. I observed that the Baltimore & Ohio Railroad tracks ran up and down the river banks, on both sides of the river, and that the county road crossed the river on a rickety wooden bridge, both approaches to which had to cross over several railroad tracks because the railroad company had its switching yards at that point.

While we were standing there, a freight train blocked the road to the bridge, and several teams of horses stopped on both sides of the train, waiting for an opportunity to get through. The train kept the road blocked for about twenty-five minutes.

With this combination of circumstances in mind, it required little imagination to see that three different parties could be interested in the building of the bridge such as would be needed to carry the weight of a streetcar.

It was obvious that the Baltimore & Ohio Railroad Company would be interested in such a bridge, because that would remove the county road from their switching tracks. It would also save them a possible accident on the crossing, to say nothing of much loss of time and expense in cutting trains to allow the wagon teams to pass.

It was also obvious that the County Commissioners would be interested in the bridge, because it would raise the county road to a better level and make it more serviceable to the public. And of course the street railway company was interested in the bridge, but it did not wish to pay the entire cost.

All of this passed through my mind as I stood there watching the freight train being cut for the traffic to pass through.

A Definite Chief Aim took place in my mind. Also a definite plan for its attainment. The next day I got together a committee of townspeople, consisting of the mayor, councilmen, and some of the leading citizens, and called on the Division Superintendent of the Baltimore & Ohio Railroad Company at Grafton. We convinced him that it was worth one-third of the cost of the bridge to get the county road off his company's tracks.

Next we went to see the County Commissioners and found them to be quite enthusiastic over the possibility of getting a new bridge by paying for only one-third of it. They promised to pay their one-third, providing we could make arrangements for the other two-thirds.

We then went to see the president of the Traction Company that owned the trolley line at Fairmont, and made him an offer to donate all the rights of way and pay for two-thirds of the cost of the bridge, providing he would begin building the line into town promptly. We found him receptive also.

Three weeks later, a contract had been signed between the Baltimore & Ohio Railroad Company, the Monongahela Valley Traction Company, and the County Commissioners of Harrison County, providing for the construction of the bridge—one-third of its cost to be paid by each.

Just two months later, the right of way was being graded and the bridge was under way. And three months after that, the streetcars were running into Lumberport on a regular schedule.

This incident meant much to the town of Lumberport, because it provided transportation that enabled people to get in and out of the town without undue effort.

It also meant a great deal to me, because it served to introduce me as one who "got things done."

Two very definite advantages resulted from this transaction. The chief counsel for the Traction Company gave me a position as his assistant, and later on it was the means of an introduction that led to my appointment as advertising manager of the LaSalle Extension University.

Lumberport, West Virginia, was then and still is a small town, and Chicago was a large city located a considerable distance away, but news of initiative and leadership has a way of taking on wings and traveling.

Although initiative and leadership were the key elements of my success, there were five of the Principles of Success that combined in the transaction I have described here: a Definite Chief Aim, self-confidence, imagination, initiative, and leadership.

It would be helpful here to take note of the part that imagination played in this transaction. For ten years, the townspeople of Lumberport had been trying to get a streetcar line built into town. It must not be concluded that the town was without any citizens of ability, because that would be inaccurate. In fact there were many able people in the town. But they had been making the mistake of trying to solve their problem through one single source, whereas there were actually three sources of solution available to them.

One hundred thousand dollars was too much for one company to assume for the construction of a bridge, but when that cost was divided among three interested parties, the amount to be borne by each was more reasonable.

The question might be asked, why did some of the local townspeople not think of this three-way solution?

In the first place, they were so close to their problem that they failed to see it from a perspective which would have suggested the solution. This is a common mistake, and one that is always avoided by great leaders.

In the second place, these people had never before coordinated their efforts or worked as an organized group with the sole purpose in mind of finding a way to get a streetcar line built into town. This is another common error made by people in all walks of life—that of failure to work in unison, in a thorough spirit of cooperation.

Being an outsider, I had less difficulty in getting cooperative action than one of their own group might have had. Too often there is a spirit of selfishness in small communities that prompts each individual to think that their ideas should prevail. It is an important part of the leader's responsibility to induce people to subordinate their own ideas and interests for the good of the project or goal.

Success is nearly always a question of your ability to get others to subordinate their own individual interests and follow a leader. The person who has the initiative, the personality, and the imagination to induce followers to accept his or her plans and carry them out faithfully is always an able leader.

Leadership, initiative, and imagination are so closely allied and so essential for success that one cannot be gainfully applied without the other. Initiative is the moving force that pushes the leader ahead, but imagination is the guiding spirit that tells him or her which way to go.

Imagination is what enabled me to analyze the Lumberport bridge problem, break it up into its three component parts, and assemble those parts into a practical working plan.

Nearly every problem may be broken up into parts that are more easily managed as parts than they are when assembled as a whole. Perhaps one of the most important advantages of imagination is that it enables you to separate all problems into their component parts and to reassemble them in more favorable combinations.

It has been said that all battles are won or lost not on the firing line but through the sound strategy, or the lack of it, used by the generals who plan the battles.

Organized effort is effort that is directed according to a plan conceived with the aid of imagination, guided by a Definite Chief Aim, and given momentum with self-confidence and initiative. These Principles of Success blend into one and become a power in the hands of a leader. Without the blending of these principles, and the initiative to pull them together and make use of them, effective leadership is impossible.

Any modern railroad bridge can be an excellent example of the value of organized effort, because it demonstrates quite simply and clearly how thousands of tons of weight may be borne by a comparatively small group of steel bars and beams which are arranged so that the weight is spread over the entire group.

Chapter Twelve

INITIATIVE, LEADERSHIP, AND SELF-RELIANCE

WHAT WOULD NAPOLEON HILL DO?

Initiative is doing the right thing without being told. Leadership is taking responsibility for doing the right thing without being told.

Napoleon Hill would recognize what needed to be done, then step forward, take charge, and assume full responsibility for the success or failure not only of *his* actions but also those of his subordinates. He would set standards for himself, and he would coach, counsel, challenge, and inspire others to share with him in achieving success.

This chapter is the fifth in a group of five related chapters focused on what might be considered the Attitude and Personality Principles. The first seven chapters in this book all share a common theme, being Methods for Working With Your Inner Mind. Then there is a slight shift in emphasis.

Beginning with chapter 8, A Pleasing Personality, the new thematic link of Attitude and Personality becomes evident, continuing through the chapters on Enthusiasm and Persistence, Self-Control, Cooperation, and finally culminating in this chapter, Initiative and Leadership.

As with the other four principles named, much of the groundwork for the principle of Initiative and Leadership has already been laid in previous chapters, allowing the editors to focus on one or two key aspects of the main subject. In the following chapter, all of the attributes and problems of leadership are reviewed, but the subject that receives the most in-depth analysis is the crucial area of decision-making.

We begin with an overview of initiative, excerpted and adapted from *Law of Success*, Lesson Five: Initiative and Leadership.

INITIATIVE AND LEADERSHIP

There is perfect coordination of thought running throughout this course. The entire seventeen lessons blend with each other so that they form a perfect chain that has been built, link by link, out of the ideas behind the development of power through organized effort.

You will find also that the same principles of psychology form the foundation of each of these lessons, although different application is made of these principles in each of the lessons.

This lesson, on Initiative and Leadership, comes after the lesson on Self-Confidence for the reason that no one could become an efficient leader or take the initiative in any great undertaking without belief in themself.

THE POWER OF INITIATIVE

Initiative and leadership are associated terms in this lesson because leadership is essential for the attainment of success, and initiative is the very foundation upon which this necessary quality of leadership is built. Initiative is as essential to success as a hub is essential to a wheel.

Initiative is that exceedingly rare quality that impels a person to do what ought to be done without being told to do it.

Elbert Hubbard expressed himself on the subject of initiative in the following words:

Elbert Hubbard was the author of the book *Message to Garcia*, which became one of the most famous books at the beginning of the twentieth century. It was a celebration of the qualities of initiative and self-reliance, told through the true story of a soldier who was given the almost impossible mission of delivering an important letter behind enemy lines, a challenge which he undertakes without question or complaint, and accomplishes in spite of the overwhelming danger.

The world bestows its big prizes, both in money and honors, for one thing, and that is Initiative.

What is Initiative? I'll tell you: It is doing the right thing without being told.

But next to doing the right thing without being told is to do it when you are told once. That is to say, "Carry the message to Garcia." Those who can carry a message get high honors, but their pay is not always in proportion.

Next, there are those who do the right thing only when necessity kicks them from behind, and these get indifference instead of honors, and a pittance for pay.

This kind spends most of the time polishing a bench with a hard luck story.

Then, still lower down in the scale than this, we have the person who will not do the right thing even when someone goes along to demonstrate and stays to see that the work is done right. This person is always out of a job, and receives deserved contempt, unless there is a rich relative in the background, in which case destiny patiently waits around the corner with a club.

To which class do you belong?

Inasmuch as you will be expected to take inventory of yourself and determine which of the factors of this course you need most, it may be well if you begin to get ready for this analysis by answering the question that Elbert Hubbard has asked: To which class do you belong?

One of the peculiarities of leadership is the fact that it is never found in those who have not acquired the habit of taking the initiative. Leadership is something that you must invite yourself into; it will never thrust itself upon you.

If you will carefully analyze all leaders whom you know, you will see that they not only exercised initiative, but they also went about their work with a Definite Chief Aim in mind. You will also see that they possessed self-confidence.

There are generally many plans through which a desired object may be achieved, and it often happens to be true that the obvious and usual methods employed are not the best.

A great philosopher once said: "Initiative is the passkey that opens the door to opportunity."

I do not recall who this philosopher was, but I know that he was great because of the soundness of his statement. [Needless to say, this philosopher was Napoleon Hill himself.]

The following is excerpted and adapted from *Think and Grow Rich*, Chapter 7: Organized Planning.

LEADERS BEGIN AS FOLLOWERS

Broadly speaking, there are two types of people in the world. One type is known as leaders, and the other as followers. Decide at the outset whether you intend to become a leader in your chosen calling, or remain a follower. The difference in compensation is vast. The follower cannot reasonably expect the compensation to which a leader is entitled, although many followers make the mistake of expecting such pay.

It is no disgrace to be a follower. On the other hand, it is no credit to remain a follower. Most great leaders began in the capacity of followers. They became great leaders because they were intelligent followers. With few exceptions, the person who cannot follow a leader intelligently cannot become an efficient leader. The person who can follow a leader most efficiently is usually the one who develops into leadership most rapidly. An intelligent follower has many advantages, among them the opportunity to acquire knowledge from that leader.

The following is excerpted and adapted from *Law of Success*, Lesson 5: Initiative and Leadership.

LEADERSHIP AND TEAMWORK

Before we go any further, let it be understood what is meant by the term *leadership* as it is used in connection with this course on the *Law of Success*. There are two brands of leadership, and one of them is as deadly and destructive as the other is helpful and constructive. The deadly brand, which leads not to success, but to absolute failure, is the brand adopted by pseudoleaders who force their leadership on unwilling followers.

The brand of leadership that is recommended throughout this course is the brand that leads to self-determination and freedom and self-development and enlightenment and justice. This is the brand that endures.

LEADERS MAKE BOLD DECISIONS QUICKLY

In Lesson Two of *Law of Success* you learned the value of a Definite Chief Aim. Here, I want to emphasize that your definite aim will never be anything else but a mere wish unless you become a person of initiative, and aggressively and persistently pursue that aim until it has been fulfilled. Your aim must be active and not passive.

You can get nowhere without persistence, a fact that cannot be too often repeated.

The difference between persistence and lack of it is the same as the difference between wishing for a thing and positively determining to get it.

To become a person of initiative, you must form the habit of aggressively and persistently following the object of your Definite Chief Aim until you acquire it, whether this requires one year or twenty years. You might as well have no Definite Chief Aim as to have such an aim without continuous effort to achieve it.

You are not making the most of this course if you do not take some step each day that brings you nearer realization of your Definite Chief Aim. Do not fool yourself, or permit yourself to be misled to believe that the object of your Definite Chief Aim will materialize if you only wait. The materialization will come through your own determination, backed by your own carefully laid plans and your own initiative in putting those plans into action, or it will not come at all.

One of the major requisites for leadership is the power of quick and firm decision!

Analysis of more than 16,000 people disclosed the fact that leaders always make ready decisions, even in matters of small importance, while followers never make quick decisions.

This is worth remembering!

The follower, in whatever walk of life you find him or her, is a person who seldom knows what he or she wants. The follower vacillates, procrastinates, and actually refuses to reach a decision, even in matters of the smallest importance, unless a leader induces him to do so.

To know that the majority of people cannot and will not reach decisions quickly, if at all, is of great help to the leader who knows what he or she wants and has a plan for getting it.

The chief reason why the follower does not reach decisions is that the follower lacks the self-confidence to do so.

The following is excerpted and adapted from *Think and Grow Rich*, Chapter 8: Decision.

LEADERS, FOLLOWERS, FAILURES

Following is a self-test designed to help you learn what kind of leader you are. After reading each of the descriptions of the attributes of a successful leader, give yourself a mental grade as to how well you have mastered each of the qualities.

If you give serious consideration to each of the questions and answer truthfully, you should find that you have learned a good deal about yourself, and you will have a very good idea of how good a leader you are.

THE 11 MAJOR ATTRIBUTES OF LEADERSHIP

1. **Unwavering courage,** based upon knowledge of yourself and your occupation. No follower wishes to be dominated by a leader who lacks self-confidence and courage. Certainly no intelligent follower will be dominated by such a leader for very long.

2. **Self-control.** The person who cannot control himself or herself can never control others. Self-control sets a strong example for your followers, which the more intelligent followers will emulate.

3. **A keen sense of justice.** Without a sense of fairness and justice, no leader can command and retain the respect of their followers.

4. **Definiteness of decision.** Those who waver in decisions show that they are not sure of themselves, and therefore cannot lead others successfully.

5. **Definiteness of plans.** Successful leaders must plan their work, and work their plans. Leaders who move by guesswork, without practical, definite plans, are like a ship without a rudder. Sooner or later they will land on the rocks.

6. **The habit of doing more than paid for.** One of the penalties of leadership is the necessity of the leaders to willingly do more than they require of their followers.

7. **A pleasing personality.** Leadership calls for respect. Followers will not respect a leader who does not grade high on all of the factors of a pleasing personality.

8. **Sympathy and understanding.** Successful leaders must be in sympathy with their followers. Moreover, they must understand them and their problems.

9. **Mastery of detail.** Successful leadership calls for mastery of the details of the leader's position.

10. **Willingness to assume full responsibility.** Successful leaders must be willing to assume responsibility for the mistakes and the shortcomings of their followers. If a leader tries to shift this responsibility, that leader will not remain the leader. If one of your followers makes a mistake, or is incompetent, you must consider that it is you who failed.

11. **Cooperation.** The successful leader must understand and apply the principle of cooperative effort and be able to induce followers to do the same. Leadership calls for power, and power calls for cooperation.

THE 10 MAJOR CAUSES OF FAILURE IN LEADERSHIP

Following are the ten most common faults of leaders who fail. It is just as important for you to know what not to do as it is to know what you should do.

After reading the explanation of each fault, measure yourself against the kind of person you think you should be.

1. **Inability to organize details.** Efficient leadership calls for the ability to organize and master details. No genuine leader is ever "too busy" to do anything that may be required of them as a leader. Whether a leader or follower, when you admit that you are "too busy" to change your plans or to give your attention to any emergency, you are admitting your inefficiency. The successful leader must be the master of all details connected with the position. That means, of course, that you must acquire the habit of relegating details to capable lieutenants.

2. **Unwillingness to render humble service.** Truly great leaders are willing, when occasion demands, to perform any sort of labor that they would ask another to perform. "The greatest among ye shall be the servant of all" is a truth that all able leaders observe and respect.

3. **Emphasis of the "authority" of leadership.** The efficient leader leads by encouraging, and not by trying to instill fear in the hearts of those who follow. If you are a real leader, you will have no need to advertise that fact. It will be apparent in your conduct—by your sympathy, understanding, fairness, and a demonstration that you know your job.

4. **Fear of competition from followers.** Leaders who fear that one of their followers may take their position are practically sure to realize that fear sooner or later. Able leaders train understudies. Only in this way can leaders multiply themselves and be at many places,

and give attention to many things, at one time. It is a fact that leaders receive more pay for their ability to get others to perform than they could possibly earn by their own efforts. A good leader may, through knowledge of the job and a magnetic personality, get followers to render more and better service than they could render without the leader's guidance.

5. **Lack of imagination.** Without imagination, the leader is incapable of meeting emergencies or of creating plans by which to guide followers efficiently.

6. **Selfishness.** Leaders who claim all the honor for the work of their followers are sure to be met by resentment. The really great leader claims none of the honors. Great leaders are content to see the honors go to their followers, because the great leaders know that most people will work harder for commendation and recognition than they will for money alone.

7. **Intemperance.** Followers do not respect an intemperate leader. You may be "one of the guys," but you won't be looked up to or admired.

8. **Disloyalty.** Leaders who are not loyal to their duty, or to those both above and below them, cannot maintain their leadership for long. Disloyalty will bring contempt. Lack of loyalty is one of the major causes of failure in every walk of life.

9. **Expectation of pay for what you "know."** The world does not pay you for what you know; it pays you for what you do with what you know, or what you can get others to do.

10. **Emphasis of title.** Competent leaders require no "title" to give them the respect of their followers. The doors to the office of a real leader are open to all and are free from formality.

The following commentary is excerpted and adapted from *Think and Grow Rich: The Workbook,* Chapter 9: Decision.

MAKE BOLD DECISIONS FIRMLY AND QUICKLY

The habit of prompt and firm decision is the first essential step in the development of initiative and leadership. The leader who hesitates between vague notions of what he or she wants to do or should do generally ends by doing nothing.

If you are a leader who changes your mind often, you will lose the confidence of those you are leading. One of the natural tendencies of human nature is willingness to follow the person with great self-confidence. If you are not sure of yourself, how can you expect others to be sure of you? No one will want to follow you if you are not sure of yourself.

Napoleon Hill's advice that you should make decisions firmly and quickly is repeated often in his writing, but he also makes it very clear that he is not advising that you jump to conclusions or act impulsively. Hill's advice is to collect all the facts, study what you have learned, then be decisive and take action. Good leaders don't procrastinate.

There are circumstances, of course, that call for slow deliberation and the examination of facts before an intelligent decision can be reached. However, after all the available facts have been gathered and organized, there is no excuse for delaying decision. The person who procrastinates cannot become an effective leader.

DECISION-MAKING QUALITIES OF A LEADER

In applying initiative and leadership, there are certain steps that are essential:

1. Know definitely what you want.

2. Build a practical plan for the achievement of what you want, making use of the counsel and advice of your Master Mind group.

Surround yourself with an organization made up of people who have the knowledge and experience essential for carrying out your definite aim.

3. Have sufficient faith in yourself and in your plans to envision your goal as a reality even before you begin to carry out your plans.

4. Do not become discouraged, no matter what obstacles you may meet. If one plan fails to work, substitute other plans until you have found the one that will work.

5. Do no guessing. Get the facts as the basis for all of your plans.

6. Do not be influenced by others to abandon your plans or aim.

7. Have no set hours of work. The leader must devote whatever hours are necessary for success.

8. Concentrate on one thing at a time. You cannot dissipate thought and energy and still be efficient.

9. Whenever possible, delegate to others the responsibility of details, but have a system for checking to see that these details are being dealt with.

10. Hold yourself accountable at all times for carrying out all of your plans, bearing in mind that if subordinates fail, it is you yourself who has failed.

HOW YOU MAKE DECISIONS

Whether you are making a major decision with ramifications that could affect your entire life, or a snap-decision between chocolate and vanilla, the important factors in determining how long you take to make the decision are how much data you think is necessary, and how much you are prepared to rely on instinct.

When faced with the need to make a decision, almost everyone reacts the same way: first, review everything you know, and second, get as much additional information as you can, keeping in mind that it is impossible to ever have all of the facts.

As you are mentally running through the facts and information, you also take into account your own personal feelings and biases. There are many decisions that do not involve absolutes, so hunches and gut-feelings can often be the deciding factor.

After juggling all of the possibilities, and going back and forth between facts and feelings, something will shift in the way you "feel" about the decision. That's when it feels right and you take action.

IN MAKING DECISIONS, LESS CAN BE MORE

Most decision-making is not like scientific experimentation in which theory after theory is tested until some consensus is reached. It would be impractical to apply such rigorous demands on most things. In fact there is research indicating that most decisions are actually made early in the process, and that the rest of the time is taken up searching for reasons to support your original gut-feeling.

In real life there is no guarantee that a decision based on more facts and information will be more correct than one based on fewer facts. Although it seems logical that the more facts you have, the better your decision will be, it is entirely possible that while you may have more facts, your interpretation of those many facts may still be incorrect. Or it could take too much time to process because having all the facts presents you with far more information, possibilities, and choices than can be reasonably dealt with, or because you've got so much to choose from that you just select the points that support your preconceived desire. Or you could just get worn down by too much to deal with.

All of these possibilities add up to delayed decisions or bad decisions because you tried to assimilate too much input.

GOOD DECISIONS AND BAD DECISIONS

Before we go any further we should point out that the chances are you are probably using the term *bad decision* incorrectly. It is likely that what you are really referring to is the bad *result* of the decision, not the decision itself. As you will see below, bad decisions are ones that are rushed and poorly conceived. Therefore, by definition, bad decisions have no place in the Napoleon Hill method.

- A good decision is one that has a clear objective, is based on appropriate research, is well thought-out, and is rational.

- A bad decision is one that may have a clear objective but it involves little research, or inappropriate facts, and it is arrived at on a whim or out of impatience.

This should make it clear why we say that bad decisions are not even worth considering in the Napoleon Hill method. If you practice the Hill method you would never make a rushed or ill-conceived decision. However, that does not mean that you may not get a bad result.

The problem is that good decisions don't always produce good results, and bad decisions don't always yield bad results. You may make a good decision that is well considered, rational, and takes into account all the available information and preferences, and you can still end up with an outcome you don't want.

On the other hand, a bad decision that isn't well thought-out, or is made on a whim, could be the one that hits the jackpot.

The lesson that you should take away from this is that you can't beat yourself up about a good decision that ends up with a bad result any more than you can take credit for a bad decision that turns out to be a winner.

BAD RESULTS DO NOT MEAN FAILURE

This is the same point that Hill made in earlier chapters when he was discussing how you should view failure. A good decision that produces a bad result is a temporary defeat, but a temporary defeat is not failure. Temporary defeats are what show you how to do it better next time. Similarly, bad results show you how to make better decisions next time.

Every problem presents you with a chance to make a decision. It's up to you whether you see a failed decision as a problem or an opportunity. You can treat it as just another annoyance that you don't want to deal with, or you can use it as an opportunity to find out what is wrong with your decision-making practices.

It is a mind-set, a state of mind, and Hill always says there is only one thing over which you have absolute control, and that is your mind.

If it is a state of mind, you can change it, because you can control what you think. If you choose, you can welcome failure as a way to learn what to do and what not to do. Failure is only temporary. Failure is a lesson you needed to learn in order to succeed. Success is built on decisions that failed. Great successes are created by those people who see the problems and turn them into opportunities.

HOW DO YOU KNOW WHEN TO CHANGE YOUR MIND?

In the chapter on your definite aim or purpose, Hill says that you should be prepared to change your aim or purpose if, after making a reasonable effort, you conclude that it is not right for you.

In the chapter on the Master Mind, Hill advises that you will almost surely make changes in your Master Mind group because you will find that some of your choices were wrong.

The question is, how will you ever know for sure when you should stick with something or when you should give up on a goal and move on to another?

The answer is, there are no magic answers. You are the person who must decide for you. It is up to you to decide what your aim or purpose will be, and for each goal you set it is up to you to make the decision at which point you should stop pursuing that goal and choose a new one.

As we have pointed out, even well-reasoned, good decisions can produce bad results. You must simply accept the fact that you may not know until after you have made a decision whether you were right or wrong. The smart move is to make contingency plans a part of your decision-making process so that you have a fall-back position in case something goes seriously wrong. That way you can stay the course with your decision, but if it becomes clear that it is producing a bad result, you are prepared to switch gears to another course of action without panicking.

In this final section adapted from *Law of Success,* Lesson Five: Initiative and Leadership, Napoleon Hill once again returns to the three primary threads that are woven into every chapter of this book: Cosmic Habit Force, Infinite Intelligence, and autosuggestion.

INSPIRE OTHERS AND INSPIRE YOURSELF

It is a well-known fact that a man learns best what he endeavors to teach others. If a person embraces a certain faith, the first thing he does is go out and try to "sell" it to others. And in exact proportion to the extent to which he impresses others does he impress himself.

In the field of salesmanship, no salesman is successful in selling others until he has first made a good job of selling himself. Stated conversely, no salesman can do his best to sell others without sooner or later selling himself that which he is trying to sell to others.

Any statement that a person repeats over and over again for the purpose of inducing others to believe it, he also will come to believe, and this holds good whether the statement is false or true.

You can now see the advantage of making it your business to talk initiative, think initiative, eat initiative, sleep initiative, and practice initiative. By so doing, you are becoming a person of initiative and leadership, for it is a well-known fact that people will readily, willingly, and voluntarily follow the person who shows by his actions that he is a person of initiative.

In the place where you work or the community in which you live you come in contact with other people. Make it your business to interest every one of them who will listen to you, in the development of initiative. It will not be necessary for you to give your reasons for doing this, nor will it be necessary for you to announce the fact that you are doing it. Just go ahead and do it. In your own mind you will understand, of course, that you are doing it because this practice will help you and will, at least, do those whom you influence in the same practice no harm.

If you wish to try an experiment that will prove both interesting and profitable to you, pick out some person of your acquaintance whom you know to be a person who never does anything that he is not expected to do, and begin selling him your idea of initiative. Do not stop by merely discussing the subject once; keep it up every time you have a convenient opportunity. Approach the subject from a different angle each time. If you go at this experiment in a tactful and forceful manner, you will soon observe a change in the person on whom you are trying the experiment. And you will observe something else of more importance still: you will observe a change in yourself! Do not fail to try this experiment. You cannot talk initiative to others without developing a desire to practice it yourself.

Through the operation of the principle of autosuggestion, every statement that you make to others leaves its imprint on your own subconscious mind, and this holds good whether your statements are false or true. You have often heard the saying: "He who lives by the sword will die by the sword." Properly interpreted, this simply means that we are constantly attracting to ourselves and weaving into our own characters and personalities those qualities that our influence is helping to create in others. If we help others develop the habit of initiative, we, in turn, develop this same habit. If we sow the seeds of hatred and envy and discouragement in others, we, in turn, develop these qualities in ourselves.

Chapter Thirteen
PROFITING BY FAILURE

WHAT WOULD NAPOLEON HILL DO?

Everyone has disappointments, everyone must face problems, and everyone suffers temporary defeats, but you never fail until you give up on yourself.

Napoleon Hill would take inventory of his assets, analyze his setbacks, and know that overcoming adversity would only make him stronger. He would face every disappointment first by being thankful that it wasn't worse, then he would throw himself back into the challenge, grateful for the opportunity to learn another valuable lesson.

Everybody loves the story of the comeback kid who loses it all, learns his lesson the hard way, pulls himself up by his bootstraps, and triumphs by turning lemons into lemonade. Trial and error is the most basic of learning methods, it is the essence of all self-help literature, and, as you will see, Napoleon Hill's own story is a classic example of the genre.

However, it was not Hill's story, but rather Andrew Carnegie's concern about the amount of time that is lost by learning through trial and error, that prompted Napoleon Hill to begin his investigation of the Principles of Success, which ultimately led him to write the bestsellers that this book is based on.

As was explained in earlier chapters, Hill first met Andrew Carnegie when he was hired to do an interview and write a story about the famed steel baron and philanthropist. During their meeting Carnegie became so impressed by Hill's perceptive mind that he invited him to spend the weekend at his estate so they could continue the discussion. Over the next few days, Carnegie carefully laid out his philosophy of success, telling Hill that he believed any person could achieve greatness if they understood this philosophy and the steps required to achieve it.

In the introduction to *Think and Grow Rich,* Napoleon Hill quotes Andrew Carnegie as saying: "It's a shame that each new generation must find the way to success by trial and error when the principles are really clear-cut."

Hill goes on to say, "It was Mr. Carnegie's idea that the magic formula, which gave him a stupendous fortune, ought to be placed within reach of people who do not have the time to investigate how others had made their money. It was his hope that I might test and demonstrate the soundness of the formula through the experience of men and women in every calling."

So, in the beginning, the reason behind Hill's research into the Principles of Success was to give readers an advantage by explaining to them the secrets of success so they didn't have to fail first in order to learn how to profit. However, by the time Hill actually wrote and published his findings, he had rethought the original intention. His research convinced him that in fact it was better to take a chance and fail, but the secret was that you must approach each failure as a possibility to learn something. If you do that, you will turn what you used to think were stumbling blocks into the steppingstones to success.

The following is excerpted and adapted from *Law of Success*, Lesson Fourteen: Profiting by Failure.

PROFITING BY FAILURE

Ordinarily *failure* is a negative term, but in this lesson the word will be given a new meaning, because it has been a very much misused word and for that reason has brought unnecessary grief and hardship to millions of people.

I will distinguish between failure and defeat, and you will see if what is so often looked upon as failure is not, in reality, just temporary defeat. Moreover, you will see if this temporary defeat is not usually a blessing in disguise. You will also learn that sound character is often the product of reversals and setbacks.

Neither temporary defeat nor adversity amounts to failure in the mind of the person who looks upon it as a teacher of some needed lesson. There is a great and lasting lesson in every reversal and in every defeat, and usually it is a lesson that could be learned in no other way.

Defeat often talks to us in a language that we do not understand. If this were not true, we would not make the same mistakes over and over again without profiting by the lessons that they might teach us. If it were not true, we would observe more closely the mistakes that other people make and we would profit by them also.

SEVEN TURNING POINTS

Perhaps I can best help you to interpret the meaning of defeat by taking you back over some of my own experiences covering a period of approximately thirty years. Seven different times within this period, I have come to the turning point that the uninformed call failure. At each of these seven turning points I thought I had been a dismal failure, but now I know that what looked to be a failure was an unseen hand that halted me in my chosen course and forced me to redirect my efforts along more advantageous pathways.

To briefly set the scene, Napoleon Hill was born into poverty in a log cabin in the mountains of southwest Virginia. He had been known as a gun-toting local hell-raiser until his stepmother's gift of a typewriter inspired him to change his ways. He graduated from the local one-room school, then attended a business college for a year to learn the skills that would qualify him as a secretary, which, at the time, was the way that young men got entry-level jobs for a career in business.

First Turning Point

After finishing a course at a business college, I took a job as a steno-grapher and bookkeeper, a position that I held for the next five years. As a result of having practiced the habit of performing more work and better work than that for which I was paid, I advanced rapidly until I was assuming responsibilities and receiving a salary far out of proportion to my age. I saved my money, and my bank account amounted to several thousand dollars. My reputation spread rapidly and found competitive bidders for my services. To meet these offers from competitors, my employer advanced me to the position of general manager of the mines where I was employed. I was quickly getting on top of the world, and I knew it.

Ah, but that was the sad part—I knew it!

Then Fate reached out and gave me a gentle nudge. My employer lost his fortune and I lost my position. This was my first real defeat, and even though it came about as a result of causes beyond my control, I didn't learn a lesson from it until many years later.

Second Turning Point

My next position was that of sales manager for a large lumber manufacturer in the South. I knew nothing about lumber, and little about
sales management, but I had learned that it was beneficial to render
more service than that for which I was paid. I had also learned that it
paid to take the initiative and find out what needed to be done without
someone telling me to do it. A good-size bank account, as well as a
record of steady advancement in my previous position, gave me all the
self-confidence I needed, with perhaps some to spare.

My advancement was rapid, with my salary having been increased
twice during the first year. I did so well in the management of sales that
my employer took me into partnership with him. We began to make
money and I began to see myself on top of the world again.

To stand "on top of the world" is a wonderful feeling, but it is
a very dangerous place to stand unless one stands very firmly, because
the fall is so long and hard if one should stumble.

But I was succeeding by leaps and bounds!

Up to that time it had never occurred to me that success could
be measured in terms other than money and authority. Perhaps this
was due to the fact that I had more money than I needed and more
authority than I could manage safely at that age.

Of course, I did not see the impending crash until it came. Mine
was a sad story, but not unlike that which many others might tell if
they would be frank with themselves.

Like a stroke of lightning out of a clear sky, the 1907 panic swept
down, and overnight it rendered me an enduring service by destroying
our business and relieving me of every dollar that I had.

The "panic" that Hill refers to is the 1907 bank failure which wiped out
many banks, brokerages, and investors. It was because of this financial collapse that legislation was enacted in 1913 to create the Federal
Reserve System.

This was my first serious defeat. I mistook it, then, for failure. But it was not, and before I complete this lesson I will tell you why it was not.

Third Turning Point

It required the 1907 panic, and the defeat that it brought me, to divert and redirect my efforts from the lumber business to the study of law. Thus, the third turning point of my life began in what most people would call failure.

I attended law school at night and worked as an automobile salesman during the day. I saw the need for trained automobile mechanics, therefore I opened an educational department in the manufacturing plant and began to train ordinary machinists in automobile assembly and repair work. The school prospered, paying me over a thousand dollars a month in net profits. [One dollar at the beginning of the twentieth century would have been worth approximately twenty dollars at the beginning of the twenty-first century.]

My banker knew that I was prospering, therefore he loaned me money with which to expand. A peculiar trait of bankers is that they will loan us money without any hesitation when we are prosperous.

My banker loaned me money until I was hopelessly in his debt, then he took over my business as calmly as if it had belonged to him. Which it did.

From the station of a man of affairs who enjoyed an income of more than a thousand dollars a month, I was suddenly reduced to poverty.

Fourth Turning Point

Because my wife's family had influence, I secured the appointment as assistant to the chief counsel for one of the largest coal companies in the world. My salary was greatly out of proportion to what was usually paid to beginners, and still further out of proportion to what I was worth, but pull was pull and I was there just the same.

It happened that what I lacked in legal skill I more than made up by performing more service than that for which I was paid and by taking the initiative and doing what needed to be done without being told to do it.

I was holding my position without difficulty. I practically had a soft berth for life had I cared to keep it. Then without consultation with my friends, and without warning, I resigned.

This was the first turning point that was of my own selection. It was not forced upon me. I saw the old man Fate coming and beat him to the door. I quit that position because the work was too easy and I was performing it with too little effort.

This move proved to be the next most important turning point of my life, although it was followed by ten years of effort that brought almost every conceivable grief the human heart can experience.

I quit my job in the legal field, where I was getting along well, living among friends and relatives, and where I had what they believed to be an unusually bright and promising future ahead of me.

As far as I am able to interpret it, I arrived at my decision to resign more because of a "hunch"—or a sort of "prompting," which I did not understand at the time—than by logical reasoning.

I selected Chicago as my new field of endeavor. I did this because I believed Chicago to be a place where one might find out if they had those sterner qualities that are so essential for survival in a world of keen competition. I made up my mind that if I could gain recognition in Chicago, in any honorable sort of work, it would prove that I had something that might be developed into real ability.

My first position in Chicago was that of advertising manager for a large correspondence school. I knew little about advertising, but my previous experience as a salesman, plus the advantage gained by rendering more service than that for which I was paid, enabled me to do particularly well.

This brings me to my fifth turning point, which was also of my own choice.

Fifth Turning Point

I had done so well as advertising manager of the correspondence school that the president of the school induced me to resign my position and go into the candy manufacturing business with him. We organized the Betsy Ross Candy Company and I became its first president.

The business grew rapidly, and soon we had a chain of stores in eighteen different cities. Again I saw my rainbow's end almost within reach, and again I believed I had at last found the business in which I wished to remain for life.

The candy business was profitable, and because I looked upon money as being the only evidence of success, I naturally believed I was about to corner that success.

Everything went smoothly until my business associate and a third man, whom we had taken into the business, took a notion to gain control of my interest in the business without paying for it. They had me arrested on a false charge and then offered to withdraw the charge on condition that I turn over to them my interest in the business.

When the time for a preliminary hearing came, the complaining witnesses were nowhere to be found. But I had them brought and forced them to go on the witness stand to tell their stories. This resulted in my vindication, and in a damage suit against the perpetrators of the injustice.

In due time I got a heavy judgment against my former business associates, and I could then have had both of them placed behind bars.

For the first time in my life I was brought face to face with the opportunity to strike back at my enemies in a manner that would hurt. Would I have my enemies jailed, or would I take advantage of this opportunity to extend them mercy, thereby proving myself to be made of different material?

Being arrested seemed, at the time, a terrible disgrace, even though the charge was false. It was not a pleasant experience, and I would not wish to go through a similar experience again, but I must admit that it was worth all the grief it cost me, because it gave me the opportunity to find out that revenge was not a part of my make-up.

Sixth Turning Point

This turning point came shortly after my dreams of success in the candy business had been shattered, when I turned my efforts to teaching advertising and salesmanship as a department of one of the colleges in the Midwest.

Some wise philosopher has said that we never learn very much about a given subject until we begin teaching it to others. My first experience as a teacher proved this to be true.

My school prospered from the very beginning. I had a resident class and also a correspondence school through which I was teaching students in nearly every English-speaking country. Despite the ravages of war, the school was growing rapidly and I once again saw the end of the rainbow within sight.

Then came the second military draft and it practically destroyed my school, as it caught most of those who were enrolled as students.

At one stroke I charged off more than $75,000 in tuition fees and, at the same time, contributed my own service to my country. [Remember, one 1917 dollar was worth approximately twenty contemporary dollars.] Once more I was penniless! Again I was forced to redirect my efforts.

But before I proceed to describe the next and last important turning point, I should mention that no single event described up to this point is, in itself, of any practical significance. The six turning points that I have briefly described meant nothing to me taken singly, and they will mean nothing to you if analyzed singly.

But take these events collectively, and they form a very significant foundation for the next turning point.

It must have been obvious to you, all through my description of the six turning points already outlined, that I had not really found my place in the world. It must have been obvious too that most, if not all, of my temporary defeats were due mainly to the fact that I had not yet truly discovered the work into which I could throw my heart and soul.

Seventh Turning Point

To describe the seventh and last of the turning points of my life, I must go back to November 11, 1918—Armistice Day, the end of the world war.

The war had left me without a penny, as I have already said, but I was happy to know that the slaughter had ceased and reason was about to reclaim civilization.

As I stood in front of my office window and looked out at the howling mob that was celebrating the end of the war, my mind went back to my yesterdays, especially to a day when a kind old gentleman had laid his hand on my shoulder and told me that if I would acquire an education I could make my mark in the world. I had been acquiring that education without knowing it.

Over a period of more than twenty years, I had been going to school at the University of Hard Knocks, as you must have observed from my description of my various turning points. As I stood in front of that window my entire past, with its bitter and its sweet, its ups and its downs, passed before me in review.

The time had come for another turning point!

I sat down at my typewriter and, to my astonishment, my hands began to play a tune on the keyboard. I had never written so rapidly or so easily before. I did not plan or think about what I was writing—I just wrote whatever came into my mind.

Unconsciously, I was laying the foundation for the most important turning point of my life, for when I finished I had prepared a document through which I would finance a national magazine that would give me contact with people throughout the English-speaking world.

What Napoleon Hill had written was a declaration of his intention to create a new magazine to be called *Hill's Golden Rule.* He ended his manifesto with the confession that although he was absolutely committed to his vision, he had no idea where he was going to get the money to launch the magazine. As was mentioned in chapter 9, the first person he read the editorial to insisted that he would finance the project, and that was how Hill finally "failed" his way into the success that he had always desired—and which would be his passion for the rest of his life.

It was in this somewhat dramatic manner that a desire which had lain dormant in my mind for nearly twenty years became translated into reality. The material out of which my knowledge was gathered is nothing more nor less than the knowledge that was forced upon me through experiences that have undoubtedly been considered by some to be failures.

This course is but the sum total of what I gathered through these "failures." If the course proves to be of value to you, as I hope it will, you may give the credit to the "failures" described in this lesson.

From the experiences described in my seven turning points, I have gathered a few golden threads of knowledge that I could have gained in no other way than through defeat.

I am glad that I have experienced much defeat. It has had the effect of tempering me with the courage to undertake tasks that I would never have begun had I been surrounded by protecting influences. Defeat is a destructive force only when it is accepted as failure. When accepted as teaching some needed lesson, it is always a blessing.

BLESSINGS IN DISGUISE

I used to hate my enemies. But that was before I learned how well they were serving me by keeping me everlastingly on the alert lest some weak spot in my character provide an opening through which they might damage me.

In view of what I have learned of the value of enemies, if I had none I would feel it my duty to create a few. They would discover my defects and point them out to me, whereas my friends, if they saw my weaknesses at all, would say nothing about them.

Failure is nature's great crucible in which she burns the dross from the human heart and so purifies the mettle of the person that it can stand the test of hard usage.

I have found evidence to support this theory in the study of the records of scores of great men, from Socrates and Christ on down the centuries to the well-known men of achievement of our times. The success of each seemed to be in almost exact ratio to the extent of the obstacles and difficulties he had to surmount.

No one ever arose from the knockout blow of defeat without being stronger and wiser for the experience.

There are a number of chapters in *Think and Grow Rich* that offer material pertinent to the concept of profiting through failure. The following is excerpted and adapted from *Think and Grow Rich,* Chapter 9: Persistence.

PERSISTENCE

Persistence is an essential factor in the procedure of transmuting desire into its monetary equivalent. The basis of persistence is the power of will.

Will-power and desire, when properly combined, make an irresistible pair.

The majority of people are ready to throw their aims and purposes overboard and give up at the first sign of opposition or misfortune. A few carry on despite all opposition, until they attain their goal. There may be no heroic connotation to the word *persistence,* but the quality is to the character of man what carbon is to steel.

YOUR TEST OF PERSISTENCE

The starting point of all achievement is desire. Keep this constantly in mind. Weak desires bring weak results, just as a small amount of fire makes a small amount of heat. If you find yourself lacking in persistence, this weakness may be remedied by building a stronger fire under your desires.

If you want a measure of your persistence, observe what happens when you start to carry out the seven steps mentioned in chapter 2 about visualizing your Definite Chief Aim. The eagerness with which you follow these instructions will indicate clearly how much or how little you really desire to accumulate money. If you find that you are indifferent, you may be sure that you have not yet acquired the "money-consciousness" that you must possess, before you can be sure of accumulating a fortune.

The following is excerpted and adapted from *Think and Grow Rich,* Chapter 1: Thoughts Are Things.

THREE FEET FROM GOLD

One of the most common causes of failure is the habit of quitting when one is overtaken by temporary defeat. Every person is guilty of this mistake at one time or another.

An uncle of R. U. Darby was caught by "gold fever" in the gold-rush days, and went west to dig and grow rich. He had never heard that more gold has been mined from the thoughts of men than has ever been taken from the earth. He staked a claim and went to work with pick and shovel.

After weeks of labor, he was rewarded by the discovery of the shining ore. He needed machinery to bring the ore to the surface. Quietly, he covered up the mine, retraced his footsteps to his home in

Williamsburg, Maryland, and told his relatives and a few neighbors of the "strike." They got together money for the needed machinery, and had it shipped. The uncle and Darby went back to work the mine.

The first car of ore was mined and shipped to a smelter. The returns proved they had one of the richest mines in Colorado! A few more cars of that ore would clear the debts. Then would come the big killing in profits.

Down went the drills! Up went the hopes of Darby and Uncle! Then something happened. The vein of gold ore disappeared!

They had come to the end of the rainbow, and the pot of gold was no longer there. They drilled on, desperately trying to pick up the vein again—all to no avail.

Finally, they decided to quit.

They sold the machinery to a junkman for a few hundred dollars, and took the train back home. The junkman called in a mining engineer to look at the mine and do a little calculating. The engineer advised that the project had failed because the owners were not familiar with "fault lines."

His calculations showed that the vein would be found just three feet from where the Darbys had stopped drilling. That is exactly where it was found!

The junkman took millions of dollars in ore from the mine because he knew enough to seek expert counsel before giving up.

"I WILL NEVER STOP BECAUSE MEN SAY NO"

Long afterward, Mr. Darby recouped his loss many times over, when he went into the business of selling life insurance. Remembering that he lost a huge fortune because he stopped three feet from gold, Darby profited from the experience by saying to himself, "I stopped three feet from gold, but I will never stop because men say 'no' when I ask them to buy insurance."

Darby became one of a small group of men who sell over a million dollars in life insurance annually. He owed his "stickability" to the lesson he learned from his "quitability" in the gold mining business.

"That experience was a blessing in disguise. It taught me to keep on keeping on, no matter how hard the going may be, a lesson I needed to learn before I could succeed in anything."

Before success comes in any man's life, he is sure to meet with much temporary defeat, and, perhaps, some failure. When defeat overtakes a man, the easiest and most logical thing to do is to quit. That is exactly what the majority of men do.

More than five hundred of the most successful men this country has ever known told me their greatest success came just one step beyond the point at which defeat had overtaken them.

The following is another of Napoleon Hill's favorite examples of a man who profited through failure. The version presented here is a compilation assembled from material that appears in *Law of Success*, *Think and Grow Rich*, and *Selling You!*

MILO C. JONES

One of the best examples of finding the seed of an equivalent benefit in failure is the story of a man of whom you may have heard, and I have no doubt that you've eaten some of the food he produced and marketed throughout the nation as the result of an adversity which would have stopped most men cold.

The man was Milo C. Jones, who owned a farm near Fort Atkinson, Wisconsin. Although he was a hard worker and his physical health was good, he seemed unable to make his small farm yield more than the bare necessities of life. Then he suffered a stroke and was stricken down with double paralysis, which deprived him of the use of every portion of his body except his brain. He was put to bed by his relatives who believed him to be a helpless invalid.

For weeks he remained unable to move a single muscle. All he had left was his mind, the one great power he had drawn upon so rarely because he had earned his living by the use of his brawn. Out of this sheer necessity he discovered the power of his mind and began to draw upon it.

Jones called his family together and told them: "I can no longer work with my hands, so I have decided to work with my mind. The rest of you will have to take the place of my hands." In this hour of his greatest adversity, Milo C. Jones used his mind—took possession of it for the first time in his life, perhaps—and out of that mind came the idea that would yield him a huge fortune.

He told his assembled family that this year they were going to start planting corn in every acre of the farm they could spare, then start raising pigs with that corn; slaughter the pigs while they are young and tender, and convert them into sausage.

The family went to work, and in a few years the trade name of Jones Little Pig Sausages became a household byword throughout the nation. Jones was the first to raise hogs specifically for producing premium sausage; prior to this innovation, sausage had always been thought of as a byproduct. The Jones company was also the first in its field to rely heavily on mail-order sales and on an aggressive national advertising program to promote its products.

Milo C. Jones lived to see himself earn a multimillion-dollar fortune from the same farm which, previous to his misfortune, had yielded him only a scant living.

Isn't it strange that so often people have to be cut down by failure and defeat before they learn they have minds capable of mastering all of their problems? Isn't it strange that Jones did not discover the Little Pig Sausage idea while he had a sound body?

The following is excerpted and adapted from *Think and Grow Rich*, Chapter 9: Persistence.

HOW TO MASTER DIFFICULTIES

What power gives men of persistence the capacity to master difficulties? Does Infinite Intelligence throw itself on the side of the person who still fights on?

These questions have arisen in my mind as I have observed men like Henry Ford, who started at scratch, and built an industrial empire of huge proportions, with little else in the way of a beginning but persistence. Or Thomas A. Edison, who, with less than three months of schooling, became the world's leading inventor and converted persistence into the talking machine, the moving picture machine, and the incandescent light, to say nothing of half a hundred other useful inventions.

I had the happy privilege of analyzing both Mr. Edison and Mr. Ford, year by year, over a long period of years, so I speak from actual knowledge when I say that I found no quality, save persistence, in either of them that even remotely suggested the major source of their stupendous achievements.

As one makes an impartial study of the prophets, philosophers, miracle men, and religious leaders of the past, one is drawn to the inevitable conclusion that persistence, concentration of effort, and definiteness of purpose were the major sources of their achievements.

Whether it is Henry Ford, Thomas Edison, R. U. Darby, Milo Jones, inventor Charles F. Kettering who says, "Failures are just practice shots," or the many entrepreneurs and celebrities mentioned in the book *The Joy of Failure,* such as Jack Welch, Mary Kay, Donald Trump, and Oprah Winfrey, every one of them is a perfect example of Napoleon Hill's creed: "Every failure or misfortune holds the seed of an equal or greater success."

HOW TO DEVELOP PERSISTENCE

There are four simple steps that lead to the habit of persistence. They call for no great amount of intelligence, no particular amount of education, and little time or effort. The necessary steps are:

1. A definite purpose backed by a burning desire for its fulfillment.

2. A definite plan, expressed in continuous action.

3. A mind closed tightly against all negative and discouraging influences, including negative suggestions of relatives, friends, and acquaintances.

4. A friendly alliance with one or more persons who will encourage one to follow through with both plan and purpose.

These four steps are essential for success in all walks of life. The entire purpose of the principles of this philosophy is to enable you to take these four steps as a matter of habit.

TAKE YOUR OWN PERSISTENCE INVENTORY

Napoleon Hill suggests that you review the following Persistence Inventory, point by point, to see how many of the eight factors of persistence you lack.

While there are no right or wrong answers, by noting your thoughts—as they are now—about each of these items, it will give you a point of reference by which to judge how your understanding changes as you study Hill's philosophy of personal achievement.

PERSISTENCE INVENTORY

1. **Definiteness of purpose.** Knowing what you want is the first and most important step toward the development of persistence. A strong motive will force you to surmount difficulties.

2. **Desire.** It is comparatively easy to acquire and maintain persistence in pursuing the object of intense desire.

3. **Self-reliance.** Belief in your ability to carry out a plan encourages you to follow the plan through with persistence. (Self-reliance can also be developed through autosuggestion.)

4. **Definiteness of plans.** Organized plans, even ones that may be weak or impractical, encourage persistence.

5. **Accurate knowledge.** Knowing that your plans are sound, based on experience or observation, encourages persistence; "guessing" instead of "knowing" destroys persistence.

6. **Cooperation.** Sympathy, understanding, and cooperation with others tend to develop persistence.

7. **Will-power.** The habit of concentrating your thoughts on making plans to attain your definite purpose leads to persistence.

8. **Habit.** Persistence is the direct result of habit. The mind absorbs and becomes a part of the daily experiences upon which it feeds. Fear, the worst of all enemies, can be overcome by forcing yourself to perform and repeat acts of courage.

IDENTIFY THE WEAKNESSES YOU MUST MASTER

Following is a list of the real enemies that stand between you and achievement. These are not only the "symptoms" indicating weakness of persistence, but also the deeply seated subconscious causes of this weakness. Study the list carefully and face yourself squarely, if you really wish to know who you are and what you are capable of doing.

As you go through the list, analyze yourself point by point, record how you measure up on the self-test scale, record the date, and make a few notes to remind yourself how you felt when you first went through this review. These are the weaknesses that must be mastered by anyone who really wants to accumulate riches:

1. Failure to recognize and to clearly define exactly what you want.

2. Procrastination, with or without cause (usually backed up with a long list of excuses).

3. Lack of interest in acquiring specialized knowledge.

4. Indecision, and the habit of "passing the buck" instead of facing issues squarely.

5.   The habit of relying on excuses instead of making definite plans by which to solve your problems.

6.   There is little remedy for the weakness of self-satisfaction, and little or no hope for those who suffer from it.

7.   Indifference, usually reflected in your readiness to compromise rather than meet opposition and fight it.

8.   The habit of blaming others for your mistakes, and accepting circumstances as being unavoidable.

9.   Weakness of desire because you neglected to choose motives that will push you to take action.

10. Willingness to quit at the first sign of defeat (based upon one or more of the six basic fears).

11. Lack of organized plans that you have written out so they can be analyzed.

12. The habit of neglecting to act on ideas, or to grasp opportunity when it presents itself.

13. The habit of wishing instead of willing.

14. The habit of compromising with poverty instead of aiming at riches. A general lack of ambition to be, to do, or to own.

15. Searching for all the shortcuts to riches. Trying to get without giving a fair equivalent, usually reflected in the habit of gambling or trying to drive unfair bargains.

16. Fear of criticism, resulting in failure to create plans and put them into action, because of what other people might think, do, or say. This is one of your most dangerous enemies, because it often exists in your subconscious mind and you may not even know it is there.

IF YOU FEAR CRITICISM

As is clear from the number of times it is mentioned in *Think and Grow Rich*, Napoleon Hill considers the fear of criticism to be one of the greatest enemies of success. In fact, the reason people have a fear of failing has more to do with their concern about what other people will think or say about them than it does with their concern for not being able to accomplish the task at hand. No one likes to try something and fail, but, more important, no one wants to be blamed for failing. Failure may make you mad at yourself, but blame and criticism diminishes you in front of others, which erodes your self-confidence.

Many people make mistakes in marriage but stay married, then go through life miserable and unhappy, because they fear criticism.

Millions of people will not go back to get an education after having left school, because they fear criticism.

Countless numbers of men and women have permitted relatives to wreck their lives in the name of family duty, because they fear criticism.

People refuse to take chances in business because they fear the criticism that may follow if they fail.

Too many people refuse to set high goals for themselves because they fear the criticism of relatives and friends who may say, "Don't aim so high, people will think you are crazy."

Although for some people the fear of being criticized can act as a motivator to succeed, for others the anxiety it causes has just the opposite effect. Like stage fright or first-time jitters, the fear of criticism can cause panic attacks, shortness of breath, rapid breathing, irregular heartbeat, sweating, nausea, and other physical symptoms.

The problem with even moderate fear of criticism is that it can keep you from being your best because it keeps you from taking chances. It's easier to go the safe route and not attract attention to yourself. But the safe idea that is not likely to be criticized is also not likely to be a big breakthrough.

The most creative ideas and the most audacious statements are the ones that are most likely to be laughed at. It's those risky ideas, the ones that someone might hate or laugh at, that usually have the best upside, but you don't put them out there because you don't want to get shot down.

For many people, the criticism doesn't even have to be directed at you. Just seeing someone else get taken down a peg is enough to keep you from wanting to suffer the same fate yourself.

The way to deal with the fear of being criticized is the same as dealing with any other fear or phobia. Psychologists may use various confrontation therapies to desensitize you, and there are drugs that might ease your anxiety, but basically the answer is, as Susan Jeffers says in the title of her bestseller: "Feel the fear and do it anyway."

What have you got to lose? What happens if you take the chance that you will be criticized?

If the downside is that you could lose your job or someone could get hurt, then the risk is probably not worth the reward.

On the other hand, if the downside is that you feel foolish for a while, but the upside is that you will achieve your burning desire, then the answer is obvious.

What would be really foolish is if you *didn't* give it a shot.

Chapter Fourteen

DOING MORE THAN PAID FOR

WHAT WOULD NAPOLEON HILL DO?

People who never do more than they are paid for, never get paid for more than they do.

Napoleon Hill would approach every task not only as a way to exceed expectations, nor just as an opportunity to highlight his abilities, but also as a personal challenge to do it better than he had ever done it before. And, like the farmer who reaps much more than he sows, Napoleon Hill would be tapping into the law of nature that ensures he would gain more than he gave.

Another of Napoleon Hill's favorite stories was about the man who was thinking about changing jobs, so he lined up a few job interviews to test the waters. The first one seemed to be going along so well that he decided to ask what salary they would offer him.

The recruiter liked the way it was going too, and he was pretty anxious to hire this new guy, so he said that they were prepared to offer him whatever he thought he was worth.

Heaving a mighty sigh and shaking his head in disappointment, the guy said, "That's no good. I'm already getting more than that where I work now!"

The habit of giving more and better service than you are paid to do, or as Napoleon Hill also called it, "going the extra mile," is not just an abstract idea that Hill arbitrarily added to his listing of the Principles of Success. He believed that it was absolutely instrumental in his personal success. If you look back at the seven turning points in the previous chapter, you will find that he mentions its importance in every one of the jobs he describes.

In fact, the first turning-point story is not really complete because it neglects to tell how important going the extra mile was in getting Hill the job in the first place. Here's the part that is missing.

Just prior to graduating from business school, Hill wrote a letter to Rufus Ayers, who was a prominent attorney, politician, mine owner, and all around "big man" in Hill's hometown of Wise, Virginia. According to Michael J. Ritt Jr., author of Napoleon Hill's biography, *A Lifetime of Riches,* this is what Hill wrote in his letter to Ayers:

> I have just completed a business college course and am well qualified to serve as your secretary, a position I am very anxious to have. Because I have no previous experience, I know that at the beginning working for you will be of more value to me than it will be to you. Because of this I am willing to pay for the privilege of working with you.

You may charge any sum you consider fair, provided at the end of three months that amount will become my salary. The sum I am to pay you can be deducted from what you pay me when I start to earn money.

Ayers read Hill's letter and decided that anyone who was that audacious deserved to be hired, properly paid, and given the chance to prove himself. To quote again from *A Lifetime of Riches*:

Hill was an instant success. He came to the office early, stayed late, and worked tirelessly in between. He was an excellent bookkeeper, fastidiously accurate and willing "to go the extra mile to render more service than compensated for"—an axiom that would one day become one of his principles for success.

The following is how Napoleon Hill introduces the concept in Lesson 9: The Habit of Doing More Than Paid For, from *Law of Success*.

THE HABIT OF DOING MORE THAN PAID FOR

It may seem to be a departure from the subject of this lesson to start with a discussion of love, but after you have completed the lesson you will understand that the subject could not have been omitted without impairing the value of the lesson.

The word *love* is used here in an all-encompassing sense. There are many objects, motives, and people that can inspire love, and one of these inspirations can be work. Great artists, for example, generally love their work.

But it is not uncommon for many people to speak of hating work, and it is easy to envision work that is dull, tiring, and emotionally unsatisfying. Work that you do merely for the sake of earning a living is seldom enjoyable. Time passes slowly, and boredom and weariness are inevitable in such circumstances.

It is possible, however, to be engaged in work that you love, work that gives you personal satisfaction and which you approach in a spirit of anticipation and excitement. When engaged in work that you love, you can labor for unbelievably long periods of time without noticing the clock, because you are focused on the challenge and the satisfaction you are getting.

Your endurance, therefore, depends very largely on the extent to which you like, dislike, or love what you are doing. This is the basis for one of the most important philosophies of this course: You are most efficient and will more quickly and easily succeed when engaged in work that you love, or work that you perform on behalf of some person whom you love.

THE MOTIVATING POWER OF LOVING WHAT YOU DO

There are many sound reasons why you should develop the habit of performing more and better service than that for which you are paid. There are two reasons, however, that transcend all the others in importance.

First, by establishing a reputation as being a person who does this, you will benefit by comparison with those around you, and the contrast will be so noticeable that there will be keen competition for your services. Whether you are preaching sermons, practicing law, writing books, teaching school, or digging ditches, you will become more valuable and you will be able to command greater pay as you gain recognition for Doing More Than Paid For.

The second reason is basic and fundamental in nature. Suppose that you wished to develop a strong right arm, and suppose you tried to do so by tying your arm to your side to give it a long rest. Would disuse bring strength, or would it bring atrophy and weakness?

You know that if you wished a strong right arm you would develop it by exercising and working it harder. Out of resistance comes strength. The strongest tree in the forest is not the one protected from the storm and hidden from the sun, but the one that stands in the open, where it is compelled to struggle for its existence against the winds and rains and scorching sun.

There's a story that should leave in your mind the importance of this lesson. This story had its setting in the city of Antioch in ancient Rome, two thousand years ago, when the great city of Jerusalem and all the land of Judea were under the oppressive heel of Rome.

The star figure of the story was a young Jewish man by the name of Ben Hur, who was falsely accused of crime and sentenced to hard labor at the galley's oar. Chained to a bench in the galley, and being forced to tug wearily at the oars, Ben Hur developed a powerful body. Little did his tormentors know that out of his punishment would grow the strength with which he would one day gain his freedom. Perhaps Ben Hur himself had no such hopes.

Then came the day of the chariot races. One span of horses was without a driver. In desperation the owner sought the aid of the young slave because of his mighty arms, and begged him to take the place of the missing driver.

As Ben Hur picked up the reins, a great cry went up from the onlookers. "Look! Look! Those arms! Where did you get them?" they howled, and Ben Hur answered, "At the galley's oar!"

The race was on. With those mighty arms Ben Hur calmly drove that charging span of horses on to victory—a victory that won for him his freedom.

Life itself is a great chariot race, and the victory goes only to those who have developed the strength of character and determination and will-power to win. It doesn't matter if we develop this strength through cruel confinement at the galley's oar, as long as we use it so that it brings us, finally, to victory and freedom.

The purpose of this lesson is to show you how to harness this law of nature—that struggle and resistance develop strength—and use it to aid you in your struggle for success. By forming the habit of doing more than what you are paid for, you will develop the strength to remove yourself from any undesirable station in life, and no one can stop you.

At this point Napoleon Hill reminds the reader of some of the ideas about laws of nature that were introduced in the opening chapter, Cosmic Habit Force.

THE LAW OF INCREASING RETURNS

The farmer carefully prepares the ground, then sows his wheat and waits while the Law of Increasing Returns produces a plant that yields many new seeds.

Were it not for this Law of Increasing Returns, there would be no advantage to be gained by sowing a field of wheat if the harvest yield did not return more than was sown.

With this "tip" from nature, consider how to apply it to the work you do or the service you render. How can your work yield returns in excess of the effort put forth?

When you do only that for which you are paid, there is nothing out of the ordinary to attract favorable comment about the transaction. But when you willingly do more than that for which you are paid, your action attracts favorable attention, and you establish a good reputation that will increase the demand for your services.

HE GOT IN THE HABIT OF CALLING ON ME

Carol Downes went to work for W. C. Durant, the head of General Motors, in a minor position yet quickly became Mr. Durant's right-hand man and the president of one of his automobile distributing companies. He promoted himself into this profitable position solely through the aid of the Law of Increasing Returns, by rendering more service and better service than that for which he was paid.

In a visit with Mr. Downes I asked him to tell me how he had managed to gain promotion so rapidly. In a few brief sentences he told the whole story.

"When I first went to work with Mr. Durant," said he, "I noticed that he always remained at the office long after all the others had gone home for the day, and I made it my business to stay there also. No one asked me to stay, but I thought someone should be there to give Mr. Durant any assistance he might need. Often he would look around for someone to bring him a letter file, or render some other trivial service, and always he found me there ready to serve him. He got into the habit of calling on me. That is about all there is to the story."

Why did Mr. Durant get into the habit of calling on Mr. Downes? Because Mr. Downes made it his business to be on hand where he would be seen. He deliberately placed himself in a position to render service that would make the Law of Increasing Returns work for him.

Was he told to do this? No.

Was he paid to do it? Yes! He was paid by the opportunity it offered for him to bring himself to the attention of the man who had it within his power to promote him.

We are now approaching the most important part of this lesson, because this is an appropriate place to suggest that you have the same opportunity to make use of the Law of Increasing Returns—by being on hand and ready to volunteer your services in the performance of work that others may shirk because they are not paid to do it.

Stop. Don't say it—don't even think it—if you have the slightest intention of using the argument "but my employer is different."

Of course yours is different. All people are different, but the majority are very much alike in being somewhat selfish. In fact they are selfish enough not to want a man such as Carol Downes to go to work for their competitor.

This selfishness may be made to serve you if you have the good judgment to make yourself so useful that the person to whom you sell your services cannot get along without you.

THE THOUSAND DOLLAR LETTER

One of the most advantageous promotions I ever received came about through an incident that seemed so insignificant at the time that it appeared to be unimportant.

One Saturday afternoon, a lawyer whose office was on the same floor as mine asked if I knew where he could get a stenographer to do some work which he was compelled to finish that day.

I told him that all of our stenographers had gone to the ball game, and that I would have been gone too had he called five minutes later, but that I would be very glad to stay and do his work.

I did the work for him, and when he asked how much he owed me I replied, "Oh, about a thousand dollars, as long as it is you; if it were for anyone else, I wouldn't charge anything." He smiled and thanked me.

Six months later, after I had entirely forgotten the incident, he called on me again and asked how much salary I was receiving. When I told him, he informed me that he was ready to pay me that thousand dollars which I had laughingly said I would charge him, and he did pay it—by giving me a position at a thousand dollars a year increase in salary.

Unconsciously, I had put the Law of Increasing Returns to work in my behalf that afternoon by giving up the ball game and rendering a service that was obviously rendered out of a desire to be helpful and not for the sake of a monetary consideration.

It was not my duty to give up my Saturday afternoon, but it was my privilege!

I have been thinking for more than twenty-five years about this privilege of doing more than you are paid for, and my thoughts have led me to the conclusion that a single hour devoted each day to rendering service for which we are not paid can be made to yield bigger returns than we receive from all the rest of the day when we are merely performing our duty.

AN AGENCEY BUILT ON INCREASING RETURNS

When I was in the advertising business, I built my entire clientele by applying the fundamentals upon which this lesson is founded. By having my name placed on the follow-up lists of various mail-order houses, I received their sales literature. When I received a sales letter or a booklet or a folder that I believed I could improve, I went right to work on it and made the improvement, then sent it back to the firm that had sent it to me, with a letter stating that this was but a sample of what I could do—that there were plenty of other good ideas where that one came from—and that I would be glad to render regular service for a monthly fee.

Invariably this brought an order for my services. On one occasion a firm was dishonest enough to appropriate my idea and use it without paying me for it, but this later turned out to be an advantage to me. A member of the firm who was familiar with the transaction started another business, and as a result of the work I had done for his former associates, for which I was not paid, he hired me at more than double the amount I would have realized from his original firm.

Thus the Law of Compensation and the Law of Increasing Returns gave back to me, and with compound interest added, that which I had lost by rendering service to those who were dishonest.

THE BEST $100 EVER INVESTED

Several years ago I was invited to deliver a lecture before the students of the Palmer School in Davenport, Iowa. My manager completed arrangements for me to accept the invitation under the regular terms in effect at that time, which were $100 for the lecture plus my travel expenses.

When I arrived at Davenport I found a reception committee awaiting me at the depot, and that evening I was given one of the warmest welcomes I had ever received during my public career, up to that time. I met many delightful people from whom I gathered many valuable facts that were of benefit to me. Therefore, when I was asked to make out my expense account so the school could give me a check, I told them that I had received my pay, many times over, by what I had learned while I was there. I refused my fee and returned to my office in Chicago feeling well repaid for the trip.

The following morning Dr. Palmer went before the two thousand students of his school and announced what I had said about feeling repaid by what I had learned, and he added: "In the twenty years that I have been conducting this school I have had scores of speakers address the student body, but this is the first time I ever knew a man to refuse his fee because he felt that he had been repaid for his services in other ways. This man is the editor of a national magazine and I advise every one of you to subscribe to that magazine, because such a man as this must have much that each of you will need when you go into the field and offer your services."

By the middle of that week I had received more than $6,000 for subscriptions. During the following two years these same two thousand students and their friends sent in more than $50,000 for subscriptions. Tell me how or where I could have invested $100 as profitably as this.

PUTTING THE LAW TO WORK

The Law of Increasing Returns is no invention of mine, nor do I lay claim to the discovery of the principles of doing more than you are paid for as a means of utilizing this law. I merely appropriated them, after many years of careful observation of those forces which enter into the attainment of success, just as you will appropriate them after you understand their significance.

You can begin this process now by trying an experiment that will open your eyes and give you powers that you did not know you had.

As you read the explanation of the experiment that Hill proposes, you may be tempted to breeze through the instructions and file them in the back of your mind as possibly an interesting idea but not anything to take too seriously. That would be wrong.

Remember what was said in the earlier chapters about laws of nature. Even if you don't know why they work, and even if they don't make logical sense to you, just like gravity or electricity, they are laws of nature, and they do what it is their nature to do.

If Napoleon Hill says that there is a Law of Increasing Returns, and if Napoleon Hill became famous for giving people advice that made them rich, maybe it isn't such a good idea to take the chance and disregard his advice. After all, even if it doesn't work, all it will have cost you is a little of your time. But if it does work, just think of the benefits you could reap.

I am going to ask you to approach this experiment with full faith that it will mark one of the most important turning points of your entire life. I am going to ask you to make the object of this experiment the removal of a mountain that is standing where your success should stand, but where it can never stand until you have removed the mountain.

And what is this mountain? It is the feeling that you have been cheated unless you receive material pay for all the service you render.

In its basic form, this feeling is usually expressed in terms something like, "I am not paid to do this and I'll be damned if I'll do it." You know the attitude to which I refer. That feeling may be unconsciously expressing itself and destroying the very foundation of your success in scores of ways that you have not observed.

During the next six months, make it your business to render useful service to at least one person every day, for which you neither expect nor accept monetary pay.

Go at this experiment with faith that it will reveal one of the most powerful laws of achieving success, and you will not be disappointed.

The rendering of this service may take any form you choose. For example, it may be rendered personally to one or more specific persons. Or it may be rendered to your employer as work that you perform after hours. Or it may be rendered to entire strangers whom you never expect to see again. It doesn't matter to whom you render this service, so long as you render it with willingness, and solely for the purpose of benefiting others.

If you carry out this experiment with the proper attitude, you will discover that you can no more render service without receiving compensation than you can withhold the rendering of it without suffering the loss of reward.

One of the most important reasons why we should always be not only ready but also willing to render service is that every time we do so, we gain an opportunity to prove to someone that we have ability.

Instead of saying to the world, "Show me the color of your money and I will show you what I can do," reverse the rule and say, "Let me show you the color of my service so that I may take a look at the color of your money if you like my service."

Make it your business to render more service and better service than that for which you are paid, and before you realize what has happened, you will find that the world is willingly paying you for more than you do!

Chapter Fifteen

THE HABIT OF SAVING: MASTERING FEAR OF POVERTY

WHAT WOULD NAPOLEON HILL DO?

The hard truth is that if you save a definite proportion of all the money you earn, you will be financially successful. If you save nothing, you are absolutely sure never to be financially independent, no matter how much your income may be.

Napoleon Hill would make his savings goal into a Definite Chief Aim, he would create a specific plan to rid himself of any vestige of poverty-consciousness, and he would focus his visualization and affirmation techniques to turn his goal into a saving habit.

The habit of saving is by far the most nuts-and-bolts of all the Principles of Success, and that is why the editors have positioned it as
the fifteenth principle, which in this book is the last of the how-to
principles. The habit of saving not only draws upon the advice and
techniques explained in each of the previous chapters, but it also
provides a practical opportunity to put them to use.

Everyone will have their own personal reasons for reading this
book, and each reader will have particular areas of their life where they
want to apply Hill's methods, but this chapter focuses on the one Definite Chief Aim that is common to everyone, and which everyone must
accomplish if they are to be truly successful.

The following is excerpted and adapted from *Law of Success*, Lesson Four: The Habit of Saving.

THE HABIT OF SAVING

To advise someone to save money, without describing *how* to save,
would be somewhat like drawing a picture of a horse and writing under
it, "This is a horse." It is obvious to all that the saving of money is one
of the essentials for success, but the big question uppermost in the
minds of the majority of those who do not save is: "How can I do it?"

The saving of money is solely a matter of habit. For that reason,
this lesson begins with a brief analysis of the law of habit.

It is literally true that an individual, through the law of habit,
shapes their own personality. Through repetition, any act indulged in
a few times becomes a habit, and the mind appears to be nothing more
than a mass of motivating forces growing out of our daily habits.

Once fixed in the mind, a habit voluntarily impels you to action. For example, follow a given route to your daily work, or to some
other place that you frequently visit, and very soon the habit has been
formed and your mind will lead you over that route without thought
on your part. Moreover, if you start out with the intention of traveling

in another direction, without keeping the thought of the change in routes constantly in mind, you will still find yourself following the old route.

LIMITATION BUILT THROUGH HABIT

Millions of people go through life in poverty and want because they have made destructive use of the law of habit. Not understanding either the law of habit or the Law of Attraction through which "like attracts like," those who remain in poverty seldom realize that they are where they are as the result of their own acts.

Fix in your mind the thought that your ability is limited to a given earning capacity and you will never earn more than that—the law of habit will set up a limitation of the amount you can earn. Your subconscious will accept this limitation, and very soon you will feel yourself "slipping" until finally you will become so hedged in by a fear of poverty that opportunity will no longer knock at your door; your doom will be sealed; your fate fixed.

On the other hand, when you thoroughly understand the law of habit, you may ensure yourself success in the great game of money-making by "playing both ends of that game against the middle."

First, through your Definite Chief Aim you set up in your mind an accurate, definite description of what you want, including the amount of money you intend to earn. Then your subconscious mind takes over this picture you have created and uses it as a blueprint or map by which to mold your thoughts and actions into practical plans for attaining the object of your chief aim or purpose.

Through the law of habit you keep the object of your Definite Chief Aim fixed in your mind until it becomes firmly and permanently implanted there. This practice will destroy the poverty-consciousness and set up in its place a prosperity-consciousness. You will actually begin to demand prosperity, you will begin to expect it, you will begin to prepare yourself to receive it and to use it wisely, thus paving the way for the development of the habit of saving.

Second, having increased your earning power, you will then make further use of the law of habit by confirming in your written statement of your Definite Chief Aim to save a definite percentage of all the money you earn.

Therefore, as your earnings increase, your savings will, likewise, increase in proportion.

By ever urging yourself on and demanding of yourself increased earning power, on the one hand, and by systematically laying aside a definite amount of all your earnings, on the other hand, you will soon reach the point at which you have removed all imaginary limitations from your own mind and you will then be well started on the road toward financial independence.

Nothing could be more practical, or more easily accomplished, than this. Form the habit of thinking and talking of prosperity and abundance, and very soon material evidence of these will begin to manifest itself in the nature of wider opportunity, and new and unexpected opportunity.

If you reverse the operation of the law of habit, by setting up in your mind the fear of poverty, very soon this fear will reduce your earning capacity.

Like attracts like! If you are in business and have formed the habit of talking and thinking about business being bad, business will be bad. One pessimist can destroy the work of half a dozen competent people, and the pessimist will do it by setting adrift in the minds of his or her associates the thought of poverty and failure.

Don't be this type of person.

One of the most successful bankers in the state of Illinois has this sign hanging in his private office:

"We talk and think only of abundance here. If you have a tale of woe, please keep it, as we do not want it."

In tens of thousands of homes, the general topic of conversation is poverty and want, and that is just what they are getting. They think of poverty, they talk of poverty, they accept poverty as their lot in life. They reason that because their ancestors had all been poor, they too must remain poor.

Poverty-consciousness is the result of the habit of thinking of and fearing poverty.

THE SLAVERY OF DEBT

Debt is a merciless master, a fatal enemy of the savings habit. Poverty alone is sufficient to kill off ambition, destroy self-confidence, and destroy hope, but add to it the burden of debt and all who are victims of these two cruel taskmasters are practically doomed to failure.

No one can do their best work, find self-expression, or carry out a definite purpose in life, with heavy debt hanging over his or her head.

It is terrible to even think of going through life like a prisoner in chains, bound down and owned by somebody else on account of debts. The accumulation of debts is a habit. It starts in a small way and grows step by step, until finally those debts take charge of one's very soul.

Those bound by the slavery of debt have no time or inclination to set up ideals. The result is that they drift downward until they eventually begin to set up limitations in their own minds, and by these they hedge themselves behind prison walls of fear and doubt from which they never escape.

The fear of poverty is one of the most destructive of the six basic fears. The person who becomes hopelessly in debt is seized with this fear, their ambition and self-confidence become paralyzed, and they sink gradually into oblivion.

Practically all people who live beyond their means are tempted to speculate with the hope that they may recoup, at a single turn of the wheel of fortune, their entire indebtedness. The wheel generally stops at the wrong place and, far from finding themselves out of debt, those who indulge in speculation are bound more closely as slaves of debt.

Fear of poverty is a negative, destructive state of mind. Moreover, one negative state of mind has a tendency to attract other similar states of mind. For example, the fear of poverty may attract the fear of ill health, and these two may attract the fear of old age, so that the victims find themselves poverty-stricken, in ill health, and actually growing old long before the time they should begin to show signs of old age.

Millions of untimely, nameless graves have been filled by this cruel state of mind known as the fear of poverty.

The following commentary is excerpted from *Think and Grow Rich: The Workbook,* Chapter 16: The Six Ghosts of Fear.

FIRST BASIC FEAR: THE FEAR OF POVERTY

Every person reading this book must face the fact that it is possible you could find yourself out on the street, living hand-to-mouth.

For some readers, the fear of poverty can be a motivating force that pushes you to succeed so it will never happen to you. For others, the fear of poverty has just the opposite effect. For them the fear of poverty keeps them from pushing themselves to succeed because the fear of losing what they have is more real than the possibility of success.

The fear of poverty can kill your adventurous spirit and turn you into a timid, overly cautious do-nothing. If you allow yourself to fear poverty, you will dwell on the fear and never see the other side. It has to be put into perspective. You must strike a balance.

What that means is that you accept poverty as one possibility, but you also recognize that riches are a possibility too. If you change from fearing poverty to desiring wealth, you will have done it.

Knowledge of what could happen and a fear of what could happen are two different things. When you have knowledge you act. When you have fear you react.

SIX SYMPTOMS OF THE FEAR OF POVERTY

1. **Indifference.** Expressed through lack of ambition, willingness to tolerate poverty and accept whatever life hands you. Also laziness, lack of initiative, imagination, and self-control.

2. **Doubt.** Generally expressed through excuses designed to cover up or apologize for your failures. Sometimes expressed as envy of those who are successful, or by criticizing them.

3. **Worry.** Usually expressed by finding fault with others, a tendency to spend beyond your income, neglect of personal appearance, nervousness, lack of poise, self-consciousness, and often the use of alcohol or drugs.

4. **Indecision.** The habit of permitting others to do your thinking; sitting on the fence.

5. **Overcaution.** The habit of looking for the negative side of every circumstance. Knowing all the roads to disaster but never searching for the plans to avoid failure. Always waiting for "the right time" to begin, instead of getting started now.

6. **Procrastination.** This symptom is closely related to overcaution, doubt, and worry. Spending more time in creating excuses than it would take to do the job. Refusal to accept responsibility. Willingness to compromise with difficulties instead of using them as steppingstones to advancement. Bargaining with life for a penny instead of demanding prosperity, opulence, riches, contentment, and happiness. Associating with those who accept poverty instead of seeking the company of those who demand and receive riches.

Fear of poverty is nothing more than a state of mind. This, coupled with the fact that everything we create begins in the form of a thought, leads us to the principle by which fear may be mastered.

You either believe that you will achieve your aim or purpose, or you fear that you will not achieve it. It must be one or the other. It is up to you to stop dwelling on the fear of what might happen, and stay focused on accomplishing your aim or purpose.

MASTER THE FEAR OF POVERTY

To whip the fear of poverty, you must take two very definite steps if you are in debt. First, quit the habit of buying on credit, then follow this by gradually paying off the debts that you have already incurred.

Being free from the worry of indebtedness, you will be ready to revamp the habits of your mind and redirect your course toward prosperity.

Any habit may be discontinued by building in its place some other and more desirable habit. The spending habit must be replaced by the saving habit by all who wish to attain financial independence.

The discontinuance of a habit leaves a hole in the mind, and this hole must be filled with some other form of habit or the old one will return and claim its place.

Adopt, as a part of your Definite Chief Aim, the habit of saving a regular portion of your income, even if it is no more than pennies a day. Very soon this habit will begin to take hold of your mind and you will actually get joy out of saving.

Some who are shortsighted are fond of pointing to the fact that no one can become rich merely by saving a few dollars a week.

This may be true enough, but the other side of the story is that the saving of even a small sum of money places one in a position where, oftentimes, even this small sum may enable one to take advantage of business opportunities that lead directly and quite rapidly to financial independence.

In the original edition of this chapter, Napoleon Hill included several charts and budgets that could put off modern readers because they are so specific to the financial conditions in the 1920s. Unfortunately, the editors of this book suffer from the same problem.

With the rollercoaster ride that the economy and the markets are on these days, any specific financial information that we might offer today could, by tomorrow, probably look just as out of date as Hill's charts do now. So instead we have chosen to stick with the basics, which can be summed up in three short sentences:

First, if you started saving just one dollar a day (and who can't spare one dollar) at the end of ten years, at 5 percent interest, because of compound interest it will have become almost five thousand dollars.

Second, if you are twenty-five years old and you start putting just $6 a day in an index fund, based on historical returns you will be a millionaire by the time you are sixty-five.

And here's the third thing to keep in mind: If you wait until you are thirty to start, it will take $10 a day in order to be a millionaire at sixty-five.

The lesson is clear: Start saving and/or investing in well balanced diversified funds, and start now! And according to Hill, that message should be . . .

. . . copied and pasted on your mirror, where it will stare you in the face every morning when you get up and every night as you retire. It should be reproduced, in letters and figures an inch tall, and placed on the walls of every public school throughout the land, where it might serve as a constant reminder to all children of the value of the savings habit.

I recall one occasion when the president of a large corporation sent me a check for $500 for an address I delivered at a banquet given for the employees, and I distinctly recall what went through my mind when I opened the letter and saw the check. I had wanted a new automobile and this check was exactly the amount required for the first payment. I had it spent before it had been in my hands thirty seconds.

Perhaps this is the experience of the majority of people. They think much more about how they will spend whatever they have than they do about saving.

The idea of saving, and the self-control and self-sacrifice that would be needed to do so, is always accompanied by thoughts of an unpleasant nature. But oh, how it thrills one to think of spending.

There is a reason for this, and it is that most of us have developed the habit of spending while neglecting the habit of saving, and any idea that seldom frequents the mind is not as welcome as the idea that frequents it often. In truth, the habit of saving can be made as fascinating as the habit of spending might seem, but not until it has become a regular, well-grounded, systematic habit. We like to do things that are often repeated, which is but another way of saying what the scientists have discovered: that we are victims of our habits.

The habit of saving requires more force of character than most people have developed, because saving means self-denial and sacrifice of amusements and pleasures in scores of different ways. For this very reason, one who develops the savings habit acquires, at the same time, many of the other needed habits that lead to success, especially self-control, self-confidence, courage, poise, and freedom from fear.

Thomas J. Stanley and William Danko, the authors of the bestseller *The Millionaire Next Door,* also stressed the connection between success and saving. This is what their research revealed:

- More than 80 percent of America's millionaires accumulated their own wealth—they did not inherit it.

- Most millionaires do not live in upscale neighborhoods. Most still live in the houses they owned when they began to accumulate their fortunes.

- Most millionaires drive mid-size American cars, not luxury Rolls-Royces. And surprisingly, one out of three always buys used cars.

- The average millionaire's income is just over $130,000. Their real wealth comes from their habit of saving 20 percent of their income.

In short, most millionaires who actually have money are not celebrities or heads of big companies. Statistically, most millionaires are just people earning a good income, who have made a habit of saving.

HOW MUCH SHOULD YOU SAVE?

Nothing in this lesson is intended as a sermon on morality. We are dealing here with cold facts which, to a large extent, constitute the materials out of which success may be created.

A few years ago I set up a lecture bureau in forty-one high schools, where I lectured once each month throughout the school season. The principals of these high schools stated that less than 2 percent of the students showed any tendency toward saving money, and an examination through the aid of a questionnaire prepared specifically for that purpose disclosed that only 5 percent of the students, out of a total of 11,000 of high-school age, believed that the savings habit was one of the essentials for success.

It is no wonder that the rich are becoming richer and the poor are becoming poorer!

We are all victims of habit. Unfortunately for most of us, we are reared by parents who have no concept whatsoever of the psychology of habit, and without being aware of their fault, most parents aid and abet their offspring in the development of the spending habit by over-indulgence with spending money, and by lack of training in the habit of saving.

The habits of early childhood cling to us all through life.

Fortunate indeed is the child whose parents have the foresight, as well as the understanding of the value of the savings habit as a builder of character, to instill this habit in the minds of their children.

It is a training that yields rich rewards.

Give the average person a $100 windfall and what will become of it? Why, the lucky person will begin to ponder how to spend the money. Dozens of things that are needed, or are perceived as being needed, will flash into that person's mind, but it is a rather safe bet that it will never occur to the recipient (unless he or she has acquired the savings habit) to make this $100 the beginning of a savings account. Before night comes, the $100 will be spent, or at least a decision will have been made as to how to spend it, thus adding more fuel to the already too bright flame of the habit of spending.

We are ruled by our habits!

It requires force of character, determination, and the power of firm decision to open a savings account and then add to it a regular, even if small, portion of all subsequent income.

There is one rule by which anyone may determine, well in advance, whether or not financial freedom and independence, which is so universally desired, is attainable. And this rule has absolutely nothing to do with the amount of your income.

The rule is that if you follow a systematic habit of saving a definite proportion of all money you earn, or receive in other ways, you are practically sure to place yourself in a position of financial independence. If you save nothing, you are absolutely sure never to be financially independent, no matter how much your income may be.

The installment plan of buying [or today, using credit cards] has become so common, and it is so easy to purchase practically anything you desire, that the tendency to spend out of proportion to your income is rapidly increasing. This tendency must be curbed by the person who has made up his or her mind to gain financial independence.

It can be done by anyone who is willing to try.

There is no virtue in keeping up with the neighbors when this means sacrifice of the habit of saving a regular part of one's income.

It is far better, in the long run, to be considered a bit behind the times than it is to go through youth, into the days of maturity, and finally into old age, without having formed the habit of systematic saving.

There is nothing quite so humiliating, that carries such great agony and suffering, as poverty in old age when personal services are no longer marketable and one must turn to relatives or to charitable institutions for existence.

A budget system should be maintained by every person, but no budget will work if the person trying to keep it lacks the courage to cut expenses on such items as entertainment and recreation. If you have so little will-power that you think it necessary to "keep up with the Joneses," then no budget system can be of service to you.

Forming the savings habit means that, to some extent at least, you must seclude yourself from all except a well-selected group of friends who enjoy you without elaborate entertaining on your part.

To admit you lack the courage to trim down your expenditures so that you can save money, even if only a small amount, is the equivalent of admitting at the same time a lack of the sort of character that leads to success.

OPPORTUNITIES THAT COME TO THOSE WHO HAVE SAVED MONEY

When the Ford automobile was perfected, during the early days of its existence, Henry Ford needed capital to promote the manufacture and sale of his product. He turned to a few friends who had saved up a few thousand dollars. These friends came to his rescue, put in a few thousand dollars with him, and later drew out millions of dollars in profits.

When Woolworth first started his 5 and 10 Cent Stores he had no capital, but he turned to a few friends who staked him and later they were paid back hundreds of thousands of dollars in profits.

Van Heusen, the famed shirt manufacturer, conceived the idea of a semi-soft collar for men's shirts, but he had not a cent to promote it. He turned to his friends who had only a few hundred dollars, and the collar made each of them wealthy.

Behind practically every great fortune you will find, as its beginning, a well-developed habit of saving money.

John D. Rockefeller was an ordinary bookkeeper when he conceived the idea of developing the oil business, which was then not even considered a business. He needed capital, and because he had developed the habit of saving, and had thereby proved that he could conserve the funds of other people, he had no difficulty in borrowing the money he needed. It may be truthfully stated that the real basis of the Rockefeller fortune is the habit of saving money that Mr. Rockefeller developed while working as a bookkeeper at a salary of $40 a month.

James J. Hill was a poor young man, working as a telegrapher at a salary of $30 a month. He conceived the idea of the Great Northern Railway System, but his idea was out of proportion to his ability to finance.

However, he had formed the habit of saving money, and on the meager salary of $30 a month had saved enough to enable him to pay his expenses on a trip to Chicago, where he interested capitalists in financing his plan. The fact that he, himself, had saved money on a small salary was considered good evidence that he would be a safe man to trust with other people's money.

There are opportunities on every corner, but they exist only for those who have ready money, or who can command money because they have formed the habit of saving.

Those who have developed the savings habit generally also have the other character attributes that go with its formation.

It may seem a cruel fact, but it is a fact nonetheless, that if you have no money, and have not developed the habit of saving, you are out of luck as far as availing yourself of the opportunity to make money is concerned.

It is a sad sight to see someone who is well along in years and self-sentenced to the wearisome treadmill of hard labor because he or she neglected to form the habit of saving money when they were younger.

The greatest thing in life is freedom! But there can be no real freedom without a reasonable degree of financial independence.

The only hope of escape from this lifelong toil which curtails freedom is to form the habit of saving money, and then live up to that habit, no matter how much sacrifice it may require.

There is no other way out for millions of people, and unless you are one of the rare exceptions, this lesson and all these statements of fact are meant for you and apply to you!

Chapter Sixteen

TOLERANCE AND INTOLERANCE

WHAT WOULD NAPOLEON HILL DO?

Remember that wars, politics, and any form of social unrest only happen because someone in some way is making a profit from it. If there was no advantage to be had, there would be no conflict.

Napoleon Hill would never allow his emotions to be manipulated for someone else's gain. He would hold fast to his principles, but he would never let them become such ingrained habits that he'd forget to question why and if he really believed in them in the first place.

Napoleon Hill was born and raised in what he described as conditions of poverty, ignorance, and superstition. "For three generations, my people had been born, lived, struggled, and died without ever having been outside the mountains of that section. There were no railroads, telephones, electric lights, or passable public highways." And there was little reason to think that anyone in the Hill clan would turn out any different.

Later in life, after Hill became famous as a public speaker, he often opened his speeches by telling his audience that theoretically he should not have been there with them. Rather, he should have been with his mountainfolk kin, carrying on feuds, killing rattlesnakes, and drinking "corn likker."

Whether it was because he actually wanted to distance himself from his humble beginnings in a part of the country that was more often than not the butt of jokes, or whether it had something to do with that other sophisticated world that Andrew Carnegie opened to him, somewhere, somehow Napoleon Hill developed a sense of right and wrong that drove him to investigate what he saw as his own character flaws. And this led him to an understanding of human nature and an attitude about race, religion, creed, and gender that was very uncommon for his day.

This entire chapter is an adaptation of the fifteenth lesson, entitled Tolerance, which appears in the original edition of *Law of Success*.

TOLERANCE

I will begin this lesson about tolerance by pointing out the two significant features of *in*tolerance.

The first is that intolerance is a form of ignorance which must be mastered before any form of enduring success can be attained. It makes enemies in business and in the professions. It disintegrates the organized forces of society in a thousand forms. It is the chief cause of all wars and a barrier to the abolition of war. It dethrones reason and substitutes mob psychology in its place.

The second is that intolerance is the chief disintegrating force in the organized religions of the world, where it plays havoc with the greatest power for good by breaking up that power into small sects and denominations that spend as much effort opposing each other as they do in destroying the evils of the world.

But this indictment against intolerance is general. Let's look at how it affects you, the individual. It is, of course, obvious that anything which impedes the progress of civilization also stands as a barrier to each individual. Stating it conversely, anything that clouds the mind of the individual and retards mental, moral, and spiritual development, also retards the progress of civilization.

All of this is an abstract statement of a great truth. And inasmuch as abstract statements are neither interesting nor informative, let us proceed to more concretely illustrate the damaging effects of intolerance.

INTOLERANCE

I will start by describing an incident that I have mentioned quite freely in practically every public address I have delivered within the past five years. But because the cold printed page has a modifying effect that makes it possible to misinterpret the incident described, I caution you not to read into it a meaning that I had not intended. You will do yourself an injustice if you neglect to study this illustration in the exact words and with the exact meaning that I have intended those words to convey.

As you read, place yourself in my position and see if you have not had a parallel experience. And if so, what lesson did it teach you?

One day I was introduced to a young man of unusually fine appearance. His clear eyes, his warm hand-clasp, the tone of his voice, and the splendid taste with which he was groomed marked him as a young man of high intellect, the typical young American college student type. As I looked him over, hurriedly studying his personality, as one will naturally do under such circumstances, I observed a Knights of Columbus pin on his vest.

Instantly I released his hand as if it were a piece of ice! This was done so quickly that it surprised both him and me.

As I excused myself and started to walk away, I glanced down at the Masonic pin that I wore on my own vest, then took another look at his Knights of Columbus pin, and wondered why a couple of trinkets such as these could dig such a deep chasm between men who knew nothing of each other.

For those who may not be familiar with the Masonic Lodge and the Knights of Columbus, Hill's story requires a little elaboration.

Freemasonry dates back to the time of the Crusades. It flourished in Europe during the Age of Enlightenment, it was influential among the founders of America, and it played a significant role in American society at the time Hill was writing *Law of Success*. Although open to all religions, in America, Masonic Lodges were largely a stronghold of pro-American Protestants.

The Knights of Columbus is a much more recent organization, having been started as a temperance society by a Catholic priest in 1881. It was named in honor of Christopher Columbus, and like the Masons, the Knights of Columbus had ceremonies and rituals, but theirs were a blend of Catholicism and American patriotism as a way to demonstrate that there was no conflict between Catholic faith and American freedom.

Because of Freemasonry's emphasis on freedom of thought, speech, and religion, and because of its secret vows, Freemasonry was long the target of condemnation by various popes, and was thus considered anti-Catholic.

On the other hand, many Freemasons held that Catholics were not true Americans because they were subject to papal decree, and therefore under the control of a foreign power.

So it was that kind of mistrust and prejudice that could cause people to react with such disdain to the symbolic meaning behind a lapel pin or watch fob.

All the remainder of that day I kept thinking of the incident, because it bothered me. I had always taken considerable pride in the thought that I was tolerant with everyone, but here was a spontaneous outburst of intolerance that proved there was something in my subconscious mind that was creating narrow-mindedness.

This discovery so shocked me that I began a systematic process of self-analysis through which I searched into the very depths of my soul for the cause of my rudeness. I asked myself over and over again why I had so abruptly released that young man's hand and turned away from him, when I knew nothing about him.

Of course the answer would always lead me back to that Knights of Columbus pin he wore, but that was not a real answer and therefore it did not satisfy me.

Then I began to do some research work in the field of religion. I began to study both Catholicism and Protestantism until I had traced both back to their beginnings, a process that I must confess brought me more understanding of the problems of life than I had gathered from all other sources. For one thing, it disclosed the fact that Catholicism and Protestantism differ more in form than they do in effect; that both are founded on exactly the same cause, which is Christianity.

But this was by no means the most important of my discoveries. My research led in many directions and forced me into the field of biology, where I learned much that I needed to know about life in general and the human being in particular. My research also led to the study of Darwin's hypothesis of evolution, as outlined in his *The Origin of Species*, and this, in turn, led to a much wider analysis of the subject of psychology than any I had previously made.

As I reached out for knowledge, my mind began to unfold and broaden with such alarming rapidity that I practically found it necessary to wipe the slate of what I believed to be knowledge, and to unlearn much that I had previously believed to be truth.

Comprehend the meaning of what I have just said. Imagine yourself suddenly discovering that most of your philosophy of life had been built of bias and prejudice, making it necessary for you to acknowledge that, far from being a finished scholar, you were barely qualified to become an intelligent student!

That was exactly the position in which I found myself. But of all the discoveries to which this research led, none was more important than that of physical and social heredity. It was through this discovery that I came to understand the cause for my action when I turned away from a man I did not know.

It was this discovery that disclosed to me how and where I had acquired my views of religion, of politics, of economics, and of many other equally important subjects. I both regret and rejoice to say that I found most of my views on these subjects without support by even a reasonable hypothesis, much less sound facts or reason.

I recalled a conversation between the late Senator Robert L. Taylor and myself, in which we were discussing the subject of politics.

"I see that you are a very staunch Democrat," he said, "and I wonder if you know why you are?"

I thought of the question for a few seconds, then blurted out this reply:

"I am a Democrat because my father was one, of course!"

With a broad grin on his face, the senator then nailed me with this response:

"Just as I thought! Now wouldn't you be in a bad fix if your father had been a horse thief?"

Too often we hold opinions that are based on no sounder a foundation than it being what someone else believes.

In the previous section Napoleon Hill says that in his search the most significant answer he learned was the importance of physical heredity and social heredity.

Hill uses the term *physical heredity* for what we today might call genetic predisposition or inherited physical traits.

By *social heredity* he means social conditioning or socialization —the methods by which one generation imposes upon the minds of the younger generation the superstitions, beliefs, legends, and ideas which it inherited from the generation that preceded it.

In the following section Hill uses physical and social heredity as a way to introduce the subject of war, and to present excerpts from a plan that he wrote and submitted to The American Peace Award.

HOW TO ABOLISH WAR: THE BACKGROUND

There are two important factors that constitute the chief controlling forces of civilization. One is physical heredity and the other is social heredity.

The size and form of the body, the texture of the skin, the color of the eyes, and the functioning power of the vital organs are all the result of physical heredity; they are static and fixed and cannot be changed, for they are the result of a million years of evolution. But by far the most important part of what we are is the result of social heredity, which is effected through our environment and early training.

Our conception of religion, politics, economics, philosophy, and other subjects of a similar nature, including war, is entirely the result of those dominating forces of our environment and training.

The Catholic is a Catholic because of their early training, and the Protestant is a Protestant for the same reason. But this is hardly stating the truth with sufficient emphasis, for it might be properly said that the Catholic is a Catholic and the Protestant is a Protestant because they cannot help it! With few exceptions, the religion of the adult is the result of their religious training during the years between four and fourteen, when their religion was forced on them by their parents or those who had control of their schooling.

A prominent clergyman indicated how well he understood the principle of social heredity when he said, "Give me the control of the child until it is twelve years old and you can teach it any religion you may please after that time, for I will have planted my own religion so deeply in its mind that no power on earth could undo my work."

The outstanding and most prominent of man's beliefs are those that were forced upon him or that he absorbed of his own volition, under highly emotionalized conditions, when his mind was receptive.

The three great organized forces through which social heredity operates are the schools, the churches, and the press. Any ideal that has the active cooperation of these three forces may, during the brief period of one generation, be forced upon the minds of the young so effectively that they cannot resist it.

At this point in the original edition, Napoleon Hill wrote an extensive section on the ramifications of the First World War, which many of his generation felt was so cruel and devastating that it shattered any idea of honor in warfare, and would spell the end of all such conflicts and introduce a new era of peace.

Five or six wars later, we know that was not to be.

Because so much of what Hill wrote in this section was directly related to people and events of the time that are now only of historical interest, the editors have chosen to excerpt only Hill's comments that pertain to his central theme of tolerance through education.

War can be eliminated not by appeal to reason but by appeal to the emotional side of humanity. This appeal must be made by organizing and highly emotionalizing the people of the different nations of the world in support of a universal plan for peace, and this plan must be forced upon the minds of the oncoming generations with the same diligent care that we now force upon the minds of our young the ideal of our respective religions.

It is not stating the possibilities too strongly to say that the churches of the world could establish universal peace as an international ideal within one generation if they would apply just one-half of the effort that they now apply in opposing one another.

In brief, if the present organized forces of the world will not lend their support to establishing universal peace as an international ideal, then new organizations must be created that will do so.

It staggers the imagination what the leading churches of all religions, the leading schools, and the press of the world could accomplish, within a single generation, in forcing the ideal of universal peace upon both the adult and the child minds of the world.

The majority of the people of the world want peace, wherein lies the possibility of its attainment!

Those who do not want peace are the ones who profit by war. In numbers, this group constitutes but a fragment of the power of the world and could be swept aside as though it did not exist, if the multitude who do not want war were organized in their objective.

In closing, it seems appropriate to apologize for the unfinished state of this essay, but it may be pardonable to suggest that the bricks and the mortar, and the foundation stones, and all the other necessary materials for the construction of the temple of universal peace have been here assembled, where they might be rearranged and transformed into this high ideal as a world reality.

ECONOMICS AND SOCIAL HEREDITY ALLIANCES

We learned many lessons of value from the world war, outrageous and destructive as it was, but none of greater importance than that of the effect of organized effort. The tide of war began to break in favor of the allied armies just after all armed forces were placed under the direction of General Foch, which brought about complete coordination of effort in the allied ranks.

Never before in the history of the world had so much power been concentrated in one group of men as that which was created through the organized effort of the allied armies. One of the most outstanding and significant facts to be found in the analysis of these allied armies is that they were made up of the most cosmopolitan group of soldiers ever assembled. Every race and religion was represented.

If they had any differences on account of race or creed, they laid them aside and subordinated them to the cause for which they were fighting. Under the stress of war, that great mass of humanity was reduced to a common level where they fought shoulder to shoulder, side by side, without asking any questions as to one another's racial or religious beliefs.

If they could lay aside intolerance long enough to fight for their lives over there, why can we not do the same while we fight for a higher standard of ethics in business and finance and industry over here? Is it only when civilized people are fighting for their lives that they have the foresight to put aside intolerance and cooperate in the furtherance of a common end?

We learned from the world war that we cannot destroy a part without weakening the whole; that when one nation or group of people is reduced to poverty and want, the rest of the world suffers too. As we also learned, cooperation and tolerance are the very foundation of enduring success.

Surely the more thoughtful and observant among us will not fail to profit, as individuals, by these great lessons.

I realize that you are probably studying this course for the purpose of profiting in every way possible, from a purely personal point of view, by the principles upon which it is founded. For this very reason, I have endeavored to apply these principles to as wide a range of subjects as possible. An important object of this course, and particularly of this lesson, is to educate more than it is to inform. It should awaken the power within you that awaits some appropriate stimulus to arouse you to action.

In conclusion, I leave with you my personal sentiments on tolerance, in the following essay which I wrote in the hour of my most trying experience, when an enemy was trying to ruin my reputation and destroy the results of a lifetime of honest effort to do some good in the world.

Tolerance

When the dawn of Intelligence shall have spread its wings over the eastern horizon of progress, and ignorance and superstition shall have left their last footprints on the sands of time, it will be recorded in the book of man's crimes and mistakes that his most grievous sin was that of intolerance!

The bitterest intolerance grows out of racial and religious differences of opinion, as the result of early childhood training. How long, O Master of Human Destinies, until we poor mortals will understand the folly of trying to destroy one another because of dogmas and creeds and other superficial matters over which we do not agree?

Our allotted time on this earth is but a fleeting moment, at most! Like a candle, we are lighted, shine for a moment and flicker out! Why can we not so live during this short earthly sojourn that when the great caravan called Death draws up and announces this visit about finished we will be ready to fold our tents, and, like the Arabs of the desert, silently follow the caravan out into the darkness of the unknown without fear and trembling?

I am hoping that I will find no Jews or Gentiles, no Catholics or Protestants, Germans or Englishmen, Frenchmen or Russians, Blacks or Whites, Reds or Yellows, when I shall have crossed the bar to the other side.

I am hoping I will find there only human souls, brothers and sisters all, unmarked by race, creed, or color, for I shall want to be done with intolerance so I may lie down and rest an aeon or two, undisturbed by the strife, ignorance, superstition, and petty misunderstandings which mark with chaos and grief this earthly existence.

Chapter Seventeen
THE GOLDEN RULE

WHAT WOULD NAPOLEON HILL DO?

Do unto others as you would have them do unto you should be more to you than a vague Sunday school memory. It is a duplicate key to Infinite Intelligence.

Napoleon Hill would do unto others not just to be polite, or in hopes that they would then do good unto him in return, but more importantly because of the good he was doing to his own subconscious. With every act, he was building his own character and becoming the kind of person who would attract to him the kind of people he himself aspired to be.

The Golden Rule was the final principle in the original edition of *Law of Success,* and even though we have added Cosmic Habit Force—the new seventeenth principle—it is perfectly appropriate that the Golden Rule should still be the final principle in this version of the Principles of Success, because the two are in effect mirror images of one another.

We begin with the following introduction adapted from *The Secret Law of Attraction as explained by Napoleon Hill.*

In reading this book, it is quite likely that at some point you were struck by the thought that there is something very familiar about the Law of Attraction's premise that if you think positively you will manifest positive things in your life, and if you think negatively you will attract negative things to yourself. Turn the words over in your mind a few times and you realize that what it is saying is not that different from the Golden Rule: "Do unto others as you would have them do unto you."

As you will learn in the following, Napoleon Hill sees much more than just a similarity in these concepts. In Hill's view they are simply different ways of stating the same basic truth. Although the Law of Attraction seems focused on your personal desires and what you think to yourself, while the Golden Rule is about what you "do unto others," Hill points out that the way you relate to others is in fact the physical manifestation of what you think to yourself.

You cannot act in any way toward someone else without first thinking about *how* you are going to act toward that person. Therefore, doing unto others so that they will do the same unto you is a perfect example of your thought transforming itself into reality. The Golden Rule and the Law of Attraction are in fact one and the same.

The entire following section is excerpted and adapted from the original *Law of Success,* Lesson Sixteen: The Golden Rule.

DO UNTO OTHERS . . .

For more than four thousand years, people have been preaching the Golden Rule as a suitable rule of conduct toward others. But while we have accepted the philosophy of it as a sound rule of ethical conduct, we have failed to understand the spirit of it or the law upon which it is based.

The Golden Rule essentially means to do unto others as you would wish them to do unto you if your positions were reversed.

There is an eternal law through the operation of which we reap what we sow. When you select the rule of conduct by which you guide yourself in your transactions with others, you will very likely be fair and just if you know that by your selection you are setting into motion a power that will run its course in the lives of others, returning finally to help or to hinder you, according to its nature.

If you fully understand that one's thoughts are transformed into reality corresponding exactly to the nature of the thoughts, it will be quite easy for you to understand the law upon which the Golden Rule is based.

You cannot divert or change the course of this law, but you can adapt yourself to its nature and thereby use it as an irresistible power that will carry you to heights of achievement which could not be attained without its aid.

It is your privilege to deal unjustly with others, but if you understand this law, you must know that your unjust dealings will come home to roost. The law does not stop by merely flinging back upon you your acts of injustice and unkindness toward others; it goes further than this—much further—and returns to you the results of every thought that you release.

Therefore, it is not enough to "do unto others as you wish them to do unto you," but you must also "think of others as you wish them to think of you."

The law upon which the Golden Rule is based begins affecting you the moment you release a thought. It is a tragedy that people have not generally understood this. Despite the simplicity of the law, it is practically all there is to be learned that is of enduring value to man, for it is the medium through which we become the masters of our own destiny.

Perhaps you have wondered why the subject of honesty has not been mentioned in this course as a prerequisite to success. If so, the answer will be found in this lesson. The Golden Rule philosophy, when rightly understood and applied, makes dishonesty impossible. It also makes all the other destructive qualities—such as selfishness, greed, envy, bigotry, hatred, and malice—impossible.

When you apply the Golden Rule, you become at the same time both the judge and the judged, the accuser and the accused. Honesty, then, begins in your own heart, toward yourself, and extends to all others with equal effect.

It is no credit to be honest only when honesty is obviously the most profitable policy so as not to lose a valuable client or be sent to jail for deception. But when honesty means a loss personally, then it becomes an honor of the highest degree to all who practice it. Such honesty has its appropriate reward in the accumulated power of character and reputation enjoyed by those who deserve it.

Those who understand and apply the Golden Rule philosophy are always scrupulously honest, not only out of their desire to be just with others but also because of their desire to be just with themselves. They understand the eternal law upon which the Golden Rule is based and they know that through this law every thought they release and every act in which they indulge has its counterpart with which they will later be confronted.

Those who understand this law would poison their own drinking water as quickly as they would indulge in acts of injustice to others, for they know that such injustice starts a chain reaction that will not only bring them physical suffering but will also destroy their characters, stain their reputations, and make it impossible for them to attain enduring success.

THE GOLDEN RULE IS AUTOSUGGESTION

The law through which the Golden Rule philosophy operates is none other than the law through which the principle of autosuggestion operates.

If all your acts toward others, and even your thoughts of others, are registered in your subconscious mind through the principle of auto-suggestion, thereby building your own character in exact duplicate of your thoughts and acts, can you not see how important it is to guard those thoughts and acts?

We are now at the very heart of the real reason for doing unto others as we would have them do unto us, for it is obvious that what-ever we do unto others we also do unto ourselves.

You cannot indulge in an act toward another person without having first created the nature of that act in your own thoughts. And you cannot release a thought without planting it in your own subconscious mind, where it becomes an integral part of your own character, modifying it in exact conformity with the nature of the act or thought.

Grasp this simple principle and you will understand why you cannot afford to hate or envy another person. You will also understand why you cannot afford to strike back, in kind, at those who do you an injustice. Likewise, you will understand the injunction "return good for evil."

Understand the law upon which the Golden Rule is based and you will also understand the law that eternally binds all mankind in a single bond of fellowship and renders it impossible for you to injure another person, by thought or deed, without injuring yourself. Similarly, the results of every positive thought and deed in which you indulge adds favorably to your own character.

Understand this law and you will then know, beyond room for the slightest doubt, that you are constantly punishing yourself for every

wrong you commit and rewarding yourself for every act of constructive conduct.

. . . AS YOU WOULD HAVE THEM DO UNTO YOU

There are people who believe that the Golden Rule philosophy is nothing more than a theory and that it is in no way connected with an
immutable law of nature. They have arrived at this conclusion because
of personal experience wherein they rendered service to others without
receiving any benefit in return.

How many have not rendered service to others that was neither
reciprocated nor appreciated? I have had such experiences many times,
and I am sure that I will have similar experiences in the future. But
I will not discontinue rendering service to others merely because they
don't reciprocate or appreciate my efforts. And here is the reason:

When I render service to another, or indulge in an act of kindness, I store away in my subconscious mind the effect of my efforts,
which may be likened to the charging of a battery. By doing such acts, I
will develop a positive, dynamic character that will attract people who
harmonize with my own character. Those whom I attract to me will
reciprocate the acts of kindness and the service that I have rendered
others. Therefore, the Law of Compensation will have balanced the
scales of justice for me, bringing back from one source the results of
service that I rendered through an entirely different source.

You have often heard it said that a salesman's first sale should be
to himself, which means that unless he convinces himself of the merits
of his wares he will not be able to convince others. Here again is this
same Law of Attraction. Enthusiasm is contagious, and when a salesman shows great enthusiasm over his wares, he will arouse in the minds
of others a corresponding interest.

You can comprehend this law quite easily by regarding yourself as a sort of human magnet that attracts those whose characters

harmonize with your own dominating characteristics and repels all who don't harmonize with you. Also keep in mind that you are the builder of that magnet, and that you may change its nature so that it will correspond to any ideal that you may wish to conform to.

Again, and most important of all, remember that this entire process of change takes place through thought. Your character is but the sum total of your thoughts and deeds.

Because of this great truth, it is impossible for you to render any useful service, or indulge in any act of kindness toward others, without benefiting. And it is just as impossible for you to indulge in any destructive act or thought without paying the penalty.

THE GOLDEN RULE IS THE LAW OF RETALIATION

Positive thought develops a dynamic personality. Negative thought develops a personality of an opposite nature.

The law of "an eye for an eye and a tooth for a tooth" is based on the same law as that on which the Golden Rule operates. This is nothing more than the Law of Retaliation. Even the most selfish person will respond to this law. They cannot help it. If I speak ill of you, even though I tell the truth, you will not think kindly of me. Furthermore, you will most likely retaliate in kind. But if I speak of your virtues you will think kindly of me and, in the majority of instances, when there is an opportunity you will reciprocate in kind.

Through the operation of this Law of Attraction, the uninformed are constantly attracting trouble and grief and hatred and opposition from others by their unguarded words and destructive acts.

Do unto others as you would have them do unto you—bearing in mind that human nature has a tendency to retaliate in kind.

Confucius must have been thinking of the Law of Retaliation when he stated the Golden Rule philosophy in somewhat this way: Do not unto others that which you would not have them do unto you.

And he might well have added an explanation to the effect that the reason for his injunction was based on that very tendency of man to retaliate in kind.

Those who do not understand the law upon which the Golden Rule is based will argue that it will not work when people are inclined toward the Law of Retaliation. If they would go a step further in their reasoning, they would understand that they are looking at the negative effects of this law, and that the selfsame law is capable of producing positive effects as well.

In other words, if you would not have your own eye plucked out, then ensure against this misfortune by refraining from plucking out the other fellow's eye. Furthermore, render the other fellow an act of kindly helpful service, and through the operation of this same Law of Retaliation he will render you a similar service.

And if he should fail to reciprocate your kindness, what then?

You will have profited nevertheless, because of the effect of your act on your own subconscious mind.

Thus by indulging in acts of kindness and always applying the Golden Rule philosophy, you are sure of benefit from one source and at the same time you have a pretty fair chance of profiting from another source.

It might happen that you would base all of your acts toward others on the Golden Rule without enjoying any direct reciprocation for a long period of time. It might also happen that those to whom you rendered those acts of kindness would never reciprocate.

In the meantime, however, you have been strengthening your own character, and sooner or later this positive character that you have been building will begin to assert itself and you will discover that you have been receiving compound interest on compound interest in return for those acts of kindness that appeared to have been wasted on those who neither appreciated nor reciprocated them.

Remember that your reputation is made by others, but your character is made by you.

One reason for being just toward others is that such action may cause them to reciprocate in kind, but a better reason is that kindness and justice toward others develops positive character in all who do so.

You may withhold from me the reward to which I am entitled for rendering you helpful service, but no one can deprive me of the benefit I will derive from the rendering of that service insofar as it adds to my own character.

In the Lord's Prayer we are admonished to forgive our enemies, but that admonition will fall on deaf ears unless the listener understands the law upon which it is based. And that law is none other than the law upon which the Golden Rule is based. It is the law through which we must inevitably reap what sow.

There is no escape from the operation of this law, nor is there any cause to try to avoid its consequences if we refrain from putting into motion thoughts and acts that are destructive.

I have incorporated this law into a code of ethics that anyone who wishes to literally follow the injunction of the Golden Rule might appropriately adopt.

MY CODE OF ETHICS

1. I believe in the Golden Rule as the basis of all human conduct. Therefore, I will never do to another person that which I would not be willing for that person to do to me if our positions were reversed.

2. I will be honest, even to the slightest detail, in all my transactions with others, not only because of my desire to be fair with them but also because of my desire to impress the idea of honesty on my own subconscious mind, thereby weaving this essential quality into my own character.

3. I will forgive those who are unjust toward me, with no thought as to whether they deserve it or not, because I understand the law through which forgiveness of others strengthens my own character and wipes out the effects of my own transgressions, in my subconscious mind.

4. I will be just, generous, and fair with others always, even though I know that these acts will go unnoticed and unrewarded, in the ordinary terms of reward, because I understand and intend to apply the law through the aid of which one's own character is but the sum total of one's own acts and deeds.

5. Whatever time I may have to devote to the discovery and exposure of the weaknesses and faults of others, I will devote more profitably to the discovery and correction of my own.

6. I will slander no person, no matter how much I may believe another person may deserve it, because I wish to plant no destructive suggestions in my own subconscious mind.

7. I recognize the power of thought as being an inlet leading into my brain from the universal ocean of life. Therefore I will set no destructive thoughts afloat upon that ocean lest they pollute the minds of others.

8. I will conquer the common human tendency toward hatred, and envy, and selfishness, and jealousy, and malice, and pessimism, and doubt, and fear, for I believe these to be the seed from which the world harvests most of its troubles.

9. When my mind is not occupied with thoughts that tend toward the attainment of my Definite Chief Aim in life, I will voluntarily keep it filled with thoughts of courage, and self-confidence, and goodwill toward others, and faith, and kindness, and loyalty, and love for truth and justice, for I believe these to be the seed from which the world reaps its harvest of progressive growth.

10. I understand that a mere passive belief in the soundness of the Golden Rule philosophy is of no value whatsoever, either to myself or to others. Therefore I will actively put into operation this universal rule for good in all my transactions with others.

11. I understand the law through the operation of which my own character is developed from my own acts and thoughts. Therefore I will guard with care all that goes into its development.

12. Realizing that enduring happiness comes only through helping others find it, that no act of kindness is without its reward, even though it may never be directly repaid, I will do my best to assist others when and where the opportunity appears.

Chapter Eighteen

THE FINAL CHAPTER

WHAT WOULD THE EDITORS DO?

Throughout this book we have focused on analyzing the technical aspects of Napoleon Hill's Principles of Success. In this final chapter we would like to offer some insight into the people and events that influenced Hill's life and the development of those principles.

This closing is divided into two parts. The first is a biographical sketch of the life and times of the author, followed by the most personally revealing story Napoleon Hill ever told. Between the two, you will learn much about the man and his philosophy.

If, as you read this biographical overview, you find yourself thinking from time to time that some of the words have a very familiar ring to them, the reason for the flashes of déjà vu is simply that this biography has been assembled by the editors from a variety of sources including some passages that also appear in earlier chapters. Those sources include excerpts from *Law of Success* and *Think and Grow Rich*, as well as editorial comments that appear in *Think and Grow Rich: The Workbook, Selling You!, Napoleon Hill's First Editions,* and *The Secret Law of Attraction as explained by Napoleon Hill.*

In assembling this final chapter our intention has been to present a fuller picture of why and how Napoleon Hill developed the Principles of Success, so for obvious reasons we have focused on his business life rather than his personal life. For those readers interested in a detailed account of all aspects of Hill's life, we recommend *A Lifetime of Riches: The Biography of Napoleon Hill,* by Michael J. Ritt Jr. and Kirk Landers, which has been very helpful to the editors of this book in understanding the influences on Napoleon Hill.

BACKWOODS BOY WITH CHEEK

Napoleon Hill, maker of millionaires, adviser to the titans of business and industry, and confidant of presidents, started out a long way from the executive boardroom or the White House. In 1883 Hill was born in a two-room log cabin in the Blue Ridge Mountains of southwest Virginia in what he described as conditions of poverty, ignorance, and superstition:

> For three generations my people had been born, lived, struggled, and died without ever having been outside the mountains of that section. There were no railroads, telephones, electric lights, or passable public highways.

And there was little reason to think that anyone in the Hill clan would turn out any different.

His mother died when Napoleon Hill was barely nine years old, and with no mother to look after the family, and with little parental supervision, young Nap turned into the local hell-raiser. Always stubborn and hot-tempered, he began carrying a six-gun stuffed into his belt, and most of the locals expected he would follow in the footsteps of the man he proclaimed as his hero: Jesse James.

Later in life, when Hill became famous as a public speaker, he often opened his speeches by telling his audience that theoretically he should not have been there with them. Rather, he should have been with his mountainfolk kin, carrying on feuds, killing rattlesnakes, and drinking "corn likker." But that all changed when Nap's father remarried and brought his new wife to live in their backwoods cabin.

Martha Ramey Banner was educated, cultured, the daughter of a physician, and the widow of a school principal, and she was little prepared for hillbilly living or a pistol-toting stepson. Something was going to change, and it wasn't going to be Martha. She vowed that she would not live in poverty, and from that moment on, the Hill clan was going to change its ways.

Within days of her arrival, Martha called her new family together and, one by one, she began planting the ideas that would inspire each of them to believe they could become more than what they were. Her influence on Napoleon would echo throughout his life.

The following excerpt from Law of Success is Napoleon Hill in his own words singing the praises of his new stepmother's influence on his family, which is made even more interesting because of the way Hill chose to write it. At that time, authors often adopted a kind of forced false modesty in which they refrained from any personal references, but in this case Hill goes so far as to write it as though it were about another family—from Kentucky instead of Virginia. We are not sure why he chose to write it in this fashion, but to anyone who knows the events of his life, there is no doubt that he is writing about his own family.

I know of a family of mountain folk who, for more than six generations, have lived in the mountainous region of Kentucky. Generation after generation of this family came and went without any noticeable improvement of a mental nature, each generation following in the footsteps of its ancestors. They made their living from the soil, and as far as they knew, or cared, the universe consisted of a little spot of territory known as Letcher County. They married strictly in their own set, and in their own community.

Finally, one of the members of this family strayed away from the flock, so to speak, and married a well-educated and highly cultured woman from the neighboring state of Virginia. This woman was an ambitious person who was well aware that the universe extended beyond the borders of Letcher County, and covered, at least, the whole of the southern states. She had heard of chemistry, botany, biology, pathology, psychology, and of many other subjects that were of importance in the field of education.

When her children reached an age of understanding, she talked to them of these subjects, and they in turn began to show a keen interest in them. One of her children is now the president of a great educational institution, where most of these subjects are taught. Another of them is a prominent lawyer, while still another is a successful physician.

Her husband, thanks to the influence of her mind, is a well-known dental surgeon and the first of his family, for six generations, to break away from the traditions by which the family had been bound.

The blending of her mind with his gave him the needed stimulus to spur him on and inspired him with ambition such as he would never have known without her influence.

It was Martha's definiteness of purpose, coupled with her enthusiasm, that would inspire each member of her new family. When she looked at her new husband, James Hill, she did not see a poor dirt farmer and part-time blacksmith. She saw a man with a genius for tinkering and an understanding of the people of the district. Soon James came to see himself that way too.

With Martha's encouragement, James left farming to become the local storekeeper and postmaster. Then one day Martha's false teeth broke and she suggested that, being as handy as he was, James could probably fix them.

The following excerpt is taken from the chapter titled Self-Confidence in *Law of Success*.

I am going to digress and break the line of thought for a moment to offer a word of advice to spouses and companions.

From having analyzed more than 16,000 people, the majority of whom were married, I have learned something that may be of value.

You have it within your power to send your mate away to his or her work, business, or profession each day with a feeling of self-confidence that will carry them successfully over the rough spots of the day and bring them home again, at night, smiling and happy.

One of my acquaintances of former years married a woman who had a set of false teeth. One day his wife dropped her teeth and broke the plate. The husband picked up the pieces and began examining them. He showed such interest in them that his wife said:

"You could make a set of teeth like those if you made up your mind to do it."

This man was a farmer whose ambitions had never carried him beyond the bounds of his little farm until his wife made that remark. She walked over and laid her hand on his shoulder and encouraged him to try his hand at dentistry. She finally coaxed him to make the start, and today he is one of the most prominent and successful dentists in the state of Virginia. I know him well, for he is my father!

According to the way Napoleon Hill told this story in his unpublished autobiography, James carved Martha a temporary plate from wood, and it worked so well that when they saw an ad for a do-it-yourself dentistry kit that read, "Fill your own teeth. For fifty cents will send enough material to fill twenty teeth," James and Martha decided to send away for it.

When it arrived, there wasn't much to it, just a couple of bent knitting needles, some chemicals, a vulcanizing kettle, and an instruction book, but James and Martha poured over the instructions until James had taught himself enough to hang out his shingle as a dentist. Though he started out self-taught, his first dental tools were made by hand in his blacksmith shop. He worked hard, gave more and better service than was expected, and James Hill became one of the most respected men in Wise County.

CONCEIVE, BELIEVE, ACHIEVE

Martha's influence was just as profound on the rest of the family. It was because of her vision and drive that Napoleon's brother Vivian worked his way from the local one-room school in their remote mountain village to a prestigious law practice in Washington, D.C., and Napoleon's stepbrother Paul followed the same course to become a highly respected surgeon.

It's unlikely that Martha thought of what she was doing in terms of visualizing a Definite Chief Aim and using autosuggestion to imprint it in the subconscious mind, but that is exactly what she was teaching her family to do. And she may never have defined the need to emotionalize the concepts that are to be imprinted in the subconscious, but, as Napoleon Hill often told his audiences, it was not uncommon for him to see his stepmother get so enthusiastic about an idea that she'd climb up on a chair to make sure she got his full attention.

This is not just an amusing anecdote about a mother's wisdom told by a devoted son. Martha Ramey Banner really did believe in focusing all of your enthusiasm on whatever you wanted to achieve. She systematically set out to teach the members of her family how to use their minds to better themselves—and they did.

And Napoleon never forgot the methods she used.

Years later, when Andrew Carnegie began introducing Hill to the wealthy and famous men who would teach him their secrets of success, Hill was more than a little surprised to find that successful entrepreneurs, inventors, and political leaders such as Henry Ford, Thomas Edison, and President Woodrow Wilson used essentially the same method his stepmother had taught him.

FROM A SIX-SHOOTER TO A TYPEWRITER

It was in her most rebellious stepson that Martha saw the greatest promise. As a boy, young Nap was known as a sometime student but a full-time troublemaker. However, in the so-called "worst boy in the county" Martha didn't see a budding juvenile delinquent, she saw a boy with boundless energy, imagination, and initiative. It was she who first told Napoleon that with his keen imagination he should be a writer, and by doing so she inspired in him a lifelong love of literature. Martha convinced him to give up his six-shooter in exchange for a typewriter, telling him, "If you become as good with a typewriter as you are with that gun, you may become rich and famous and known throughout the world."

Her faith and encouragement turned young Nap's life around, and by the age of fifteen he was submitting stories to the local newspapers. Although he was more of a truant than a student before Martha took him in hand, with her encouragement Napoleon Hill became a devoted student. So much so, that at the one-room schoolhouse in his hometown of Wise, Virginia, for years after he was remembered as the "talent of the school." He went on to graduate from the local two-year high school, then headed about a hundred miles down the road to Tazwell, Virginia, to attend the business college.

The Tazwell business school had a one-year curriculum geared to teaching young men the basic accounting and office skills needed to get hired as a male secretary, which in those days was the prime entry-level job. It was expected that from there you would learn the business and climb the corporate ladder, and that's exactly what Hill did. After completing the course, he checked out his options and decided that Rufus Ayers owned the corporate ladder he would climb.

Ayers had made a fortune in banking and in the coal-mining industry, and he'd become one of the wealthiest and most powerful men in Virginia. Following is an excerpt from the letter of application that Hill wrote to Rufus Ayers, which was also quoted previously:

> I have just completed a business college course and am well qualified to serve as your secretary, a position I am very anxious to have. Because I have no previous experience, I know that at the beginning working for you will be of more value to me than it will be to you. Because of this I am willing to pay for the privilege of working with you.
>
> You may charge any sum you consider fair, provided at the end of three months that amount will become my salary. The sum I am to pay you can be deducted from what you pay me when I start to earn money.

Ayers was intrigued enough by this self-assured young man that he offered him a job, including a salary, and over the next two years Hill met and exceeded all expectations.

The following is our brief version of what happened, with details based on Hill's notes for his unpublished autobiography:

In 1902, after Hill had been promoted to chief clerk at one of Rufus Ayers' coal mines, the manager of the mine and his brother, who was cashier of a bank owned by Ayers, had gone on a drinking spree. At one of their later stops at a hotel, the brother dropped a loaded revolver he was carrying and it discharged, killing a bellboy.

Hill heard the news almost immediately and went to the hotel. He learned that the brother had left the bank the previous day and hadn't returned. Rushing to the bank, Hill found the vaults open and money scattered everywhere. He then wired the news to Ayers, who told him to count the money and charge Ayers's own account for any shortage.

Standing there in the midst of thousands of dollars, Napoleon Hill faced a moral crossroad: He could take any amount of money he wanted, and there would be nobody to contradict his story. Or, he could put all of the money back in the safe where it belonged.

He counted it, found that no money was missing, and informed Ayers. Impressed by Hill's honesty, Ayers instantly promoted him to replace the manager—making this nineteen-year-old the youngest manager of a mine and in charge of three hundred and fifty men.

UNPACKING HIS TYPEWRITER AGAIN

Even though he had risen so quickly and accomplished so much within Ayers' company, Hill came to the realization that it was a family firm and there were two sons who were way ahead of him in line to occupy the top management positions. That, plus his admiration for Rufus Ayers' skills in legal matters, prompted Hill to quit his job so he could pursue a career as a lawyer.

After three years in the coal industry, Napoleon Hill returned to his studies by enrolling at Georgetown Law School in Washington, D.C. In order to put himself through law school, Hill concluded that his best opportunity was to apply for a job as a writer for *Bob Taylor's Magazine*.

Napoleon Hill was well aware of Robert L. Taylor as the past governor of Hill's home state of Virginia. Taylor had since become the publisher of his own magazine, a Washington-based publication that specialized in inspirational stories for those striving to get ahead in business, and writing for such a magazine seemed to Hill like something he would be perfect at.

Robert Taylor had heard of Napoleon Hill as a bright young man who'd made quite a name for himself back home in Virginia. That intrigued Taylor enough to meet with the self-declared journalist, and he found that he not only liked him, but he also liked Hill's proposal to write a series of success profiles. His first choice was to interview Andrew Carnegie, and that's how Hill managed to secure that fateful first meeting.

NAPOLEON HILL MEETS ANDREW CARNEGIE

As a young man determined to make a name for himself in the world of business, it was only natural that Napoleon Hill would have read about the Law of Attraction in the popular books of the day associated with the New Thought Movement. And this concept became more than just a passing interest on that day in the fall of 1908 when Hill was ushered through the door of the magnificent 64-room mansion at the corner of Fifth Avenue and 91st Street in New York City. He was awe-struck by the opulence that surrounded him as he stood in the grand foyer of Andrew Carnegie's Georgian manse, waiting for the butler to escort him to the library where he was to meet with the famed steel tycoon and philanthropist.

Hill had been granted three hours in which to interview Andrew Carnegie. However, by the end of the allotted time, Carnegie had become so taken with the intelligence of this intense young man that he kept extending their meeting, until the interview that had started on Friday finally came to an end the following Monday. Hill's entire career as an author is the result of what he learned from Andrew Carnegie at that meeting.

During their three-day marathon, Andrew Carnegie set forth in detail his personal philosophy of wealth and success. It was a philosophy that drew upon some of the ideas championed by the New Thought Movement—particularly the concept of the Law of Attraction—but Carnegie's version was tempered with the practical lessons learned by having raised himself out of poverty to create one of the greatest fortunes the world has ever known.

ANDREW CARNEGIE

Andrew Carnegie was born in Scotland and was thirteen when he emigrated to America with his parents in 1848. He took his first step onto the ladder of success by quitting his job as a bobbin boy in a cotton mill, earning $1.20 a week, and getting a job as a Western Union telegraph messenger boy. That move put him in a position where he could teach himself to operate a telegraph key, which led to him being hired as personal telegrapher and secretary to the head of the Pennsylvania Railroad. From there he worked his way up through the ranks until he achieved the position of superintendent of the Pittsburgh division.

A great believer in the role that railroads would play in America's future, Carnegie was an early investor in the Pullman company, which became the leading manufacturer of railway cars. It was Carnegie's investment in Pullman, plus some successful real estate ventures, that provided him the capital to go into business for himself.

In 1865, as the civil war was coming to an end, Carnegie tendered his resignation to the Pennsylvania Railroad in order to start his own company that would go into the business of building iron bridges for the railroads. From building iron bridges it was a short step to the manufacturing of rails, then locomotives, which led him to acquire control of his own iron and steel mills, then his own coal fields to supply his smelters, then his own ore boats and his own rail lines to haul the ore and coal. Because of the vertical integration of Carnegie's various companies, and because he insisted on using the most up-to-date and efficient manufacturing methods, he was able to sell top-grade steel at a lower price than his competitors. By 1899 he managed to drop the price of steel from $140 a ton to $20 a ton, and the Carnegie Steel Company then controlled about 25 percent of the iron and steel production in America.

In 1901 Andrew Carnegie was persuaded to sell his company to J. P. Morgan for $400 million (which would be comparable to approximately $8 billion at the beginning of the twenty-first century). It was Carnegie's company that Morgan used as the lynchpin in the creation of a new company that became the industrial giant U.S. Steel.

From the 1870s until his death in 1919, Andrew Carnegie strove to match his outstanding business success with his even greater philanthropic largesse. He built public libraries, endowed colleges, provided funding for schools and churches, and created numerous foundations, trusts, and institutions for the advancement of human rights, world peace, ethics, conflict prevention, and all levels of education, science, and the arts.

By almost every measure, Andrew Carnegie was one of the most successful men in the world.

THE NEW THOUGHT MOVEMENT

Coinciding with Hill's formative years and with Carnegie's rise to wealth and success, a philosophical trend called the New Thought Movement —based on the power of positive thinking—was gaining influence in America. Phineas Quimby, generally acknowledged as the father of the movement, was a healer and a practitioner of hypnosis who came to believe that the healing he was able to effect was not caused by him, but rather it was being done by the power of the patient's own mind.

Quimby's theory that the power of thought can produce change in the real world was not original to him, but because his sphere of friends and associates included a number of influential people, his ideas began to have a significant impact. New Thought began to emerge as a movement around 1850, and reached its zenith from the turn of the century through the 1930s.

One of Quimby's patients, author Warren Felt Evans, was so impressed by the way he was cured that he wrote a number of books about "mental science" and its application in healing. Learning of the technique, William James, the father of American psychology, wrote and lectured on what he called "the mind cure."

Another of Quimby's patients, Mary Baker Eddy, adapted belief in the power of the mind as the basis of the Christian Science Church and, in turn, her associate Emma Curtis Hopkins went on to teach the philosophy to Myrtle and Charles Filmore, who founded the Unity Church. Hopkins also taught Ernest Holmes, who founded the Church of Religious Science.

Although the early offshoots of Quimby's work were primarily concerned with using the power of the mind to effect healing in the body, others in the movement focused on the Law of Attraction's ability to create not only health but also wealth and success.

Often expressed by the phrase "like attracts like," this concept proposes that positive thoughts held in the mind attract positive results in reality.

The emphasis on self-improvement brought to the movement writers such as Ralph Waldo Trine who wrote *Character Building—Thought Power.* Charles Haanel wrote the still-in-print classic *The Master Key System.* William Watkins Atkinson wrote more than one hundred books on the subject, including *Thought Vibration or the Law of Attraction in the Thought World.* Orison Scott Marden wrote fifty books, with such titles as *Every Man a King* and *Pushing to the Front.* Marden was also the creator and publisher of *Success Magazine* which, except for a brief hiatus, was still on the stands in 2010—one hundred and fifteen years after its first issue. Also influential in the New Thought Movement was Wallace Wattles, whose 1906 book *The Science of Getting Rich* would be credited a century later by Rhonda Byrnes as one of her major inspirations when she created her video program *The Secret.*

However, by far the most successful and enduring of all the books that speak to the power of the Law of Attraction are *Law of Success* and *Think and Grow Rich,* by Napoleon Hill.

NAPOLEON HILL LEARNS THE CARNEGIE SECRET

For three days Napoleon Hill listened as Andrew Carnegie explained the secret of his extraordinary success. And it is significant that "the secret" was exactly the way Carnegie phrased it: singular, not plural. Although there were a number of factors that figured in Carnegie's success—and over three days and nights he covered an enormous range of subjects and explained a wide variety of ideas—to Carnegie they were all aspects of the one secret.

When Napoleon Hill published his first book based on what he had learned from Andrew Carnegie, Hill made certain that Carnegie's point of view was clear even in the title. Despite the fact that the book details sixteen separate principles, it was intentionally titled *Law of Success.* Singular, not plural.

Later, when Hill wrote his classic, *Think and Grow Rich,* the first sentence he wrote was about the Carnegie secret.

> In every chapter of this book, mention is made of the money-making secret that has made fortunes for the exceedingly wealthy men whom I have carefully analyzed over a long period of years.
>
> The secret was first brought to my attention by Andrew Carnegie. The canny, lovable old Scotsman carelessly tossed it into my mind when I was but a boy. Then he sat back in his chair, with a merry twinkle in his eyes, and watched carefully to see if I had brains enough to understand the full significance of what he had said to me.

Fortunately, Napoleon Hill did have the brains to understand the significance of what Carnegie was saying, and before the weekend was over he would have the chance to prove it.

> It was Mr. Carnegie's idea that the magic formula, which gave him a stupendous fortune, ought to be placed within reach of people who do not have the time to investigate how others had made their money.
>
> It was his hope that I might test and demonstrate the soundness of the formula through the experience of men and women in every calling.

At the time of their meeting, it had been seven years since Andrew Carnegie had sold his business holdings to J. P. Morgan and devoted himself to public service and to his many philanthropic pursuits. In

Napoleon Hill he saw the possibility to advance one of these pursuits. To quote from *A Lifetime of Riches,* Napoleon Hill's biography, Carnegie told Hill:

> My early days of youth were cursed with poverty and limited opportunity, a fact with which all who know me are acquainted. I am no longer cursed by poverty because I took possession of my mind, and that mind has yielded me every material thing I want, and much more than I need. But this power of the mind is a universal one, available to the humblest person as it is to the greatest.
>
> It's a shame that each new generation must find the way to success by trial and error, when the principles are really clear-cut.

Carnegie went on to explain that one of his greatest passions was to guide the development of a comprehensive, written philosophy of success that could be understood and used by the average person. He told Hill he believed that to do it properly would require a series of lengthy, in-depth interviews with hundreds of the most successful leaders in every walk of life, as well as extensive research, testing, and analysis that could take as long as twenty years to complete. Then, in his famously blunt fashion, Carnegie turned to Hill and asked if Hill felt that he was equal to the task.

Surprised to be put on the spot, but still caught up in Carnegie's lofty vision, Napoleon Hill's answer was an unreserved yes. This was an answer that displayed a self-confidence which would be sorely tested a minute or two later when it became clear that Carnegie was not offering to pay Hill to work on the project.

Carnegie explained that his own contribution to the creation of this philosophy would be to introduce Hill to the most successful and influential men in the world so Hill could learn directly from them the secret of their success. Carnegie again made it clear that he would make the introductions and cover the necessary travel expenses, but Hill's reward would not be a salary. Rather, it would be in the doors that would be opened to him, in the special knowledge that he would become privy to, and finally, in the satisfaction and accolades he would receive for bringing to the world the first philosophy of individual achievement.

Though Napoleon Hill wasn't quite sure how he would manage it, he reaffirmed his commitment to take on the project and see it through to the end.

It took Hill twenty-nine seconds to accept Carnegie's proposal. Carnegie had been timing him, and he told Hill afterward that had it taken him more than sixty seconds to make the decision he would have withdrawn the offer, for "a man who cannot reach a decision promptly, once he has all the necessary facts, cannot be depended upon to carry through any decision he may make."

Shortly thereafter, Andrew Carnegie began to arrange for Hill to meet with and study the most successful and powerful people of the day.

Hill was granted unprecedented access to interview and thoroughly investigate the business practices, personal influences, and private lives of the most successful businessmen, industrialists, inventors, scientists, authors, artists, and leaders of every kind.

Andrew Carnegie wanted Napoleon Hill to prove to himself that the secret he had explained to him was not just some eccentric millionaire's harebrained idea. He wanted Hill to convince himself that even though each of these famous and successful men had their own ways of doing things, the secret that helped them rise to the top was the same secret that Carnegie had revealed to Hill during their three-day meeting.

And that was how Napoleon Hill became the central figure in the process of analyzing the Carnegie secret in order to devise a practical method for the average person to use in creating their own success.

FINALLY FINDING HIS DEFINITE CHIEF AIM

As was explained in the section on Napoleon Hill's seven turning points, over the next ten years Hill launched companies in the lumber business, the candy business, and the automobile industry; he acted as legal counsel to a power company, created sales and advertising courses, became an educator, a lecturer, a writer.

And all the while he continued meeting with and studying the greatest business leaders in the world including Henry Ford, Thomas Edison, Alexander Graham Bell, Harvey Firestone, John D. Rockefeller, the Wright brothers, F. W. Woolworth, Luther Burbank, Marshall Field, and even President Theodore Roosevelt, President William Howard Taft, and President Woodrow Wilson for whom Hill became one of the first dollar-a-year men who advised the president during the First World War.

Andrew Carnegie died in 1919, but this seed he had planted continued to bear fruit, as the leaders of business and industry—whom Hill had met through Carnegie—in turn introduced Hill to other equally important figures who agreed to tell him the secrets of their success.

At this point we return to an excerpt from *Law of Success* that was presented in part in the chapter on Enthusiasm. This is Hill's explanation of how he started his first magazine, which is reprinted again here to set up the complete version of the editorial that launched his career as an author.

To describe the seventh and last of the turning points of my life, I must go back to November 11, 1918—Armistice Day, the end of the world war. The war had left me without a penny, as I have already said, but I was happy to know that the slaughter had ceased and reason was about to reclaim civilization.

As I stood in front of my office window and looked out at the howling mob that was celebrating the end of the war, my mind went back to my yesterdays, especially to a day when a kind old gentleman had laid his hand on my shoulder and told me that if I would acquire an education I could make my mark in the world. I had been acquiring that education without knowing it.

Over a period of more than twenty years, I had been going to school at the University of Hard Knocks, as you must have observed from my description of my various turning points. As I stood in front of that window my entire past, with its bitter and its sweet, its ups and its downs, passed before me in review.

The time had come for another turning point!

I sat down at my typewriter and, to my astonishment, my hands began to play a tune on the keyboard. I had never written so rapidly or so easily before. I did not plan or think about what I was writing—I just wrote whatever came into my mind.

Unconsciously, I was laying the foundation for the most important turning point of my life, for when I finished I had prepared a document through which I would finance a national magazine that would give me contact with people throughout the English-speaking world. So greatly did that document influence my own career, and the lives of tens of thousands of other people, that I believe it will be of interest to the students of this course. Therefore, I am reproducing it just as it appeared in *Hill's Golden Rule* magazine, where it was first published:

A PERSONAL VISIT WITH YOUR EDITOR

I am writing on Monday, November eleventh, 1918. Today will go down in history as the greatest holiday.

On the street, just outside of my office window, the surging crowds of people are celebrating the downfall of an influence that has menaced civilization for the past four years.

The war is over. Soon our boys will be coming back home from the battlefields of France. The lord and master of brute force is nothing but a shadowy ghost of the past!

Two thousand years ago the son of man was an outcast, with no place of abode. Now the situation has been reversed and the devil has no place to lay his head.

Let each of us take unto himself the great lesson that this world war has taught: namely, only that which is based upon justice and mercy toward all—the weak and the strong, the rich and the poor, alike—can survive. All else must pass on.

Out of this war will come a new idealism—an idealism that will be based on the Golden Rule philosophy; an idealism that will guide us, not to see how much we can "do our fellow man for," but how much we can do for him that will ameliorate his hardships and make him happier as he tarries by the wayside of life.

Emerson embodied this idealism in his great essay, Compensation. Another great philosopher embodied it in these words, "Whatsoever a man soweth, that shall he also reap."

The time for practicing the Golden Rule philosophy is upon us. In business as well as in social relationships, he who neglects or refuses to use this philosophy as the basis of his dealings will but hasten the time of his failure.

And while I am intoxicated with the glorious news of the war's ending, is it not fitting that I should attempt to do something to help preserve, for the generations yet to come, one of the great lessons to be learned from William Hohenzollern's effort to rule the earth by force?

I can best do this by going back twenty-two years for my beginning. Come with me, won't you?

It was a bleak November morning, probably not far from the eleventh of the month, that I got my first job as a laborer in the coal mine regions of Virginia, at wages of a dollar a day. A dollar a day was a big sum in those days; especially to a boy of my age. Of this, I paid fifty cents a day for my room and board.

Shortly after I began work, the miners became dissatisfied and commenced talking about striking. I listened eagerly to all that was said. I was especially interested in the organizer who had organized the union. He was one of the smoothest speakers I had ever heard, and his words fascinated me.

He said one thing, in particular, that I have never forgotten; and, if I knew where to find him, I would look him up today and thank him warmly for saying it. The philosophy which I gathered from his words has had a most profound and enduring influence upon me.

Perhaps you will say that most labor agitators are not very sound philosophers, and I would agree with you if you said so. Maybe this one was not a sound philosopher, but surely the philosophy he expounded on this occasion was sound.

Standing on a dry goods box, in the corner of an old shop where he was holding a meeting, he said:

"Men, we are talking about striking. Before you vote I wish to call your attention to something that will benefit you if you will heed what I say.

"You want more money for your work, and I wish to see you get it, because I believe you deserve it. May I not tell you how to get more money and still retain the goodwill of the owner of this mine?

"We can call a strike and probably force them to pay more money, but we cannot force them to do this and like it. Before we call a strike, let us be fair with the owner of the mine and with ourselves; let us go to the owner and ask him if he will divide the profits of his mine with us fairly.

"If he says yes, as he probably will, then let us ask him how much he made last month and if he will divide among us a fair proportion of any additional profits he may make if we all jump in and help him earn more next month.

"He, being human like each of us, will no doubt say, 'Why, certainly boys, go to it and I'll divide with you.' It is but natural that he would say that.

"After he agrees to the plan, as I believe he will if we make him see that we are in earnest, I want every one of you to come to work with a smile on your face for the next thirty days. I want to hear you whistling a tune as you go into the mines. I want you to go at your work with the feeling that you are one of the partners in this business.

"Without hurting yourself you can do almost twice as much work as you are doing, and if you do more work, you are sure to help the owner of this mine make more money. And if he makes more money he will be glad to divide a part of it with you. He will do this for sound business reasons if not out of a spirit of fair play.

"If he doesn't, I'll be personally responsible to you, and if you say so I'll help blow this mine into smithereens! That's how much I think of the plan, boys! Are you with me?"

They were, to the man!

The following month every man in the mines received a bonus of twenty percent of his month's earnings. Every month thereafter each man received a bright red envelope with his part of the extra earnings in it. On the outside of the envelope were these printed words: Your part of the profits from the work which you did that you were not paid to do.

I have gone through some pretty tough experiences since those days of twenty-odd years ago, but I have always come out on top—a little wiser, a little happier, and a little better prepared to be of service to my fellow men, owing to my having applied the principle of performing more work than I was actually paid to perform.

It may be of interest to you to know that the last position I held in the coal business was that of assistant to the chief counsel for one of the largest companies in the world. It is a considerable jump from the position of a common laborer in the coal mines to that of assistant to the chief counsel—a jump that I never could have made without the aid of this principle of performing more work than I was paid to perform.

I wish I had the space to tell you of the scores of times that this idea of performing more work than I was paid to perform has helped me over rough spots.

Many have been the times that I have placed an employer so deeply in my debt, through the aid of this principle, that I got whatever I asked for, without hesitation or quibbling, without complaint or hard feelings, and what is more important, without the feeling that I was taking unfair advantage of my employer.

I believe most earnestly that anything a man acquires from his fellow man, without the full consent of the one from whom it is acquired, will eventually burn a hole in his pocket, or blister the palms of his hands, to say nothing of gnawing at his conscience until his heart aches with regret.

As I said in the beginning, I am writing on the morning of the eleventh of November, while the crowds are celebrating the great victory. Therefore, it is but natural that I should turn to the silence of my heart for some thought to pass on to the world today—some thought that will help keep alive in the minds of Americans the spirit of idealism for which they have fought and in which they entered the world war.

I find nothing more appropriate than the philosophy which I have related. To get this philosophy into the hearts of those who need it, I shall publish a magazine to be called *Hill's Golden Rule.*

It takes money to publish a national magazine, and I haven't very much of it at this writing. But before another month shall have passed, through the aid of the philosophy that I have tried to emphasize here, I shall find someone who will supply the necessary money and make it possible for me to pass on to the world the simple philosophy that lifted me out of the dirty coal mines and gave me a place where I can be of service to humanity. The philosophy which will raise you, my dear reader, whoever you may be and whatever you may be doing, into whatever position in life you may make up your mind to attain.

Every person has, or ought to have, the inherent desire to own something of monetary value. In at least a vague sort of way, every person who works for others (and this includes practically all of us) looks forward to the time when he will have some sort of a business or a profession of his own.

The best way to realize that ambition is to perform more work than one is paid to perform. You can get along with but little schooling; you can get along with but little capital; you can overcome almost any obstacle with which you are confronted, if you are honestly and earnestly willing to do the best work of which you are capable, regardless of the amount of money you receive for it.

It was in this somewhat dramatic manner that a desire which had lain dormant in my mind for nearly twenty years became translated into reality. During all that time I had wanted to become the editor of a newspaper. Back more than thirty years ago, when I was a very small boy, I used to "kick" the press for my father when he was publishing a small weekly newspaper, and I grew to love the smell of printer's ink.

As I have stated, this editorial was written with enthusiasm. I took it to a man of my acquaintance, and with enthusiasm I read it to him.

I had hardly finished reading this editorial when the man to whom I read it—the first and only person to whom I had shown it—said:

"I can tell you where you are going to get the money, for I am going to supply it."

And he did!

HE WROTE THOUSANDS OF WORDS EVERY MONTH

The person to whom Napoleon Hill showed the finished essay was George B. Williams, a Chicago printer he had met while working at the White House, and by early January of 1919, *Hill's Golden Rule* magazine was on the newsstands. It was a sellout.

The first issue was forty-eight pages. In the beginning, with no money to pay anyone else, Hill wrote and edited every word himself, changing his writing style for each article as well as using a variety of pen names.

To Napoleon Hill it seemed that this magazine was the fulfillment of everything he had dreamed of and worked for. It gave him a national platform for the secrets of success he had learned from his years of researching the most successful men in America, and it also allowed him to teach the lessons he had learned from his own business triumphs and failures. *Hill's Golden Rule* was in every way an extension of him, his talent, his philosophy, and his passion.

Then, in the late summer of 1920, Hill discovered that Williams had gone behind his back and contrived to seize control of the magazine. At first Williams offered to pay Hill off—if he would sign an agreement promising to get out of publishing. Hill refused. But when the October issue came out, he saw that his name had been removed from the masthead. He was devastated.

For about a month. Then he got mad. Then he got even.

Within two months Hill moved from Chicago to New York City and raised enough money to launch a new publication, *Napoleon Hill's Magazine,* the foundation of which was again the Golden Rule, but it also expanded into presenting many of the Principles of Success that would become the basis of Hill's later books. The first issue hit the stands in April, and by the September issue it was clear that he had accomplished the almost unheard-of feat of launching a magazine that would be profitable in its first year!

The magazine's acceptance and nationwide success also led to an increase in demand for Napoleon Hill to appear as a speaker and motivator, which led to even greater success for the magazine.

At the same time, Hill was working with one of the inmates of the Ohio State Penitentiary to develop a correspondence course which he proposed to offer to the prison systems to encourage prisoner rehabilitation.

Most everything Hill did during this time was successful, and the success of the prison program was significant. But the greed of two members of the board of directors, one of which was the prison chaplain, caused a scandal that eventually led in 1924 to the demise of not only the educational rehabilitation programs but also Hill's pride and joy, *Napoleon Hill's Magazine,* as well as numerous other successful offshoot ventures.

FINDING THE SEED OF THE NEXT SUCCESS

Between 1918 and 1924, Hill had launched and published two monthly magazines—*Hill's Golden Rule* and *Napoleon Hill's Magazine.* It was the need to fill the pages of his magazines that prompted Hill to begin committing to paper the principles behind the secret of success which he had learned from Carnegie's famous friends, and to turn his own personal triumphs and failures into lessons.

In these magazine articles, Hill honed his theories, refined his arguments, and polished his presentation of the success philosophy for the common man that Andrew Carnegie had envisioned.

Although he was deeply depressed over the loss of *Napoleon Hill's Magazine* and the unfair criticisms that were leveled against him personally, Hill followed his own advice, searched for the hidden benefit, and found it in the lessons he had learned from the actual failure itself.

He moved to Cleveland and convinced some local businessmen that he would put up the expertise if they would put up the cash to launch a new learning institution to be called the Metropolitan Business College.

With Hill beating the publicity drum, the college enrollment soon reached capacity, which gave Hill the freedom not only to teach at his own college but also to launch a series of extracurricular lectures.

It was in Canton, Ohio, at one of his speaking engagements, that Napoleon Hill met the publisher of the *Canton Daily News,* Don Mellet.

Like Carnegie before him, Don Mellet was fascinated by Hill's intellect and intensity. The two men clicked, Mellet's newspaper took over the sponsorship of Hill's lectures, and, using the paper as the base, they launched a syndicated column offering Hill's business advice.

Because of his increasingly high profile, Hill's fame as a lecturer continued to grow and his column began to have an impact on readers, which unfortunately brought him into conflict with the mob.

In 1926 Mellet's reporters learned that Prohibition gangsters were selling narcotics and bootleg liquor to schoolchildren in Canton, and members of the local police force were being bribed to do nothing about it. Mellet was outraged and wrote an exposé in the *Canton Daily News,* while Hill contacted the governor to implement a state investigation of the corrupt police department.

Although it was hard slogging because most of the local officials were too intimidated to stand up to the gangsters, Hill and Mellet were finally getting close to an indictment when Mellet was ambushed outside his home and assassinated by a gangster and a renegade cop.

That would very likely have been Hill's fate too if he had not been delayed by car trouble. When he finally arrived back home he received a phone call from that same cop, warning him that he had one hour to get out of town.

Hill left without even packing. He got in his car and headed for the hills. Literally. He drove all night until he found himself in the familiar shoals and hollers of the Blue Ridge Mountains of West Virginia. He made contact with some relatives who offered to take him in, and spent most of the next year in a deep depression, living in fear for his life and hiding out with his kinfolk in the mountains of Virginia.

Then, in one long night of self-therapy, Napoleon Hill took hold of his mind, banished his depression, pulled himself together, borrowed money from his brother-in-law, went to Philadelphia, and convinced a publisher to help him publish the philosophy of success he had been working on for all those years.

LAW OF SUCCESS FINALLY PUBLISHED

In 1928 Hill published his first book based on what he referred to as the Carnegie secret. It was called *Law of Success* and it was the culmination of his twenty years of research into the habits of more than one hundred of the most successful individuals in America, as well as more than 16,000 interviews with average working people, business managers, and entrepreneurs.

In what proved to be a brilliant marketing idea, the first edition was published as eight separate but interconnected volumes. No one had ever seen anything like it before. It was a phenomenon, a masterwork in eight parts, and it was a runaway bestseller.

For the next year, Napoleon Hill and his family were on top of the world. Royalties poured in, Rolls-Royces were purchased, and a lavish compound in the Catskill Mountains was acquired with the intention of creating a university and retreat where people could come from around the world to study Napoleon Hill's Philosophy of Personal Achievement and take courses in the Science of Success.

A year later—when the market crashed in 1929 and the Great Depression hit—Napoleon Hill declared it his personal mission to turn the tide by creating a variety of self-help programs. And though book sales dried up, he hit the road once again, depleting his resources to support his lectures and programs. However, try as he might, it soon became disappointingly apparent that it was going to take more than one man to do it.

The Depression worsened, and when Franklin Delano Roosevelt was elected president he reached out to Napoleon Hill for help. Although Hill was as broke as everyone else, just as he had done when he worked for President Wilson, he refused to accept any money for his work for the government and President Roosevelt. During the Depression he became a close confidant of the president, helping to guide FDR in his efforts to revitalize America. It is said that it was Hill who gave Roosevelt the famous line "We have nothing to fear but fear itself."

Throughout the 1930s and his days at the White House, Hill had continued his research into the Principles of Success. In 1937, as America was finally beginning to see glimmerings of hope that the Depression might end, Hill convinced his publisher that America now needed a book to help shake off the mental and emotional stigma of those terrible times.

It had been nine years since the publication of *Law of Success,* and after having spent those years working with many of the next generation's most influential people, Napoleon Hill updated and re-organized his research. By this time the total number of interviews collected by Hill or his associates had grown to 25,000 individuals. More than 500 of those were personal, in-depth interviews with the wealthiest and most influential entrepreneurs and leaders who were instrumental in America's recovery and rise to greatness.

Hill went back, rewrote and revised key sections from *Law of Success*, adapted some of his earlier magazine articles, and condensed his research which he fashioned into a single volume that he titled *Think and Grow Rich.* The appeal of this new book was so great that even during the Depression years it sold millions of copies, and it continued to sell through war or peace, and boom or bust, until it became the best-selling success book ever published.

When America entered the Second World War, Napoleon Hill was too old for active duty, so he offered his services to the defense industry. He worked with both the government and private industry to boost production of military materials, he mediated labor disputes, and he continued to create lecture series and radio programs which spread his influence even further. The result of all his years of exhaustive research had made Hill one of the best-selling authors in history and one of the most influential voices in America.

In the late 1940s, as the soldiers began to return home from war, it seemed as though America was waking up again and people were eager to make up for lost time and get back to being successful. Once again, the Napoleon Hill philosophy was perfect for the times. And so was Napoleon Hill.

He moved to Los Angeles, he continued to lecture and write, he expanded his career as a motivational radio broadcaster, and he began to collect the accolades and degrees that come with a long and distinguished career.

By 1951, at the age of 67, Napoleon Hill began to think about slowing down, so he started to cut back on his bookings for the following year. Then, at what was going to be one of his final lectures, he met the famed Chicago insurance millionaire, W. Clement Stone. Their rapport was instant—and so powerful that they made a deal then and there to work together to bring Hill's philosophy to the next generation.

W. Clement Stone had been a devotee of Napoleon Hill's philosophies since he first read *Think and Grow Rich* in 1938. The owner of an insurance company selling one-dollar travel policies, Stone had purchased many thousands of copies of the book, making it required reading for each of his thousands of salespeople.

In 1952 Stone's friend and dentist, Dr. Herb Gustafson, had recommended Napoleon Hill as speaker for a dental convention in Chicago. It was to have been one of Hill's last public engagements, and Gustafson invited Stone to attend.

When they met, Stone told Hill of the numerous copies he had bought of *Think and Grow Rich,* and said he attributed his success and great wealth to that book. In *A Lifetime of Riches,* author Michael Ritt says that to Hill it "was an endorsement of his life's work, and it came from a man who was more than accomplished—Stone was, in Hill's eyes, an empire builder cut from the same mold as the giants of early twentieth-century American industry whose philosophies had provided the basis for Hill's Principles of Success."

W. Clement Stone's primary goals were to increase his business from a $32-million enterprise to $100 million and, personally, to use his wealth and knowledge to "create a better world for this and future generations." He called this his "magnificent obsession."

They were philosophically in perfect harmony. Stone persuaded Hill to forget about retirement, and by the end of the luncheon they had created the foundation for what would become the strongest Master Mind Alliance of Hill's career. To further spread Hill's message, Stone would manage his activities and provide financial backing.

Within a year they had launched Napoleon Hill Associates; they published new books by Hill including *How to Raise Your Own Salary* and *The Master Key to Riches*; they reissued Hill's earlier bestsellers; and they co-authored a new bestseller, *Success Through a Positive Mental Attitude*. They also launched *Success Unlimited* magazine, created the Science of Success home-study courses, made television programs, radio shows, a documentary film—*A New Sound in Paris,* which showed the amazing change that happened when the entire town of Paris, Missouri, adopted the Napoleon Hill philosophy—and they both crisscrossed America speaking, teaching, giving interviews, and spreading the philosophy to as many people as possible.

During that period Hill also reorganized Stone's sales program, which proved to be so successful that he astounded the business world by growing Stone's Combined Insurance Company from $32 million to $100 million—and meeting Stone's primary goal.

The success of their business partnership and Master Mind Alliance continued until 1961—always with a handshake, never a contract. Their friendship continued throughout the rest of Hill's life.

There has perhaps never been a greater example of "coordination of knowledge and effort, in a spirit of harmony, between two or more people for the attainment of a definite purpose." The sheer volume of work and scope of influence achieved in a ten-year period by Napoleon Hill and W. Clement Stone leaves little question as to the power and importance of a Master Mind Alliance.

In 1962, Napoleon Hill and his wife, Annie Lou Hill, established The Napoleon Hill Foundation, dedicated to "making the world a better place in which to live." The Foundation continues the work of imparting Napoleon Hill's philosophy of personal achievement to social-service agencies, educators, minority groups, prison inmates, businesses, and individuals. Napoleon Hill died on November 8, 1970, at the age of eighty-seven.

When W. Clement Stone passed away on September 3, 2002, at the age of one hundred, Stone's company, now known as Aon Corporation, had revenues of $2 billion a year, and W. Clement Stone had personally given more than $275 million to various charitable and philanthropic organizations. Stone would trace much of his company's success to the man he lured out of retirement in 1952.

This concludes the editors' brief biography of Napoleon Hill. To continue our exploration of the influences that shaped his life and philosophy, we offer the following story written by Napoleon Hill about one of the most important people ever to enter his life, his son Blair.

The following is excerpted and adapted from *Think and Grow Rich,* Chapter 2: Desire. In it you will not only find every one of the Seventeen Principles of Success, but you will also find why Napoleon Hill knew, without any doubt, that the Principles of Success work.

DESIRE OUTWITS MOTHER NATURE

As a fitting climax to this chapter, I wish to introduce one of the most unusual persons I have ever known. I first saw him twenty-four years ago, a few minutes after he was born. He came into the world without any physical sign of ears, and the doctor admitted, when pressed for an opinion on the case, that the child might be deaf and mute for life.

I challenged the doctor's opinion. I had the right to do so. I was the child's father. I, too, reached a decision and rendered an opinion, but I expressed the opinion silently, in the secrecy of my own heart. I decided that my son would hear and speak. Nature could send me a child without ears, but nature *could not induce me to accept* the reality of the affliction.

In my own mind I knew that my son would hear and speak. How? I was sure there must be a way, and I knew I would find it. I thought of the words of the immortal Emerson, "The whole course of things goes to teach us faith. We need only obey. There is guidance for each of us, and by lowly listening, we shall hear *the right word*."

The right word? *Desire!* More than anything else, I desired that my son should not be a deaf mute. From that desire I never receded, not for a second.

Many years previously I had written, "Our only limitations are those we set up in our own minds." For the first time, I wondered if that statement were true. Lying on the bed in front of me was a newly born child, without the natural equipment of hearing. Even though he might hear and speak, he was obviously disfigured for life. Surely, this was a limitation which that child had not set up in his own mind.

What could I do about it? Somehow I would find a way to transplant into that child's mind my own burning desire for ways and means of conveying sound to his brain without the aid of ears.

As soon as the child was old enough to cooperate, I would fill his mind so completely with a burning desire to hear, that nature would, by methods of her own, translate it into physical reality.

All this thinking took place in my own mind, but I spoke of it to no one. Every day I renewed the pledge I had made to myself, not to accept a deaf mute for a son.

As he grew older, and began to take notice of things around him, we observed that he had a slight degree of hearing. When he reached the age when children usually begin talking, he made no attempt to speak, but we could tell by his actions that he could hear certain sounds slightly.

That was all I wanted to know! I was convinced that if he could hear, even slightly, he might develop still greater hearing capacity. Then something happened which gave me hope. It came from an entirely unexpected source.

We bought a Victrola. When the child heard the music for the first time, he went into ecstasies, and promptly appropriated the machine. He soon showed a preference for certain records, among them, "It's a Long Way to Tipperary." On one occasion, he played that one piece over and over, for almost two hours, standing in front of the Victrola, *with his teeth clamped on the edge of the case.* The significance of this self-formed habit of his did not become clear to us until years afterward, for we had never heard of the principle of "bone conduction" of sound at that time.

Shortly after he appropriated the Victrola, I discovered that he could hear me quite clearly when I spoke with my lips touching his mastoid bone, at the base of the brain. These discoveries placed in my possession the necessary media by which I began to translate into reality my burning desire to help my son develop hearing and speech. By that time he was making stabs at speaking certain words. The outlook was far from encouraging, but desire backed by faith knows no such word as *impossible.*

Having determined that he could hear the sound of my voice plainly, I began, immediately, to transfer to his mind the desire to hear and speak. I soon discovered that the child enjoyed bedtime stories, so I went to work, creating stories designed to develop in him self-reliance, imagination, and a *keen desire to hear and to be normal.*

There was one story in particular, which I emphasized by giving it some new and dramatic coloring each time it was told. It was designed to plant in his mind the thought that his affliction was not a liability, but an asset of great value. Despite the fact that all the philosophy I had examined clearly indicated that every adversity brings with it the seed of an equivalent advantage, I must confess that I had not the slightest idea *how* this affliction could ever become an asset. However, I continued my practice of wrapping that philosophy in bedtime stories, hoping the time would come when he would find some plan by which his handicap could be made to serve some useful purpose.

Reason told me plainly that there was no adequate compensation for the lack of ears and natural hearing equipment. Desire backed by faith pushed reason aside, and inspired me to carry on.

As I analyze the experience in retrospect, I can see now, that my son's *faith in me* had much to do with the astounding results. He did not question anything I told him. I sold him the idea that he had a distinct *advantage* over his older brother, and that this advantage would reflect itself in many ways.

For example, the teachers in school would observe that he had no ears, and, because of this, they would show him special attention and treat him with extraordinary kindness. They always did. His mother saw to that, by visiting the teachers and arranging with them to give the child the extra attention necessary. I sold him the idea, too, that when he became old enough to sell newspapers (his older brother had already become a newspaper merchant), he would have a big advantage over his brother, for the reason that people would pay him extra money for his wares, because they could see that he was a bright, industrious boy, despite the fact he had no ears.

We could notice that, gradually, the child's hearing was improving. Moreover, he had not the slightest tendency to be self-conscious because of his affliction. When he was about seven, he showed the first evidence that our method of servicing his mind was bearing fruit. For several months he begged for the privilege of selling newspapers, but his mother would not give her consent. She was afraid his deafness made it unsafe for him to go on the street alone.

Finally, he took matters in his own hands. One afternoon, when he was left at home with the servants, he climbed through the kitchen window, shinnied to the ground, and set out on his own. He borrowed six cents in capital from the neighborhood shoemaker, invested it in papers, sold out, reinvested, and kept repeating until late in the evening.

After balancing his accounts, and paying back the six cents he had borrowed from his banker, he had a net profit of forty-two cents. When we got home that night, we found him in bed asleep, with the money tightly clenched in his hand.

His mother opened his hand, removed the coins, and cried. Of all things! Crying over her son's first victory seemed so inappropriate. My reaction was the reverse. I laughed heartily, for I knew that my endeavor to plant in the child's mind an attitude of faith in himself had been successful.

His mother saw, in his first business venture, a little deaf boy who had gone out in the streets and risked his life to earn money. I saw a brave, ambitious, self-reliant little businessman whose stock in himself had been increased a hundred percent, because he had gone into business on his own initiative, and had won.

The transaction pleased me, because I knew that he had given evidence of a trait of resourcefulness that would go with him all through life. Later events proved this to be true. When his older brother wanted something, he would lie down on the floor, kick his feet in the air, cry for it—and get it. When the "little deaf boy" wanted something, he would plan a way to earn the money, then buy it for himself. He still follows that plan.

Truly, my own son has taught me that handicaps can be converted into steppingstones on which one may climb toward some worthy goal, unless they are accepted as obstacles, and used as alibis.

The little deaf boy went through the grades, high school, and college without being able to hear his teachers, except when they shouted loudly, at close range.

He did not go to a school for the deaf. We would not permit him to learn the sign language. We were determined that he should live a normal life, and associate with normal children, and we stood by that decision, although it cost us many heated debates with school officials.

While he was in high school, he tried an electrical hearing aid, but it was of no value to him, due, we believe, to a condition that was disclosed when the child was six, by Dr. J. Gordon Wilson of Chicago, when he operated on one side of the boy's head, and discovered that there was no sign of natural hearing equipment.

During his last week in college (eighteen years after the operation), something happened which marked the most important turning point of his life. Through what seemed to be mere chance, he came into possession of another electrical hearing device, which was sent to him on trial. He was slow about testing it, due to his disappointment with a similar device.

Finally he picked the instrument up, and more or less carelessly, placed it on his head, hooked up the battery, and lo! as if by a stroke of magic, his lifelong desire for normal hearing became a reality! For the first time in his life he heard practically as well as any person with normal hearing. "God moves in mysterious ways, His wonders to perform."

Overjoyed because of the changed world which had been brought to him through his hearing device, he rushed to the telephone, called his mother, and heard her voice perfectly. The next day he plainly heard the voices of his professors in class, for the first time in his life! Previously he could hear them only when they shouted at short range. Now he heard the radio. He heard the talking pictures. For the first time in his life, he could converse freely with other people, without the necessity of their having to speak loudly. Truly, he had come into possession of a changed world. We had refused to accept nature's error, and by persistent desire, we had induced nature to correct that error, through the only practical means available.

Desire had commenced to pay dividends, but the victory was not yet complete. The boy still had to find a definite and practical way to convert his handicap into an *equivalent asset.*

Hardly realizing the significance of what had already been accomplished, but intoxicated with the joy of his newly discovered world of sound, he wrote a letter to the manufacturer of the hearing aid, enthusiastically describing his experience. Something in his letter, something which perhaps was not written on the lines, caused the company to invite him to New York. When he arrived, he was escorted through the factory, and while talking with the chief engineer, telling him about his changed world, a hunch, an idea, or an inspiration—call it what you wish—flashed into his mind. It was *this impulse of thought* which converted his affliction into an asset, destined to pay dividends in both money and happiness to thousands for all time to come.

The sum and substance of that impulse of thought was this: It occurred to him he might be of help to the millions of deafened people who go through life without the benefit of hearing devices, if he could find a way to tell them the story of his changed world. Then and there, he reached a decision to devote the remainder of his life to rendering useful service to the hard of hearing.

For an entire month, he carried on an intensive research, during which he analyzed the entire marketing system of the manufacturer of the hearing device, and created ways and means of communicating with the hard of hearing all over the world for the purpose of sharing with them his newly discovered "changed world." When this was done, he put in writing a two-year plan, based upon his findings. When he presented the plan to the company, he was instantly given a position, for the purpose of carrying out his ambition.

Little did he dream, when he went to work, that he was destined to bring hope and practical relief to thousands of deafened people who, without his help, would have been doomed forever to deaf mutism.

There is no doubt in my mind that Blair would have been a deaf mute all his life, if his mother and I had not managed to shape his mind as we did.

When I planted in his mind the desire to hear and talk and live as a normal person, there went with that impulse some strange influence which caused nature to become bridge-builder, and span the gulf of silence between his brain and the outer world.

A burning desire has devious ways of transmuting itself into its physical equivalent. Blair desired normal hearing; now he has it! He was born with a handicap that might easily have sent one with a less defined desire to the street with a bundle of pencils and a tin cup.

The little "white lies" I planted in his mind when he was a child, by leading him to believe his affliction would become a great asset on which he could capitalize, has justified itself. Verily, there is nothing, right or wrong, which belief, plus burning desire, cannot make real. These qualities are free to everyone.

In all my experience in dealing with men and women who had personal problems, I never handled a single case which more definitely demonstrates the power of desire. Authors sometimes make the mistake of writing of subjects of which they have but superficial, or very elementary knowledge. It has been my good fortune to have had the privilege of testing the soundness of the power of desire, through the affliction of my own son.

I planted in my son's mind the desire to hear and speak as any normal person hears and speaks. That desire has now become a reality. I planted in his mind the desire to convert his greatest handicap into his greatest asset. That desire has been realized. The modus operandi by which this astounding result was achieved is not hard to describe.

It consisted of three very definite facts. First, I mixed faith with the desire for normal hearing, which I passed on to my son. Second, I communicated my desire to him in every conceivable way available, through persistent, continuous effort, over a period of years. Third, HE BELIEVED ME.

I believe in the power of desire backed by faith, because I have seen this power lift men from lowly beginnings to places of power and wealth; I have seen it rob the grave of its victims; I have seen it serve as the medium by which men staged a comeback after having been defeated in a hundred different ways; I have seen it provide my own son with a normal, happy, successful life, despite nature's having sent him into the world without ears.

Through some strange and powerful principle of "mental chemistry," which she has never divulged, nature wraps up in the impulse of strong desire "that something" which recognizes no such word as *impossible*, and accepts no such reality as failure.

This concludes the excerpt taken from Chapter 2: Desire, in *Think and Grow Rich*. On the following pages you will find a series of self-analysis questions devised by Napoleon Hill and excerpted from Chapter 15: How to Outwit the Six Ghosts of Fear, also from *Think and Grow Rich*.

SELF-ANALYSIS QUESTIONS

If you are reading this book to learn how to grow rich, you should examine yourself very carefully to determine whether you are susceptible to negative influences. If you neglect this self-analysis, you will give up your right to attain the object of your desires.

Make your analysis searching. As you read the following questions, be tough on yourself. Go at the task as carefully as you would if you were searching for any other enemy you knew was waiting to ambush you. You must deal with your own faults as you would with a real and serious enemy.

The following list of questions is designed to help you see yourself as you really are. You should read through the list now, then set aside a day when you can give adequate time to go through the list again, and thoroughly answer each question.

When you do this, I advise that you read the questions and state your answers aloud so you can hear your own voice. This will make it easier for you to be truthful with yourself.

Do you complain often of "feeling bad," and if so, what is the cause?

Do you find fault with other people at the slightest provocation?

Do you frequently make mistakes in your work, and if so, why?

Are you sarcastic and offensive in your conversation?

Do you deliberately avoid associating with anyone, and if so, why?

Do you suffer frequently with indigestion? If so, what is the cause?

Does life seem futile and the future hopeless to you? If so, why?

Do you like your occupation? If not, why not?

Do you often feel self-pity, and if so, why?

Are you envious of those who excel you?

To which do you devote the most time—thinking of success or of failure?

Are you gaining or losing self-confidence as you grow older?

Do you learn something of value from all mistakes?

Are you permitting some relative or acquaintance to worry you? If so, why?

Are you sometimes "in the clouds" and at other times in the depths of despondency?

Who has the most inspiring influence on you, and for what reason?

Do you tolerate negative or discouraging influences that you could avoid?

Are you careless of your personal appearance? If so, when and why?

Have you learned to ignore your troubles by being too busy to be annoyed by them?

Would you call yourself a "spineless weakling" if you permitted others to do your thinking for you?

How many preventable disturbances annoy you, and why do you tolerate them?

Do you resort to alcohol, drugs, cigarettes, or other compulsions to "quiet your nerves"? If so, why do you not try will-power instead?

Does anyone "nag" you, and if so, for what reason?

Do you have a definite major purpose, and if so, what is it and what plan do you have for achieving it?

Do you suffer from any of the six basic fears? If so, which ones?

Have you developed a method to shield yourself against the negative influences of others?

Do you use autosuggestion to make your mind positive?

Which do you value most, your material possessions or your privilege of controlling your own thoughts?

Are you easily influenced by others, against your own judgment?

Has today added anything of value to your stock of knowledge or your state of mind?

Do you face squarely the circumstances that make you unhappy, or do you sidestep the responsibility?

Do you analyze all mistakes and failures and try to profit by them, or do you take the attitude that this is not your duty?

Can you name three of your most damaging weaknesses? What are you doing to correct them?

Do you encourage other people to bring their worries to you for sympathy?

Do you choose, from your daily experiences, lessons or influences that aid in your personal advancement?

Does your presence have a negative influence on other people as a rule?

What habits of other people annoy you most?

Do you form your own opinions, or do you permit yourself to be influenced by other people?

Have you learned how to create a mental state of mind with which you can shield yourself against all discouraging influences?

Does your occupation inspire you with faith and hope?

Are you conscious of possessing spiritual forces of sufficient power to enable you to keep your mind free from all forms of fear?

Does your religion help to keep your mind positive?

Do you feel it your duty to share other people's worries? If so, why?

When others offer you free, unsolicited advice, do you accept it without question, or analyze their motive?

If you believe that "birds of a feather flock together," what have you learned about yourself by studying the friends you attract?

What connection, if any, do you see between the people with whom you associate most closely and any unhappiness you may experience?

Could it be possible that some person whom you consider to be a friend is, in reality, your worst enemy because of their negative influence on your mind?

By what rules do you judge who is helpful and who is damaging to you?

Are your intimate associates mentally superior or inferior to you?

How much time out of every twenty-four hours do you devote to:

- your occupation
- sleep
- play and relaxation
- acquiring useful knowledge
- plain wasted time

Who among your acquaintances:

- encourages you most
- cautions you most
- discourages you most
- helps you most in other ways

What is your greatest worry? Why do you tolerate it?

What, above all else, do you most desire? Are you willing to subordinate all other desires for this one, and how much time daily do you devote to acquiring it?

Do you change your mind often? If so, why?

Do you usually finish everything you begin?

Are you easily impressed by other people's business titles, college degrees, or wealth?

Are you easily influenced by what other people think or say about you?

Do you cater to people because of their social or financial status?

Whom do you believe to be the greatest person living? In what respect is this person superior to yourself?

How much time have you devoted to studying and answering these questions? (At least one day is necessary for the analysis and the answering of the entire list.)

If you have answered all these questions truthfully, you know more about yourself than the majority of people. Study the questions carefully, come back to them once each week for several months, and be astounded at the amount of additional knowledge of great value to yourself you will have gained by the simple method of answering the questions truthfully. If you are not certain about the answers to some of the questions, seek the counsel of those who know you well, especially those who have no motive in flattering you, and see yourself through their eyes. The experience will be astonishing.

FIFTY-FIVE FAMOUS ALIBIS BY OLD MAN "IF"

People who do not succeed have one distinguishing trait in common. They know all the reasons for failure, and have what they believe to be airtight alibis to explain away their own lack of achievement.

Some of these alibis are clever and a few of them are justifiable by the facts. But alibis cannot be used for money. The world wants to know only one thing: Have you achieved success?

A character analyst compiled a list of the most commonly used alibis. As you read the list, examine yourself carefully and determine how many of these alibis you use. Remember, the philosophy presented in this book makes every one of these alibis obsolete.

If I didn't have a wife and family . . .

If I had enough "pull" . . .

If I had money . . .

If I had a good education . . .

If I could get a job . . .

If I had good health . . .

If I only had time . . .

If times were better . . .

If other people understood me . . .

If conditions around me were only different . . .

If I could live my life over again . . .

If I did not fear what "they" would say . . .

If I had been given a chance . . .

If I now had a chance . . .

If other people didn't "have it in for me" . . .

If nothing happens to stop me . . .

If I were only younger . . .

If I could only do what I want . . .

If I had been born rich . . .

If I could meet "the right people" . . .

If I had the talent that some people have . . .

If I dared to assert myself . . .

If only I had embraced past opportunities . . .

If people didn't get on my nerves . . .

If I didn't have to keep house and look after the children . . .

If I could save some money . . .

If the boss only appreciated me . . .

If I only had somebody to help me . . .

If my family understood me . . .

If I lived in a big city . . .

If I could just get started . . .

If I were only free . . .

If I had the personality of some people . . .

If I were not so fat . . .

If my real talents were known . . .

If I could just get a "break" . . .

If I could only get out of debt . . .

If I hadn't failed . . .

If I only knew how . . .

If everybody wasn't against me . . .

If I didn't have so many worries . . .

If I could marry the right person . . .

If people weren't so dumb . . .

If my family were not so extravagant . . .

If I were sure of myself . . .

If luck were not against me . . .

If I had not been born under the wrong star . . .

If it were not true that "what is to be will be" . . .

If I did not have to work so hard . . .

If I hadn't lost my money . . .

If I lived in a different neighborhood . . .

If I didn't have a "past" . . .

If I only had a business of my own . . .

If other people would only listen to me . . .

If—and this is the greatest of them all—I had the courage to see myself as I really am, I would find out what is wrong with me and correct it. And I know that something must be wrong with the way I have done things, or I would already have the success that I desire. I recognize that something must be wrong with me, otherwise I would have spent more time analyzing my weaknesses and less time building alibis to cover them.

Building alibis to explain away failure is a national pastime. The habit is as old as the human race, and is fatal to success. Why do people cling to their pet alibis? The answer is obvious. They defend their alibis because they create them. Your alibi is the child of your own imagination. It is human nature to defend your own brainchild.

Previously you may have had a logical excuse for not having forced life to come through with whatever you asked. That alibi is now obsolete because you are in possession of the Master Key that unlocks the door to life's riches.

The Master Key is intangible, but it is powerful. It is the privilege of creating, in your own mind, a burning desire for a definite form of riches. There is no penalty for the use of this key, but there is a price you must pay if you do not use it. The price is failure. There is a reward of stupendous proportions if you put the key to use. It is the satisfaction that will come to you when you conquer self and force life to pay whatever is asked.

Highroads Media, Inc. is the publisher of more books and audiobooks by Napoleon Hill than any other publisher in the world. Other titles available:

REVISED & UPDATED EDITIONS
Think and Grow Rich: The 21ˢᵗ-Century Edition (hardcover)
Think and Grow Rich: The 21ˢᵗ-Century Updated Edition (softcover)
Think and Grow Rich: The 21ˢᵗ-Century Edition Workbook (softcover)
Law of Success: The 21ˢᵗ-Century Edition (softcover; single volume)
The Secret Law of Attraction as explained by Napoleon Hill (hardcover)
Selling You! (softcover)

LEATHER-BOUND, GILT-EDGED
COLLECTOR'S EDITIONS
Think and Grow Rich (single volume)
Law of Success (available in four volumes)
Napoleon Hill's First Editions (single volume)

THE *THINK AND GROW RICH* SUPERSET
A SPECIALLY BOUND 2-BOOK EDITION
which includes the softcover editions of:
Think and Grow Rich: The 21ˢᵗ-Century Updated Edition
Think and Grow Rich: The 21ˢᵗ-Century Edition Workbook

AUDIOBOOKS AVAILABLE ON CD
Think and Grow Rich: The 21ˢᵗ-Century Edition (unabridged audiobook)
Think and Grow Rich (unabridged and abridged audiobook editions)
Think and Grow Rich: Instant Motivator (original audiobook)
Law of Success (four-volume unabridged audiobook set)
Law of Success (abridged audiobook; single volume)
The Secret Law of Attraction as explained by Napoleon Hill (unabridged audiobook)
Selling You! (abridged audiobook)
Selling You! (unabridged audiobook)
Your Right to Be Rich (unabridged audiobook)
Napoleon Hill's Keys to Success (unabridged and abridged audiobooks)
Believe and Achieve (abridged audiobook)
The Richest Man in Babylon & The Magic Story (original audiobook)
A Lifetime of Riches: The Biography of Napoleon Hill (abridged audiobook)

For more information about Napoleon Hill books and audiobooks, contact:
Highroads Media, Inc., 6 Commerce Way, Arden, NC 28704
telephone: (323) 822-2676; fax: (323) 822-2686
email: highroadsmedia@sbcglobal.net
visit us at our website: www.highroadsmedia.com